THE WISDOM OF THE SERPENT

The Myths of
Death, Rebirth, and Resurrection

PATTERNS OF MYTH

Alan W. Watts, General Editor

I. MYTH AND EXPERIENCE

ALPHA The Myths of Creation by Charles H. Long
THE WISDOM OF THE SERPENT The Myths of Death, Rebirth,
and Resurrection by Joseph L. Henderson and Maud Oakes
THE TWO HANDS OF GOD The Myths of Polarity by Alan W. Watts

II. THE HUMAN IMAGE

MYTHS OF THE HERO (in preparation)
MYTHS OF THE ROYAL FATHER (in preparation)
MYTHS OF THE GODDESS (in preparation)

THE WISDOM OF
THE SERPENT

The Myths of Death,

Rebirth, and Resurrection

BY

JOSEPH L. HENDERSON
and MAUD OAKES

GEORGE BRAZILLER

NEW YORK

1963

ACKNOWLEDGMENTS

We are indebted to the Bollingen Foundation for their collaboration in making available quotations and photographs from their publications, to N. Rambova for the loan of photographs and for her textual advice, and to Giles Healy for making photographic reproductions.

For permission to reprint excerpts from source materials in this volume, the authors wish to thank the following:

George Allen & Unwin Ltd.—for selection from *The Nine Songs* by Arthur Waley; and The Macmillan Company for selections from *Three Ways of Thought in Ancient China* by Arthur Waley. First published in 1939 by George Allen & Unwin Ltd. Copyright under the Berne Convention.

Arthur J. O. Anderson and Charles E. Dibble—for selections from their transl. of *Florentine Codex* by Fray Bernardino de Sahagun.

Basil Blackwell (Oxford, England) for selection from *Cumaean Gates* by W. F. Jackson-Knight.

Bollingen Foundation—for selections from *Myths and Symbols in Indian Art and Civilization* by Heinrich Zimmer; *Yoga: Immortality and Freedom* by Mircea Eliade; *Essays on a Science of Mythology* by C. G. Jung and K. Kerényi; *The Great Mother* by Erich Neumann; *The I Ching, or Book of Changes* by Richard Wilhelm, tr. by Cary F. Baynes; "The Malekulan Journey of the Dead" by John Layard and "Dream Symbols of the Individuation Process" by C. G. Jung from *Spiritual*

Disciplines (Eranos Yearbooks, No. 4); *The King and the Corpse* by Heinrich Zimmer; *African Folktales and Sculpture* by Paul Radin and James Johnson Sweeney; *The Road of Life and Death* by Paul Radin; *Philosophies of India* by Heinrich Zimmer; and Joseph Campbell for selections from his "The Symbol Without Meaning" from the *Eranos Jahrbuch* XXVI.

Cambridge University Press for "The Thunder Rite" from *Themis* by Jane Ellen Harrison.

Clarendon Press, Oxford for selection from *Babylonian Epic of Creation* by S. Langdon.

Padraic Colum for selections from his *Myths of the World*.

Doubleday and Company, Inc. for selections from *Mythologies of the Ancient World* edited by Samuel N. Kramer. Copyright © 1961 by Doubleday & Company, Inc. Reprinted by permission.

Éditions Payot, Paris for selections from *Le Chamanisme et les techniques archaïques de l'extase* by Mircea Eliade.

Farrar, Straus & Co., Inc. for selection from *The Dance of Shiva* by Ananda Coomaraswamy. Copyright © 1957 by The Noonday Press, Inc. Reprinted by permission of Farrar, Straus & Co., Inc. and Mrs. Ananda Coomaraswamy.

Funk & Wagnalls Company, Inc. for selection from *Standard Dictionary of Folklore, Mythology and Legend,* Vol. I.

Harper & Row, Publishers—for selections from *Birth and Rebirth* by Mircea Eliade; *Sumerian Mythology* by Samuel Kramer; and The Harvill Press Ltd. for selections from *Myths, Dreams and Mysteries* by Mircea Eliade.

George G. Harrap & Co. Ltd. for selections from *Myths of the Hindus and Buddhists* by Nivedita and Coomaraswamy.

The Hokuseido Press Co., Ltd. for selection from *Zen in English Literature* by R. H. Blyth.

Hutchinson & Co. (Publishers) Ltd. for selection from *The Tarot of the Bohemians* by Papus. Reprinted by permission of William Rider & Co.

A. Klasens for selection from "A Magical Statue Base" in his *In The Museum of Antiquities at Leiden.*

Oxford University Press for selections from *The Tibetan Book of the Dead* and *The Tibetan Book of the Great Liberation,* both ed. by W. Y. Evans-Wentz.

Pantheon Books, Inc. for selection from *Grimm's Fairy Tales*. Copyright 1944 by Pantheon Books, Inc. Printed by permission.

Philosophical Library, Inc. for selection from *A Dictionary of Symbols* by J. E. Cirlot.

Princeton University Press for selections from—*Light From the Ancient Past* by Jack Finegan, Copyright © 1946 by Princeton University Press; and *Ancient Near Eastern Texts* by James Pritchard, Copyright 1950, 1955 by Princeton University Press.

G. P. Putnam's Sons and Paul Hamlyn Publishers for selection from *Larousse Encyclopedia of Mythology*. © 1959 Batchworth Press Ltd.

Sheed & Ward, Inc. and the Harvill Press Ltd. for selections from *Images and Symbols* by Mircea Eliade. © in the English translation Harvill Press Ltd. 1961, published by Sheed & Ward, Inc., New York.

D. B. Taraporevala Sons & Co. Private Ltd. for selection from *Epics, Myths and Legends of India* by P. Thomas.

Thames and Hudson Ltd. for selections from—*Gods of the North* by Brian Branston; and *Gods of the Greeks* by Karl Kerényi.

University Books, Inc. and John M. Watkins (London) for selections from *Fragments of a Faith Forgotten* by G. R. S. Mead.

University of Chicago Press for selections from *The Gilgamesh Epic and Old Testament Parallels* by Alexander Heidel. Copyright 1946 by the University of Chicago.

University of Oklahoma Press for selections from—*The Aztecs* by Alfonso Caso, tr. Lowell Dunham. Copyright 1958 by the University of Oklahoma Press; and *The Sacred Pipe, Black Elk's Account of the Seven Rites of the Oglala Sioux* by Joseph Epes Brown. Copyright 1953 by the University of Oklahoma Press.

Vanguard Press, Inc. for selections from—*Myth and Ritual in Christianity* by Alan W. Watts; and *Burning Water: Thought and Religion in Ancient Mexico* by Laurette Sejourne. Reprinted by permission of the publisher, Vanguard Press, Inc.

The Viking Press for selections from *The Bible of the World* edited by Robert O. Ballou. Copyright 1939 by Robert O. Ballou; and Martin Secker and Warburg Ltd. for selection from *The Masks of God: Primitive Mythology* by Joseph

Campbell. Copyright 1959 by Joseph Campbell. Reprinted by permission of The Viking Press, Inc.

John M. Watkins (London) for selections from *The Hymn of the Robe of Glory* by G. R. S. Mead.

To the Memory of
Professor C. G. Jung

EDITOR'S FOREWORD

NOTHING IS MORE provocative than the idea of death. It is because men know that they will die that they have created the arts and sciences, the philosophies and religions. For nothing is more thought-provoking than the thought which seems to put an end to thought: "What will it be like to go to sleep and never wake up?" Irresistibly this seems to suggest a corollary: "Where and who was I before my father and mother conceived me?" For the unthinkable-after-death appears to be the same as the unthinkable-before-birth, so that if once I came out of nothing, the odds are that I can come again and again. Nothing seems to create something by implication, just as low implies high. This is why the cycle of birth, death, and rebirth is about the most basic theme of myth and religion. Joseph L. Henderson approaches this problem, not so much as the historian or the anthropologist, as the psychiatrist watching his patients work out this perennial problem in their dreams and fantasies. It is here that the formation of mythology continues even in our curiously pragmatic and anti-poetical culture, and, as Maud Oakes's anthology shows, its themes are the same as ever.

Surveys of the world's mythologies have usually classified their materials by regions, describing the myths of the Greeks and Romans, of the Norsemen, the Egyptians, or the Hindus —as if these racial, nationalistic, and geographical categories were the really significant divisions of the subject. But what would be the significant divisions in a survey of the world's birds? Would it be of major importance to stress the difference between American and European sparrows, or between sparrows and thrushes? Birds, plants, minerals, and other natural phenomena seem to be discussed more usefully by divisions of form or behavior than of locality.

To the extent, however, that a specific region is the cradle of a particular culture, and to the extent that myths are phenomena of cultures, the regional classification has its merits. But it should be supplemented by some other method, by a horizontal classification superimposed upon a perpendicular, and for this reason it has seemed important to discuss world mythology in terms of its themes or, to use C. G. Jung's word, its archetypes. Such an approach is therefore naturally indebted to Jung, to his provocative idea that myths are natural phenomena which grow out of the mind more or less uniformly in all places, just as the human body is of one essential pattern in China and Peru.

Yet in inviting authors to contribute to this series I have not restricted myself to those who are formally Jungian. I have tried to get as wide a variety of opinion as the thematic approach to mythology will permit.

The plan of the series is to publish, first, three volumes under the general title of *Myth and Experience* and having to do with mythological themes which treat of the ultimate structure and dynamics of the cosmos—the myths of creation, the myths of death and resurrection, and the myths of polarity. These will be followed by three volumes with the general title of *The Human Image* and dealing with myths in which the universe is understood in terms of anthropomorphic images, so that the themes here will be the father god, the goddess, and the hero.

Each volume is primarily an anthology of texts and images—i.e., photographs of works of art, ritual objects, and the like—presented with introduction and running commentary.

It is not, however, the intention of the series to serve as a sort of reference encyclopedia with each volume a compendium of all the principal myths of the given type. What was desired here was a more imaginative treatment of the material, and thus the contributing authors were selected accordingly.

ALAN W. WATTS

TABLE OF CONTENTS

INITIATION AS PSYCHIC LIBERATION   184

MYTHS OF RESURRECTION   202

LIST OF PLATES

dino de Sahagun, *Historia de las Cosas de Nueva España* (Mexico, 1829). Photo: *From collection of Maud Oakes.*

12b. Sacrifice of youth impersonating Tezcatlipoca. *Ibid.*

13. The Great Mother. *Courtesy of Peabody Museum, Harvard University.*

14. Demeter and Kore. Museum, Eleusis. Photo: *Alinari.*

15. Pārvatī, the Thunder Goddess. *Courtesy of the Smithsonian Institution, Freer Gallery of Art, Washington 25, D.C.*

Plates 8–15 follow page 134.

16. Wheel of Mother Nature. From a French manuscript. *Courtesy of Bibliothèque Nationale.* Photo: *The Warburg Institute, London.*

17. Ancestor image. From John Layard, "The Malekulan Journey of the Dead" in Joseph Campbell, ed., *Papers from the Eranos Yearbooks,* Vol. 4, *Spiritual Disciplines* (New York: Bollingen Series XXX, 1960).

18. Gilgamesh with herb of immortality. From C. G. Jung, *Symbols of Transformation* (Zurich: Rascher Verlag, revised ed., 1952; New York: Bollingen Series XX, *The Collected Works of C. G. Jung,* Vol. 5, 1956).

19. Coffin of Amenapet. *Courtesy of The Louvre, Paris.* Photo: *N. Rambova.*

20. Wall painting from tomb of Rameses IX. *Photo courtesy of N. Rambova.*

21. Baptism of King Seti I. Photo: *From collection of Maud Oakes.*

22. Le Baptême. Mosaic. From *L'Art en Grece* (Paris: Cahiers d'Art Editions, 1934). Photo: *From collection of Maud Oakes.*

23. Birth of Dionysus. Reprinted by permission of G. P. Putnam's Sons and Batchworth Press Ltd. from *Larousse Encyclopedia of Mythology.* © 1959 Batchworth Press Ltd. Photo: *From collection of Maud Oakes.*

24. The Moon Boat. Stele from India. *Photo courtesy of Dr. Stella Kramrish.*

Plates 16–24 follow page 166.

LIST OF LINE DRAWINGS

THE WISDOM OF THE SERPENT

The Myths of
Death, Rebirth, and Resurrection

INTRODUCTION

by Joseph L. Henderson

I. THE FEAR OF DEATH

Not so very many years ago, in his *Varieties of Religious Experience,* William James foreshadowed an entirely new psychological relativity toward religious experience. Ignoring theology, he brought to his readers the benefit of an impartial and, above all, accepting attitude to all forms of religious experience. He did not consider some as higher or lower, better or worse than others, and although a good many were experiences reported by pathological individuals he did not interpret these experiences themselves as being essentially healthy or deranged. It is with this attitude that I should like to approach the subject of death; in fact, the subject of death and resurrection as a whole. It is a subject which defies our ever finding the ultimate truth but one around which cluster a variety of symbolic representations by which the living have sought to approach the end of life in a meaningful way. Of course it must be recognized that the first reaction of most people to the thought of death is not symbolic but painfully literal. What will happen to Me when I die? And for this we must postulate a personal reaction appropriate to the individual disposition of each person who faces the fear of death, which is at bottom the ego's fear of the unknown. So it seems to me from a psychological point of view.

In the contrast between the universal and the personal experience of what is unknown we may find the conditions necessary to explore the eternal mystery of death. To this end we shall review traditional patterns of belief and compare them with experiences of modern individuals. The selected texts provide us at the outset with a rich yield from the records of mankind concerning death and its correlates, rebirth and resurrection, which I as a psychologist and psychotherapist will use along with case material to illustrate and I hope reinterpret for contemporary minds some aspects of this eternal theme. If we may postulate that the fear of death is basically fear of the unknown, there would seem to be no limit to the images of foreboding or hope which can be projected by a fearful ego into it.

Surprisingly, therefore, I think it can be demonstrated from the diverse material at our disposal that the combinations are not infinite but conform to certain rather simple designs. Whenever we find the theme of death, whether in recurrent myths or modern dreams, we find that it is never seen to stand alone as a final act of annihilation. Apart from extreme forms of pathological depression or of infantile sadism, death is universally found to be part of a cycle of death and rebirth, or to be the condition necessary to imagine transcendence of life in an experience of resurrection. Somewhere between the myths of death and rebirth and the myths of death and resurrection we find abundant evidence for another theme in which the experience of death and rebirth is central —the theme of initiation. Initiation provides the archetypal pattern by which the psyche, whether in individuals or in groups of people, is enabled to make a transition from one stage of development to another and therefore brings the theme of death and rebirth into close relation to problems of education whether in a religious or a secular sense.

Viewed from the only absolute standpoint we have, that is, of being still alive, we can therefore regard fear of death as being fear of change, or fear of growing up, or fear of becoming independent of the claims of the material world, or a mixture of all three.

In order to make our study broad enough to do justice to such widely separated groups as are represented by the claims of pragmatists on the one hand or by metaphysicians on the other, we have above all to postulate the existence of a symbol-forming tendency in all people, irrespective of race, creed, geography, and historical period, common to Buddhists or Christians, African Pygmies or Kwakiutl Indians. The same symbols may be found to have equal importance in the dream life of both modern New Yorkers and the inhabitants of Communist China. C. G. Jung's famous concept, the "collective unconscious," has given a necessary modern label to the universal source of the products of symbolism; but now what, fifty years ago, appeared to be only "unconscious" has progressively come to express itself in the consciously or half-consciously realized data of archetypal images and their corresponding patterns of behavior.

But the concept of the unconscious is still relevant, especially in this material, since as far as we know the fear of death is derived from an archetypal pattern whose total extent can never be made visible in this life; the image is present, but the actual experience is forever withheld, and we try to know and yet do not know its full meaning. All the rest is symbol, which we are then justified in accepting as hypothetically real in the absence of further knowledge. Partially enlightened, but still full of doubt and curiosity, humanity continues to fear death and yet longs for a deliverance from life appropriate to the symbol of its choice.

A way of learning more and experiencing more of this symbolic life is provided by modern studies of comparative mythology, but we have to be cautious about which one of several uses we choose to make of this. We may, as Neumann warns us, fall into an introverted negative way which "leads through the experience of heavens and hells to a merger of the two; it moves farther and farther from consciousness to ecstatic demolition of the ego."[1] In contrast to this way there is another way equally to be avoided. This is the "outward mysticism of extroversion . . . and culminates in a pantheistic or panentheistic seizure in which the ego is overpowered." Beyond these two choices there is a third choice "bound up with unity of being" which "corresponds to development of personality . . . the man of this phase is in the world and outside it, at rest and in creative motion, attached to the numinous and also at home in himself."[2]

The winding course a person must follow before attaining such an ideal philosophical position is shown in the contrasting themes of the separate chapter headings. The chief difference between the cosmic cycle and the nature cycle is, very roughly, the difference between a masculine creative agency (Shiva) and a feminine creative agency (Inanna). This division of archetypal configurations seems basic to any understanding of mythology, while the interaction of the two provides one of the germinal points of psychological development of an individual nature. This can be seen in the symbolism of the unconscious of modern people as well as in the traditional myths.

Out of this interaction there comes into being a type of mythology which is no longer exclusively masculine or feminine but a mixture of both, appealing to men or women either in rites of tribal societies or in the dreams of modern individuals. This is the archetypal pattern of initiation with its eternal theme of death and rebirth, sometimes associated with entrance into the life of a significant group, sometimes experienced in a lonely individual rite of vision. This rite of vision leads us to the most remote and single form of all initiation—shamanism—with its other-worldly capacity for liberation. Lastly, the themes of rebirth and resurrection, so differently illustrated in the changing myths, lead to a recurrent dilemma experienced by modern people as the need to choose symbols of containment in the meaningful group, or symbols of liberation of a transcendent, individual nature.

This necessarily poses an ultimate question as to whether these two kinds of symbols must remain separate or whether they may on some transpersonal level be joined and reconciled. Examples of this attempt at reconciliation comprise the substance of the final chapter.

II. DEATH AND REBIRTH
AS COSMIC PATTERN:
THE DANCE OF SHIVA

There is a marvelous collection of stories from India telling about the eternal cycles of death and birth, or of death and rebirth, as a timeless series of events supposed to occur and recur without the faintest suggestion of any end in view. This is the subject of the Dance of Shiva. We are confronted with the astonishing assertion that the movement of the dance represents "the release of . . . souls of men from the snare of illusion," and the "place of the dance, the centre of the universe, is within the heart."[1] This sounds clear enough at first, but, as we read further accounts of the dance, we begin to capture its sinister undertone which means that freedom from illusion is not to be achieved without death, and this gloomy prospect is then answered by the promising reference to that something which can be centered in the living human heart as rebirth.

This all comes out more clearly in Zimmer's account of Shiva as the great destroyer-god. His dance "bears traits suggesting some cosmic war-dance, designed to arouse destructive energies and to work havoc on the foe; at the same time it is the triumphant dance of the victor."[2] One myth "represents Shiva as the conqueror of a great demon who had assumed the shape of an elephant. The god, having forced his opponent to dance with him, continued until the victim fell down dead, then flayed him, donned his skin as a kind of mantle, and finally, wrapped in his blood-dripping trophy, executed a horrendous dance of victory. Against this sinister background, however, there flash the divine, youthful limbs, agile, delicate, and graceful, moving with their measured solemnity; and in these is the beautiful innocence of the first athletic powers of young manhood."[3] Here the lineaments of death and rebirth reveal themselves more clearly still. But the paradox of Eastern cosmic consciousness is overwhelming to the Western intellect, nursed as it has been for nineteen centuries in Judeo-Christian stories about the destruction of evil and the ultimate triumph of good to be experienced on the way to a heaven composed of final things. Perhaps therefore we have to look somewhat farther or deeper into this matter of death and rebirth to find its applicability and its rationale for modern man.

A variation of the Dance of Shiva will be remembered by those who saw the great Hindu dancer Uday Shankar, who fascinated Western audiences of the 1930's. In his version of the myth, we saw the god awaken from a state of timeless contemplation in response to the elephant demon's attempt to abduct Shakti, the god's divine consort. Rescuing her from the demon, Shiva prepared for the dance of death while Shakti procured for him the lightning which he hurled from his golden fingertips against the adversary. After the demon had fallen down, overcome at last in the fateful struggle, Shiva did not in this case execute "a horrendous dance of victory"; instead he calmly danced the destruction and creation of the world, and straight away retired once more into his natural state of inner contemplation in the cross-legged position of the divine ascetic. Here we experience in its living force the truth of Zimmer's final comment upon the meaning of the Dance of Shiva* where he says that "destruction—Shiva—is only the negative aspect of unending life."[4] And so, following the necessary act of destroying the evil demon,

* See p. 78.

he wills the destruction of the world in order to recreate it. There is no question here of merely submitting to a painful ordeal nor of overcoming evil with good, but rather of subordinating good and evil both to a higher law ritually expressed in the conscious act which affirms the equal validity and the cyclic succession of destruction making way for creation, in order to reestablish the harmony that can exist between man and the universe. It is not man who has to placate an all-powerful god in this story, but the god who has to put himself in order after the chaos engendered by the strife of opposites. And there is no end to this cycle which will be repeated throughout eternity in the dance of death and rebirth.

The Western world has also had its myths of destruction with an equivalent myth of recreation, expressed either as rebirth or resurrection, or as the return of the dead to life, providing an echo of the Eastern belief in transmigration or reincarnation. But nothing we have in our cultural tradition seems quite to equal the overwhelming power of the destructive and its inevitable and unending power of rebirth as do the Eastern mythical systems. They are not myths only, but systems of thought placing their myths in categories which give them a certain relativity to each other and make such absolute mythical systems as the stories of Genesis, the Olympian or Scandinavian Gods seem bigoted or infantile by comparison. For example, the eternal recurrence of the death and rebirth cycle is only one of four "kinetic ideas" which Eliade describes as bringing us "to the core of Indian spirituality:"

(1) The law of universal causality which connects man with the cosmos and condemns him to transmigrate indefinitely. This is the law of *Karma*.

(2) The mysterious process that engenders and maintains the cosmos and, in so doing, makes possible the "eternal return" of existences. This is *māyā*, cosmic illusion, endured (even worse—accorded validity) by man as long as he is blinded by ignorance, *avidya*.

(3) Absolute reality, "situated," somewhere beyond the cosmic illusion,

. . . and pure Being, the Absolute . . . the Self (*atman*), the transcendent, the immortal, the indestructible, *Nirvana.**

(4) The means of attaining Being, the effectual techniques for gaining liberation. This corpus means Yoga.[5]

From the very beginning it is man, not God who is the prime mover of his spiritual life and development, with some innate power to "appropriate another *mode of being* transcending the human condition. This is as much as to say that, for India, not only is metaphysical knowledge translated into terms of *rupture* and *death* ('breaking' the human condition, one 'dies' to all that was human); it also necessarily implies a consequence of a mystical nature: *rebirth to a nonconditioned mode of being*. And this is liberation, absolute freedom."[6]

Though asserted as from a position of unassailable logic, this formulation is very heady stuff, at least to Western minds. It has therefore tended either to be branded as mystical nonsense or else believed with fanatical devotion. But there is a growing band of Western people who are more cautiously accepting the challenge of ancient Hindu philosophy in an effort to see whether their own powers of spiritual comprehension can verify their attempts to rescue themselves from our kind of *avidya*. These philosophers, psychologists, religious historians, and members of the lay public have found in their own experience a meeting of East and West which arrives at some beginning of synthesis.

This movement began from the time of Schopenhauer's publication of *The World as Will and Idea* in the early part of the nineteenth century. Schopenhauer was one of the first Western philosophers to be influenced directly by knowledge of Eastern religions, specifically by Anquetil-Duperron's translation of the *Upanishads*. Schopenhauer described "will" as a blind creative urge essentially destructive and chaotic except where intellect can make some partial sense of it. He saw that human life is not just order and purpose, as other philos-

* See "The Death of Buddha," p. 216.

ophers and psychologists of the age of enlightenment had assumed. Jung tells us that Schopenhauer "brought an answer to the world which thousands had been obscurely groping for and for which they had looked to the empiricists in vain. This new note is the voice of human suffering."[7] We can verify this statement as being also true of Eastern philosophy, if we recall Eliade's description of *māyā,* where he says that the experience of such a cosmic illusion is also synonymous with suffering, which the ancient Hindus took as being the inevitable lot of human life in a state of *avidya.* The pessimistic nature of Schopenhauer's philosophy began to take on a brighter color as the nineteenth century turned into our own because, as Thomas Mann[8] so brilliantly shows, Schopenhauer's philosophy led to the discovery of that hidden reservoir of vital energy which psychologists opened with therapeutic intent to meet the suffering psyche of modern man.

First came Freud's conception of this vital source as the *libido,* with its pleasure-producing instincts derived from the general unconscious (Id) and after this his formulation of its self-inhibiting counter-instinct (death wish). Primarily a medical man, Freud naturally saw the unconscious as a combination of instincts which must, according to the rationale of this discipline, be eventually reduced to biologically verifiable entities. Jung, on the other hand, from a background of philosophy and psychiatry, originally saw the unconscious much as the Hindus had described *māyā;* as an interplay of the forces of destruction and creation, and in this sense, he saw what Schopenhauer had seen—that there is in modern Western man a fundamental split between the intellect and the blind will or unconscious. Later he viewed the unconscious differently and saw also that the libido, which implied an oversimplification of some sort of sex instinct, was part of a larger objective psychic dynamis, which he called psychic energy. Psychic energy was described as purposeful and capable of producing the effect of order from the otherwise chaotic contents of the unconscious.

What came to be seen chiefly by Jung was increasingly verified by other psychologists; namely that the unconscious contained archetypal images which promoted recreation and integration as well as destruction. This could be seen also as a natural rhythm of change, a process by which images of death were succeeded by images of rebirth in a cycle or series of cycles. This was not merely a repetition of life-affirming or life-denying instincts, but seemed, rather, to come from a definite source of energy whose flow was conditioned not by mere chance but by psychic necessity. Other characteristics of the unconscious which had long been known in Oriental and in ancient Greek philosophy became apparent. The tendency towards repetition carried with it the promise of "an eternal return of all things" (*apokatastasis*) and the tendency for one image or tendency to turn into its opposite and back again (*enantiodrama*). As a final stage in the development of these observations, it became clear that the "kinetic ideas," described by Eliade as constituting the core of Indian spirituality, also applied to the modern unconscious.

Besides the fateful determination of *māyā* there appeared to exist a principle capable of transcending the ignorance of the unconscious state and achieving, if only periodically, a state of *being in consciousness.* Jung spoke of a *transcendent function of the psyche,* capable of making unconscious contents accessible to consciousness, and of *the Self* as the center of a kind of awareness independent of the ego, arrived at by a process of individuation. And so, with the concept of individuation as a transformation of ego-consciousness into self-consciousness, the parallelism of modern psychology with Eastern philosophy became complete.

But the means of attaining this state of self-identity differed, as it still does, between the East and the West. In the East it was to be achieved by Yoga or Zen as a discipline for gaining spiritual liberation; in the West it has remained a psychotherapeutic procedure utilizing dream interpretation and the products of active imagination to attain self-realization on whatever plane of existence best seems to favor psychic health. Far from needing liberation or detachment, the Western "patient" or "analysand" needs to reexperience or to experience perhaps for the first time the phenomenal world in his own way, and this is individuating no less than liberation from the power of *māyā* would be. In other words, the ego has an essential place in the process of individuation as an evaluatory and discriminatory function.

There is also considerable difference between our Western conception of the Self and the Eastern conception of Atman. For the East the supreme ground of Being, Atman, is suprapersonal and completely transcendent, rendering its possessor capable of maintaining an attitude of selfless nonattachment to all wishes or compulsions of the ego. The Western Self, in contrast, is personal as well as impersonal. Through the ego it is attached to life in a meaningful and fateful way, while its transcendent aim relates it to the higher goal of individual differentiation from collective social patterns. In this sense individuation, therefore, involves the experience of conflict between the claims of the ego and the claims of the self. Resolution occurs only at the nodal points of life where harmony can be established between these two claims by the creation of a reconciling symbol which performs its work by joining in a totally spontaneous or unexpected fashion the images of attachment with images of what is liberating for a transcendent experience. In these significant moments a man may become, as Wordsworth says, "true to the kindred points of heaven and home."

III. DEATH AND REBIRTH
AS CYCLES OF NATURE:
THE DESCENT OF INANNA

Certain great myths have a universality of meaning for groups of people belonging to a given tribe
or traditional culture in a certain period of history. By culture contact these myths influence each other and may reflect
in the historical sense either a period of evolution or a period
of retrogression. Analytical psychology has shown that what
is true of myths in the collective sense is also true in the individual sense. A single person may step out of his culture
pattern at any time, producing dreams or acts which bring
again to life myths which might have been thought to be dead
or outgrown; and he too may show regressive trends. Kerényi
describes the basis of this spontaneous myth-forming tendency
in general; it is "a particular kind of material contained in
tales about gods and god-like beings, heroic battles and journeys to the underworld—'mythologem' is the best Greek word
for them—tales already well known but not unamenable to
further reshaping. Mythology is the *movement* of this material: it is something solid and yet mobile, substantial and yet
not static, capable of transformation."[1]

One of these great mythologems is told in the story of
the Sumerian goddess Inanna, more commonly known as the
Babylonian Ishtar. She descended to the underworld, the
land of No Return, experienced death, and achieved the im-

possible return to life again. This is the basic myth but there is also an important variant (pp. 20-24) . The chief characteristic of the variant to the descent of Inanna lies in the nature of her mission to the underworld. Here the journey is a kind of mystery in which Inanna accomplishes the quest of herself and emerges as one reborn from a symbolic sacrifice and death. In the Babylonian variant, we are told that the goddess went to the Land of No-Return to procure the life of her son-lover, Tammuz, he who yearly came to life in the springtime as a vegetation god and subsequently died again before his next renewal in a cycle which recurred endlessly year after year.

Fig. 1—The cow-headed Isis-Hathor watering the sacred grain from which the resurrected soul of Osiris arises. This emphasizes his transcendence of the nature cycle and the archetype of the Great Mother. From bas-relief at Temple of Isis at Philae, Egypt.

The yearly repetition of an event of this type is expressed also in the myth of Demeter and Persephone. During the winter months Persephone is imprisoned in Hades, during which time her mother is disconsolate, refusing to promote the birth or growth of all living things. The rest of the year, when mother and daughter are reunited, is characterized by abundant fertility. This also is the pattern of the mother goddesses and their son-lovers, Inanna and Tammuz, Isis and Osiris, Cybele and Attis, Aphrodite and Adonis. While the common denominator of all these myths is the death and yearly rebirth of the vegetation from which mankind in the ancient Near East drew sustenance, we may also perceive another older pattern, surviving in the Cretan Bronze Age culture, of a mother goddess of wild life, the Mountain Mother, later known as Artemis or Dea Artio, who was a kind of protectress of the hunt. She is shown in works of art surrounded by young male attendants, young men in arms who guard a holy child, the Kouretes with their future Kouros (leader) who was to become in later traditions Dionysos, Apollo, or even Zeus himself.

The element of sacrifice and sacrament, of dismemberment or immolation, which is so common in all the myths of the dying and resurrecting gods whether as youths or maidens, is reflected in Inanna's descent, by her willingness to make the sacrifice of the symbols of worldly power (her garments and jewels) during six or seven stages into the place of death. She is ready to risk all for an uncertain return to life reborn. What is chiefly remarkable is that the myth of rebirth never fails; the ravished daughter or the dead son-lover is always resuscitated: Inanna, though "turned into a corpse" and "hung from a stake," is always brought back to life. In this respect the mythologem of death and rebirth as sacrifice differs from the mythologem of death and rebirth as initiation, though they have many features in common. This will be discussed later on.

Besides the yearly vegetation cycle, these stories include

the human experience of a love-death which bears a strong likeness to the Hindu stories associated with Shiva or Kali. In these, the eternal recurrence of all things becomes an endless tapestry of destruction and creation in the preconscious or dreamlike world known as *māyā*. In this sense Inanna's descent is seen as a reenactment of this eternal drama; yet it also contains features of a shamanistic attempt to pierce the veil of *māyā* and experience a moment of truth beyond good and evil. Mankind in the dreamlike unconsciousness of the illusory world merely longs for the secret of eternal youth but is not prepared to die for it. Through the mother goddess' sacrificial act, so beautifully told in the Isis and Osiris myth where the mother gathers together the dismembered limbs* of her consort and brings life to them again, the unconsciousness of mankind is partially redeemed and its dissociated elements reintegrated. But this would not, *could* not, take place without some universal consent of collective man to experience the mythologem in its entirety. And so it is unquestionably true that there must have existed that ritual performance so liberally reported by Sir James Frazer in *The Golden Bough:* Throughout ancient Europe and the Near East those bands of wailing women must have roamed the countryside in early summer mourning for the dead Tammuz in an expression of the most vital religious impulse of its time. At Eleusis alone, we know the mysteries celebrating Demeter's recovery of the lost Persephone were enacted regularly for over 2000 years.

Dimly at first but more clearly as one continues to read these accounts, it becomes apparent that we must be dealing with a form of religious belief which places its whole value upon the mythologem of the mother-and-son or mother-and-daughter in a highly ambivalent relationship. Although love and devotion are the outward attitudes of these couples, the awful truth of their mutual destructiveness comes out all too plainly in the stories of the great mother-witches, Kali, In-

* See *Lemminkainen*, p. 121.

anna, or Hecate, who exult in destroying their loving victims and apparently see no inconsistency in again restoring them to life and love. Harding tells us specifically that Inanna brought about the death of Tammuz, although in other versions it is some mother surrogate. For example in the Greek myth "Adonis was killed by a bear, one of the animals sacred to Aphrodite, his mother . . . so that in the myth Adonis is really killed by one aspect of his own mother . . ."[2] But the horror of these stories is misleading. If there were not a symbolic dismemberment there could never be a reintegration of the old parts, and there would be no new life pattern to replace the old one grown anemic by feeding only upon goodness. Furthermore, the sacrifice is not always so castrating as it seems. In one version of the Tammuz myth the youth does not go to death as a sacrificial victim but as a conquering hero.

> Arise then, go, hero, the road of 'No-Return'—. . . .
> He goeth, he goeth, to the bosom of the earth—
> He will cause abundance for the land of the dead . . . .
> At the call of the Lord,
> (Go), hero to the distant land which is unseen.[3]

But there was a strong tribal resistance to the rites of the Great Goddess on the part of the ancient Jews, a singularly tough and highly religious pastoral people. It appears that the ritual of death and rebirth was outlawed from the religious conventions of the Jews, not because it was such a bloody business but because of its feminine changeableness and the fear of orgiastic sex associated with the popular rites of the Great Goddess. They accordingly referred to the great river valley civilizations as "the whore of Babylon" or "the flesh-pots of Egypt." Later we shall see that this proceeded not from any narrow prudery but from a different religious need in which the instincts of the mother and her repetitive compulsion of sacrifice could be sublimated to achieve a more permanent attitude of devotion to the Holy Spirit. Meanwhile it led to great inner tension, forcing a repression of those natural longings of Jewish patriarchal figures to bring the feminine principle of love into their religious life to soften the harsh law of obedience to the will of the Lord God (Yahweh). At least in earlier times before the Exodus they seem to have been aware of the sacrifice they had to make and to have given it veiled expression as a need for honoring somehow, in spite of everything they held ethically dear, the principle of death and rebirth.

This conflict and its resolution has been told with great psychological sensitivity in the Old Testament story of Joseph. Because he was especially dear to his father, Jacob, as Rachel's son Joseph was a mother's son in a family of father's sons (the brothers of Joseph were sons of the first wife, Billah). In re-telling this ancient story, Thomas Mann[4] has collected evidence for believing that the famous coat of many colors was really Rachel's wedding garment. For Joseph to possess this enraged his brothers much as a group of college students today would be enraged if one of their number appeared in women's clothes and expected to have his transvestitism accepted. But they presumably threw him into the pit, as it says, because of the deeper offense to the principle of patriarchy of which they were not quite sure enough themselves at this early stage of their tribal development. It might have meant that Jacob intended to give the first right of inheritance to a man who would establish a matriarchal tradition, which for them would embody the horror of incest. According to Mann, the symbolism of this event carries with it more than a suggestion of that ritual of dismemberment, a death followed by a re-birth which parallels the myth of Tammuz. Although there is no representative of the mother goddess in this story, her place is taken by Jacob's inner feeling for Rachel in that kind of psychological displacement so commonly found in people who have lost faith in the efficacy of a collective symbol and are reduced to finding its surrogate in a personal relationship. We are told how Jacob even feared lest the young Joseph might espouse the feminine principle before becoming a man, as if he realized his own inner weakness in this respect might come to the surface in his son.

When Joseph's lot was mitigated by his being sold into slavery, and he had become part of Potiphar's household in Egypt, the same pattern was repeated, this time in relation to Potiphar's wife, who embodied more appropriately the power of the doubtful feminine principle. More conscious of the danger to his masculinity, Joseph then acted from his patriarchal heritage and rejected her love (this, too, seen by Mann as the expression of a significant ritual act as well as of a personal problem). But he was none the less punished by coming as close as he did to her, and we are shown how a different form of punishment was also the same, mythically speaking. His being thrown into prison by Potiphar represented a second ritual death from which he then emerged as if reborn to be chief steward of Pharaoh, whose dream he had succeeded in interpreting correctly. This was the dream of the seven fat and seven lean kine corresponding to the seven years of abundance and the seven years of famine, which Neumann tells us points to the underworld journey of the soul. "The seven dwellings of the underworld are seven aspects of the Feminine, to whose sphere belongs Osiris, the moon, as lord, son and fecundator of the goddess. For this reason Chapter CXLVII of the Book of the Dead, the chapter of the seven houses, is followed by the chapter of the seven cows and their bull on which fertility depends . . ."[5] The parallel with the seven stages of Inanna's journey is obvious, and we can readily see how Joseph was conditioned in his responses to the events of his life by a secret knowledge of the feminine principle.

At this point the story of Joseph changes as one might imagine the mythologem of the Great Goddess to have changed in response to the influence of the growing religion of the Father. By saving his father and brothers from starvation and giving them a temporary home in Egypt, he restored his masculine identity as a product of his own tribal society. Yet because of his deviant life he had stepped out of the patriarchal line of inheritance as one of the children of Israel. Indirectly through Joseph, nevertheless, they had received the full benefit of his experience of death and rebirth through the power of the Great Goddess, however veiled.

At other points throughout the Old Testament, briefly in the Song of Solomon and especially the story of Ruth,* the feminine principle reappears as a valid image in its own right. In other cases, while there are exceptional women, there is no image of Woman strong enough to rescue womankind from second class citizenship in this society. What the story of Joseph so satisfactorily illustrates, however, is that the women do not necessarily suffer in this society, for they at least can experience the joys of giving birth to a new generation of real men, for which they receive abundant approval. It is the men who suffer from a loss of the capacity for inner renewal which the mysteries of Inanna or of Isis made available to all who felt moved to accompany her on her journey to the Land of No-Return and then return to a life renewed. For all those who had to foreswear this ultimate boon, the wish for deliverance had to be indefinitely postponed and became a longing for immortality, a resurrection in a life hereafter, made possible only by the future appearance of a "messiah," or savior who could reconcile the law of the prophets with the archetype of renewal. Finally in Christianity the father-son religion had to insist upon resurrection of the body as the only possible kind of survival, whereas the mother-son religion insisted upon rebirth in this life as the prototype for any future life to come.

Thomas Mann's retelling of an ancient story is an example of how any basic mythologem survives its time and place of origin and can come to life again with the right stimulus either from without or within. The story of Joseph can be retold today with a renewed meaning for the modern Christian, especially the Protestant, or for anyone who has

---

* I am indebted to Yehezchel Kluger for this observation elaborated in his seminar on The Book of Ruth given in San Francisco.

lived through the Puritan form of patriarchalism which in the nineteenth century gave rise to the philosophy of dialectical materialism with its implication that science combined with industry would provide the royal road to achieving all possible human satisfactions. This was constructed upon the solid foundation of the French Enlightenment in the eighteenth century when (during the French Revolution) the Goddess of Reason was enthroned in Notre Dame cathedral in Paris. Such a repression of the true spirit of the feminine in favor of a false-masculine intellectual ideal must eventually break out in a form of irrational moodiness as we see in modern neurotics suffering from this type of hypertrophy of the masculine superego. And so it did collectively after the eighteenth century in the Romantic Movement.

But liberating as this was in many ways, it overreached itself, becoming already somewhat past its prime before 1850. Then set in the industrial age with its Victorian prejudices and repressions and the feminine principle had no other way of expressing itself ultimately than in producing a new race of militant feminists who did not champion the real cause of the Great Goddess but merely her false-masculine rights. In response to this, men have reacted with pseudo-feminine pettiness or with the development of an estheticism which sought retrogressively to revive the lost feminine image. This state of affairs left us in the twentieth century with a confusion of identity which has increasingly made women doubt themselves as women and men as men.

It is this condition of a confusion of the sexes which modern psychologists find so prevalent and makes their work as therapists so sought after today. Freudianism first clarified this problem and then proceeded to obscure it again by assuming that the problem was a confusion of sexual (that is, genital) identity. The Jungian and neo-Freudian schools recognized this error and have to a considerable extent helped to correct it. But there is still a vast semiconscious prejudice that all psychological problems would be swept away if the sexual life

could be put in good working order. What is still not sufficiently known is that modern people are not suffering so
much from a confusion of sex as of gender,* and this is com-
plicated by the embarrassing fact that all men and women
capable of mature reflection upon their psychic constitution
discover they are basically two in one, male and female.

With this background perhaps we can see why a retelling
of the story of Joseph might have a new relevance in our time
since it shows a man who suffers from this very confusion as
to his gender and is forced through the circumstances of his
background and birth to have to acknowledge both sides.
Through the need to reconcile the conflict between them he
also discovers painfully at first, more gracefully as time goes
on, how the feminine image belongs within and is not to be
lived in action which would bring him harm or harm to
others. This knowledge would correct the one-sidedness of
the beautiful Tammuz who is the yearly victim of his too-
feminine beauty and never achieves heroic stature as a man.

It is unnecessary to present the case histories of modern
people in whom this identical problem is found since it has
been so thoroughly done by Jung and certain of his followers,[6]
but I should like to emphasize the particular point which has
relevance for our study of myths of death and rebirth. No one
can change his gender or even develop the other, undeveloped
half without experiencing some form of the death and rebirth
archetype by which change is made possible; and then one
does not remain just a vainglorious egotist straining to over-
compensate for feelings of inferiority. By some form of mythological reasoning, modern man appears to need to find his
feminine counterpart just as modern woman seeks again her
own appropriate self-image.

What of the masculine image for the woman; does she
need an appropriate masculine figure to promote her wel-
fare as men appear to need the feminine image? This ques-

* I am originally indebted to A. S. Gibb for this observation in *In Search
of Sanity*, Farrar & Rinehart, 1942.

tion is, I think, partially answered by the myth of Inanna, who is shown to be willing to accomplish the underworld journey to regain her masculine soul-image: "My god Damu," or "hero! son—my faithful lord . . . thou who (art) my heavenly light . . ." so chants an ancient hymn of lamentation for Tammuz. Although she knows the secret of the great round of destruction and creation and the mystery of giving birth, she does not know how to champion her cause in the realm of the spirit. For this she needs a hero, a god-man who can find his way toward the heavenly light and lead her to it.

In some such way I have come to understand that part of the Isis-Osiris myth in which the mourning Isis gathers the dismembered parts of Osiris' body from the ends of the earth to bring life to them again, but nowhere finds his generative organ, the phallus. For the accomplishment of the lower mystery too she needs a fruitful power of the masculine and, no matter how great she may become as a deity, she cannot conceive without the phallus.

In a symbolism which does justice to the biologically sexual phase of life but quickly transcends it, we find ithyphallic deities such as Thoth in Egypt or Hermes in Greece, as the spiritual messengers necessary to guide the souls of the dead to their resting place. And Thoth is the symbolic messenger of the life that has died to this world of material things or the illusion of *māyā* and seeks rebirth into the life of the spirit. As such he is the mediator between the masculine and feminine deities. In the account of an Egyptian magic spell* Isis calls upon Thoth to provide magic power to cure Horus, her son, from poisoning by his elder brother. Here she wants him restored to life not just as a son-lover (though a trace of this symbolism persists). She wants him not for herself but because she sees in him "the avenger of his father." Horus, we know, is the great Egyptian hero figure who slew the monster, Typhon, and so we see in this account the mythologem of the hero at one of the moments of its birth. Thoth comes

* See *The Death and Rebirth of Horus*, p. 107.

to the rescue as "the eldest son of Re with the command of Atum, the father of the gods." In the end he "lives for his mother" like Tammuz and all the fertility gods, but he is something more, a hero in his own right for ". . . Re in heaven vouches for him, his father watches over him" even while "the magic power of his mother is his protection."

Thus we see the mother goddess opening herself to the power of the youthful hero with willingness to give up her possessive power over the masculine. In so doing, as the prototype of every woman, she frees herself for an experience of the higher mystery of the masculine to bring something to her she could not find by herself. In the myth I have mentioned as well as in the truest form of the Demeter-Kore myth (in which the masculine principle is represented by a heroic youth called Triptolemus), we perceive a beneficent interaction between masculine and feminine. The masculine principle makes its impression upon the feminine without the goddess having to relinquish any of her loving maternal qualities. These mother goddesses, as Jane Harrison has observed, still maintain the full dignity of the feminine order of being, which in a later, more strongly patriarchalized period they lost, becoming "abject and amorous."[7]

It is at this point, I think, that we can see that we are talking about men as well as about women, and that for both the youthful hero represents the effective power of ego-consciousness to prevent regression to archaic modes of functioning and to ensure an evolving mythologem. This may mean progress in a historical sense, but it means almost the reverse where, instead of going upward into higher stratifications of Father worship, ego-consciousness must descend to the lower depths to obtain that secret wisdom of the feminine godhead embodied in such fearful manifestations as Ereshkigal, Queen of the Dead in Babylonian mythology, or the mysterious Turquoise Woman of the Navaho Indians. Here we find that a male deity or hero figure also may descend to recover a feminine consort and that later he too must lose his possessive power over her. We find this in the myth of Orpheus' descent to reclaim Eurydice from death.

Another, more basic, form of this myth comes from Japan where a primordial couple, Izanagi and Izanami, are separated by her (significantly!) sacrificial death.

Under the earth it is very dark; but Izanagi finally meets his wife and offers to bring her back with him. Izanami begs him to wait at the door of the subterranean palace, and not to show a light. But the husband loses patience. He lights a tooth of his comb and enters the palace where, by the flame of his torch, he perceives Izanami in process of decomposition. Seized with panic, he takes flight. His dead wife pursues him, but Izanagi manages to escape by the same way that he had gone down under the earth and casts a great rock down over the aperture. Husband and wife talk together for the last time, separated from each other by this rock. Izanagi pronounces the sacramental formula for separation between them, and then goes up to heaven; while Izanami goes down forever into the subterranean regions.[8]

Eliade then tells us, "She becomes Goddess of the dead and this corresponds to what is generally the case with chthonic and agricultural Goddesses, who are divinities of fecundity and, at the same time, of death, of birth, and of re-entry into the maternal bosom."[9]

Here we see a different dénouement since, unlike Inanna's descent which ends successfully in obtaining renewal of life for the dead Tammuz, the primal father does not resuscitate his dead wife. On the contrary, their separation was fatally intended to become absolute, which he acknowledges by pronouncing the "sacramental formula of separation." So there is symmetry between the two myths when we remember that the earth goddess as Inanna also had to give up her possive hold upon the image of her son-lover and become, like mother Isis, content to produce heroes who went their way and achieved an autonomy of the masculine. She then remained goddess of the chthonic depths of life as her husband became God of Heaven.

This polarity is basic to any conception of mythology, and

from such a vantage point we are permitted to see the myth-ologem of the Great Goddess in its true perspective viewed historically. Eliade wisely warns us, however, not to take "history" too literally. There was apparently a primordial state of being before hierogamy denoted by a single complete an-drogynous divinity or original oneness of being (Urmono-theismus) which corresponds to the cultures and religions of the food-gathering peoples (represented today in the oldest Australians, the Pygmies, the Fuegians).

When the means of existence changed, that is, when men had learnt how to hunt big game, and women had found out how to cultivate plants, the *Urkultur* gave birth to two more complex and clearly dis-tinct forms of society, the totemic society in which man was predomi-nant, and on the other hand the matrilocal and matriarchal society where women were predominant. It was in the latter that the worship of the Earth-Mother originated and reached its highest development. . . . We do not know whether the matriarchate ever existed as an inde-pendent cycle of culture—in other words, whether a certain stage in the history of mankind was ever characterized by the absolute ascendency of woman and by an exclusively feminine religion. It is more prudent to say that matriarchal *tendencies* or *predispositions* are manifest in certain religions and social customs. It is true that certain social struc-tures—for example, uterine descent, matrilocalism, the avunculate and gynaecocracy—show the social, juridical and religious importance of woman. But *importance* does not mean absolute *predominance*.[10]

From this historico-cultural viewpoint, we see that the Earth Mother was a very old divinity, but not the original divinity any more than the Sky Father was. Both representa-tives of femininity or masculinity were subject to an original primordial condition which was a "neuter and creative whole-ness." When therefore we reread the story of Inanna's descent without any Tammuz in view but only her own immolation and self-regeneration, can we hypostasize a condition wherein the feminine principle descends to its original condition without help of the masculine and sinking into its own depths becomes self-regenerative? The seven phases of her journey,

FIG. 2—Seven virgins being transformed from trees—a transformation of the cycle of nature to the human state.

at each stage of which she relinquishes the symbols of her conscious power, correspond to the phases of the moon which link her with a feminine awareness which penetrates more deeply into the unconscious world of prehistory than anything associated with agriculturally-oriented goddesses. Here the symbol is not that of a woman at all but the shell, the pearl, or the great sea snail. This is the quality of the feminine which achieves rebirth through its own intrinsic creativeness without any fecundating agent.

In China, the symbolism of the oyster denotes the "sacredness of the Moon." In the treatise *Lu shi ch'un ts'is* of the third century B.C., we read, "The moon is the root of all that is *yin;* when the moon is full, the *pang* and *ko* mussels are full; all *yin* things are abundant (waxing); when the moon is dark (the last day of the moon) the *pang* and *ko* mussels are empty." Mo-Tsi, of the fifth century B.C., after having observed that the pearl oyster *pang* is born without help of the male, adds: "Therefore, that the *pang* can at length bear the pearl* is because it concentrates wholly upon its *yin* force."

Besides being a talisman used in magic and medicine, the pearl played a part in Christianity and Gnosticism. "A tradition of Eastern origin explains the birth of the pearl

* See *The Hymn of the Robe of Glory*, p. 153.

as the child of lightning penetrating into a mussel, the pearl thus being the result of union between Fire and Water. St. Ephrem makes use of this ancient myth to illustrate the Immaculate Conception as well as the spiritual birth of the Christ in the baptism of Fire . . . and the pearl was the supreme Iranian symbol of the saviour."[12]

Thus we see that the creative power of the feminine spirit, as virgin, antedates or transcends the idea of hierogamy since it approximates the original "neuter creative wholeness" of the primordial state. Here extremes meet, since this is also the way of the savior through whom the human material state of being may be redeemed. In an absolutely unexpected reversal of the mythologem, rebirth leads to resurrection in an image of the pearl as a unifying symbol, embodying the paradox that the changeable feminine moon, in a process of transformation, becomes a symbol for the constancy of spiritual grace. In a text of pseudo-Macrobius, ". . . those who wear and possess the pearl will live and reign with the Christ for all eternity" (pp. 148-49). And, "In the famous Gnostic scripture, the *Acts of Thomas*, the quest of the pearl symbolises the spiritual drama of the fall of man and his salvation . . . the Pearl represents, on the one hand, the fallen soul of man in the world of darkness, and on the other, the 'Saviour saved' himself."

Perhaps it is not too bold a flight of the imagination to conjecture that this kind of talisman, as sacred vessel or precious stone originally associated with the original mystery of the feminine, but ultimately appropriated by the masculine to symbolize the highest type of spiritual insight, was in early medieval Europe known as the Holy Grail. And if so we continue to dream of its wonderful power of ensuring rebirth.

The relevance of this to our modern condition is clearly stated by Harding:

To us of the West these things are mysteries only dimly sensed. We cannot speak of them with certainty, but at the same time we cannot ignore the fact that modern poetry and art and the dreams of and fantasies of many people today agree with the religious teachings of the past. . . . They tell of a path for renewal which is new in our day but old in actual fact, a path of redemption through the things that are lowest, which is the fundamental teaching of the moon religions, and of the worship of the feminine principle.[13]

One of these ancient sources is not so much religious as philosophical and even psychological in its connotation of a highly pragmatic application of the feminine principle in the affairs of everyday life. This is the second hexagram of the *I Ching,* the Chinese *Book of Changes,* of which it says:

K'un. The Receptive.

This hexagram is made up of broken lines only. The broken line represents the dark, yielding, receptive primal power of yin. The attribute of the hexagram is devotion; its image is the earth. It is the perfect complement of *The Creative*—the complement, not the opposite, for the Receptive does not combat the Creative but completes it. It represents nature in contrast to spirit, earth in contrast to heaven, space as against time, the female-maternal as against the male-paternal. However, as applied to human affairs, the principle of this complementary relationship is found not only in the relation between man and woman but also in that between prince and minister and between father and son. Indeed, even in the individual this duality appears in the coexistence of the spiritual world and the world of the senses . . . .

The Judgement.

The Receptive brings about sublime success
Furthering through the perseverance of a mare.
If the superior man undertakes something and tries to lead,
He goes astray;
But if he follows, he finds guidance . . . .
Quiet perseverance brings good fortune.[14]

IV. PERSONAL ENCOUNTER: THE WISDOM OF THE SERPENT

We have seen in the preceding sections how an archetypal image associated with a tradition of religious thought existing thousands of years ago at a great geographical distance can influence and even transform a whole philosophy. But this diffusion of a spiritual tradition could not take hold in an alien culture if people were not ripe for its reception. It is precisely this readiness of modern man to receive the wisdom of the ancient East or the ancient cultures of the Mediterranean West which so quickly transferred it from philosophy into psychology and helped transform psychology from an intellectual movement into a therapeutic movement which could touch the lives of actual people. In turn, it was from the unconscious depths of such ordinary people that the new knowledge gained its true sanction and found its indigenous direction in Western culture. And we are still learning.

The archetype of death and rebirth has become in our time a kind of touchstone for the understanding of certain important psychological experiences of which I should like to present a brief example. In my psychiatric practice I have frequently noticed that when people have what is called euphemistically "a breakdown," this term is a mild reference to what feels to the patient like a death. Still more euphemistically we say such a person is "sick." None of our terms goes the whole way as they would if they did justice to the condition from which such people suffer.

I was once forced to hospitalize a patient, not because she was insane but because of an unalterable conviction that she was going to die. In trying to understand what she meant by death I gradually found that death meant to her fear of losing her mind. Being in a hospital was important to her because if she was going to go mad this was obviously the place to do it, where no one would be shocked by such things. Up to this time she was quite rational in her description of herself as one who needed psychiatric care, but her delusion that she was going to die introduced a new element which both horrified and fascinated her. I was inclined to think she was right in equating fear of death with fear of insanity and that the sheer logic of her conviction was forcing her into a state of schizophrenic dissociation which could lead to the destruction of the integrity of her ego. But the expected dissociation did not occur. Instead she went on thinking she was going to die, and this was so real that the hospital attendants noticed the physiological symptoms of such fear, rapid pulse, sweating, etc., far beyond the usual neurotic symptoms of anxiety. And so in her symptom complex she experienced for many weeks all the horror of Shiva-the-destroyer or confrontation with the Queen of the Dead without any mitigation except during occasional periods of sedation.

During the period of hospitalization this patient passed out of my care temporarily. I did not see her again for several months until she again came to consult me to understand better what she had passed through. She was quite well again, but with a wary attitude toward the unconscious and toward anything which might arouse a condition of emotional stress. She feared music especially which might evoke the dangerous mood she had passed through of feeling that everything was in a state of dynamic movement, perpetually changing from one aspect to another. I asked what had happened to the mood of death in which I had last seen her, and she replied this had passed when one day she could let herself die, figuratively speaking. It had been a kind of letting go, a diving into the depths until she hit the bottom, and then she said she had been able to come up again and after that she could come back to life. She felt like a different person, one who has been not just renewed but changed in the process, and because this change was so new she felt the need of holding onto it with great care lest it get away from her.

In the light of these happenings it became quite fruitful to review her dream and fantasy material preceding her breakdown, and there we found a most accurate picture of the whole process, of all she had to go through in symbolically dying and then being reborn. The subject of death was foreshadowed by a powerful dream in which she was threatened by attack from a white cobra. The bite of a poisonous snake is a frequent symbol for the fear of death or insanity or both, and this was, as we have seen, the dual fear of this woman.

Most snakes representing death also represent the souls of the dead, and they are only dead to this life; they live a heightened and more important life in the other world to which they have retreated. As such, they are the ghosts or ancestral figures, or mythical, primal titanic men who walked the earth in former times. Although impersonating death in its ghostly aspect, they are also the harbingers of that life which springs anew from the original source of all things. It is significant that these men are represented as being white like the dream cobra, not black as the most appropriate shade with which to represent death. This white is an ambiguous color and would seem to embody just that spirit of paradox which is the essence of the death and rebirth experience, as if to indicate that white is black as life is death and death is life renewed. Because the experience of death and rebirth is so unified, so immediate and so unique, it seems as if the imagery of dreams does not know how to represent it at first except as the simultaneous conjunction of two opposites. A black snake is what my patient or I would have been most likely to expect to represent the experience of the death she was to undergo; but the dream says it is not black but white, as though to predict that this would be the kind of death which would end in rebirth.

Nonetheless the dream snake was quite sinister enough, and there was no doubt that this albino was sacred in its deadliness, something to avoid if possible. Although not actually bitten by the snake, the woman felt she had come close to that kind of death dealt out by the ancient Erinys or Furies, which is like madness. In so doing both she and I understandably failed to recognize at first its possible transforming power.

The next stage was represented by fantasies and dreams showing my patient's wish to submit uncritically to the archetypal powers of the unconscious which she represented in a series of colored pictures. In one she is represented as a leaf floating on a serpentine stream; in another she is seen as a completely passive naked girl suspended in foaming water in a U-shaped container, which was without visible walls, the whole apparently floating in a deep blue watery medium, with nothing to protect her from dissolving into it. This was followed by a picture called *The Mirror,* in which a circular design of all colors blending with each other in a confusing way was surrounded by a circular frame composed of two interlacing serpents, yellow and green. From experience, I have found that green and yellow as colors represent the fruitfulness of nature and here they show the tendency of the sinister whiteness of death to be transformed into a life-giving image. The many colors, radiating from a central point and mingling with each other, provided an iridescence of color characteristic of the state of rebirth at its moment of inception. In alchemical lore this is referred to as *the peacock's tail,* or iridescence of color seen in the black chaotic original substance in the alembic as this turns by heat into the next stage of the great work.

The change from black or white to all-colors represents

the change from death to new life, according to the alternation found in the cycle of nature in its archetypal form. In
turn this means that what was dead comes alive if it receives
the appropriate treatment in the appropriate container. Psychologically, we see this symbolism repeated whenever a
person in a state of despair or depression or the fear of dissociation can trust the container provided by the therapist
until this change can come about (*Deo concedente,* as the
alchemist insists). It was in this case my patient's doubt and
my own early lack of knowledge of symbolism which made
it impossible for us to contain the whole process until it could
undergo a transformation sufficient to rescue her from the
terrors of the unconscious, and we had to fall back upon the
mental hospital. But in the end the unconscious symboliza-
tion itself provided an archetypal container sufficient to carry
her across the danger point, and this image then provided me
with that measure of hope which ultimately allowed me to
reassure her that she would come back to safety and to sanity
again. This was a dream of a raft of serpents intertwined like
a wicker lattice upon which she could rest.* In contrast to
the threatening cobra, these snakes provided a platform of
security over and above the engulfing waters as though that
same symbol which initially appeared to destroy life here
serves the function of preserving it.

The snake as a symbol of rebirth following death is an
ancient, yet ever-present conception which can be traced
through endless patterns of sculpture, painting, verse, and the
myths of gods, demi-gods, or heroic mortals. This is so because
during its yearly period of hibernation the snake sheds its skin
and reappears as if renewed. The wisdom of the serpent, which
is suggested by its watchful lidless eye, lies essentially in mankind's having projected into this lowly creature his own secret
wish to obtain from the earth a knowledge he cannot find in

---

* See *The Disappearance of Quetzalcoatl,* p. 162, for reference to a raft
of serpents. This whole myth is a myth of initiation, in which death is represented by sleep or drunkenness or sacrifice (as of breaking the flutes), while
rebirth is represented by the quest for everlasting life.

waking daylight consciousness alone. This is the knowledge of death and rebirth forever withheld except at those times when some transcendent principle, emerging from the depths, makes it available to consciousness.

For this reason, analytical psychology postulates the existence of a transcendent function of the psyche which has the power to relate contents of the unconscious to consciousness in a healing symbol. This is less likely to be represented by the poisonous rattler or cobra than by the harmless green tree-

FIG. 3—An early Greek representation of Hermes with his pointed cap, caduceus, and rod, performing his ritual function as guide or leader of souls. This means he is the master of initiation from life to death or from death to life. Terra-cotta vase, Attic.

snake which is coiled around the staff of Aesculapius, Greek god of healing, and so has continued into our own day as a sign representing the medical profession. The green and yellow snakes entwined around the mirror in my patient's fantasy appear to denote this healing principle from nature which replaced the lethal cobra of her original dream.* The mirror itself was born out of a need of the unconscious psyche to present her with a healing image, and the many colors shone forth as the iridescent coloring might show on a spinning gramophone record in the sunlight. What was in itself dark and opaque became in this case illumined by that special light once called by Paracelsus the light of nature (*lumen naturae*).

The first phase of this woman's experience was therefore symbolized by the cobra which brought the certainty of death in a psychological sense; the second phase was symbolized by the healing serpents of rebirth. But this second phase, though immensely reassuring and intoxicating, was also felt by my patient to be unreliable, emotionally unstable, and she feared returning to it much as a Hindu Yogin would fear to be swallowed again by his own desirousness into the eternal succession of deaths and rebirths, the endless return of all things in the state of ignorance known as *māyā,* the eternal illusion of nature. Having seen beyond the limits of this world, he seeks to transcend it in the attainment of a superior consciousness leading to nonattachment from all we mean by the interplay of opposites given in the realm of the collective unconscious. And so in this woman's fantasy the raft of serpents on which she lay could carry and then transport her to her condition of change where she hoped to consolidate her newly won self-awareness. But in what specific psychological sense was she changed?

It is almost impossible to describe such a change without

* See following pages for reference to the lethal or transforming power of the serpent:

seeming to reduce it to an utterly banal occurrence. If I were to say her change occurred as a prelude to the menopause and that she was freed to give up some biological clinging to youth for the sake of acquiring some degree of detachment and inner security, this would be true but it would merely provoke a reaction of indifference appropriate to any psychological reduction. When ten million women are going through the same experience, one woman's experience of the change of life hardly seems worth singling out for special comment. Yet if one does manage to understand one single person's experience on a significantly impersonal level, its nature may be clarified far more intensively than it could be in compiling the statistical report of a multitude. In this case her change lay in the ability to see in her transition from maturity to late middle age a revival and recapitulation of an earlier transition from girlhood to early maturity. It was like growing up again and learning to shed that fear of death which is really a fear of life. But in this second period of transition a new element appeared which tested her faith much more strongly than the first. Instead of a symbolic death leading to real life, she was now faced with the need to affirm a life leading to real death. Hence the need for an experience of transcendence in which her fears for the safety of her personal ego might be liberated for an experience of the Self (Brahman Atman).

The raft of entwined serpents suggests this kind of transcendence much as the Naga serpents of India or the caduceus of Hermes in ancient Greece represent the original source of all intuitive wisdom of psychic life. This is not synonymous with the highest liberation of the master Yogis for whom the symbol of transcendence is conveyed by the wild gander. The snake is the root of this power still contained in the unconscious. Insofar as it becomes conscious, it implies no certain knowledge but only an intuition of liberation for the suffering ego emerging from the coils of illusion in the world of blind passion, and so is a kind of hermetic finger pointing the way to some sort of spiritual salvation.

Common both to my patient's memory of her early experience of emergence from girlhood to maturity and to her present experience is the symbol of rebirth with its paradoxical meaning, death-in-life or life-in-death, comprising one archetypal event which makes the transition possible. The psychological impact of this experience would not be complete, however, without mentioning one thing, seemingly very ordinary, but absolutely indispensable if rebirth is to be any more than a psychic inflation. This is the simple variety of human feeling which knows how to love life in a new way, with the capacity to suffer meaningfully while the change takes place. Here the great danger would be that the transition be made too abruptly. One sees this in manic-depressive insanity where a meaningless period of depression changes suddenly into gloriously intoxicating euphoria, which is, however, arrived at without any transitional period through which suffering leads meaningfully to a more permanent reaffirmation of the life to come.

V. INITIATION
AS A SPIRITUAL EDUCATION

We have seen that the ultimate triumph of new life over death which is associated with the Great Goddess may be extended also to the myth of the hero at its inception. The youthful Horus, Heracles, Theseus, Siegfried, or Balder, whatever his name or homeland, is successful in overcoming the powers of darkness and emerges as one victoriously reborn at the moment of the rising sun. But as that same sun must set in the afternoon, so the hero-figure must die and his hope of permanent apotheosis be frustrated in the end. I have suggested that this may denote psychologically the transitory power of ego-consciousness over the inertia of the collective unconscious, wonderful beyond measure at the beginning of each new phase of development, especially through childhood into maturity, but quite unreliable when it comes to providing the consciousness of a process of individuation, which is so necessary for living the second half of life appropriately. To put it another way, the heroic mode of behavior at any age, having accomplished its purpose of helping the ego to overcome the negative force of unconsciousness, is superseded by another myth and another pattern of behavior whereby consciousness of ego is transformed into consciousness of self.

This transformation is made possible by a special archetype which is known in various outer manifestations as the rites of passage[1] appropriate for traversing each stage of essential development throughout life. Nor does it stop there. From the earliest sources of knowledge concerning the ritualistic behavior of prehistoric man, we find evidence of rites of passage performed to conduct the souls of human beings (and totem animals) into death as well as to initiate the young into life. It is not surprising then to find the essence of this rite expressed in a unique myth of death and rebirth, the whole mythologem of which illustrates the archetype of initiation.

FIG. 4—An initiation ordeal as a ritual operation with the initiate lying on a couch in a cave, the master of initiation standing over him, and a kneeling figure as a prayerful attendant behind. Outside we see an archer and a dog suggesting the guide and protector of the underworld journey. The seven-pointed star stamps the ritual as an initiation. Neo-Assyrian seal.

We have already made some acquaintance with the archetypal pattern in the ritual journey of Inanna to the underworld in the seven stages of her sacrificial descent. Seven is the number most commonly associated with initiation, a number seeming to denote the steps or stages of an inner, as opposed to an outer, journey. Initiation is derived from the Latin *in ire,* "to enter into,"[2] and therefore primarily denotes a temporary withdrawal from outer actions, especially adventures of the heroic sort. Submission is the characteristic of initiation, but it is not apathy or weakness; it contains a strong element of the archetypal "trial and strength" carried over from the heroic phase of life. This is exemplified in the symbol of the seven stages represented as seven rungs of a ladder leading to Heaven, so that the journey may be an ascent as well as a descent. As Inanna's descent represented an initiation into the secrets of the underworld as Great Mother, so ascent was made possible by the creative act of a Great Father (Father Enlil of the "great above") who made the earth-men (*Kurgarru* and *Kalaturru*) capable of transmitting to the corpse of Inanna the food and water of life (*pulhu* and *melammu*).

As I have previously indicated we should not, however, consider that initiation always implies success in reaching the goal of its descent or its ascent. By its very nature it is highly doubtful. The way is precarious and as in the stories of Gilgamesh, Gawain, and other famous initiants the trial is one which initially fails (*initiation manqué*). There are no certain goals in sight. Eliade tells us "In a number of cases the original meaning of the climb—symbolic ascent to Heaven—seems to have been lost, yet the rite continues to be performed, for the memory of celestial sacrality remains even when the Celestial Beings have been completely forgotten."[3] And so it is also the other way round. Initiation to the underworld is often symbolized by a swallowing monster. Nothing may be said about a Mother Goddess in the puberty initiations, but the novices are nevertheless ritually tortured (that is, symbolically dismembered) as an expression of initiatory death, with the implied goal of spiritual transmission.

Leaving aside the question of initiatory ascent, and its connection to shamanism and to Yoga, let us examine in detail some of the commoner initiatory symbols of descent and return to life. Certainly in the practice of modern psychotherapy we are struck with the very frequent theme of descent associated with passing a test which allows the patient, in dream or fantasy, to cross a threshold presumably from the world of his conscious life to the unconscious in a meaningful way for the cure of some psychoneurotic disorder. I have already spoken of the snake as a particularly significant symbol for the life of the unconscious. In its sinuous, unpredictable movement it frequently illustrates the indirect, non-rational approach to the unconscious, most necessary if anything new is to be learned. A patient of mine, at the beginning of an analysis which promised to take her quite deep, saw in a dream a snake intricately coiled like an endless knot lying on the ground in the path she was about to take down a mountainside. It seemed to me to configure the archetypal symbol of the labyrinth of which so many fascinating examples have been recovered from prehistoric rock paintings and modern stone-age ritual practices still employed in the initiation rites.

In John Layard's *The Malekulan Journey of the Dead,** we see a remarkable parallel to Inanna's descent in the encounter of the initiate with a Female Devouring Ghost, Le-Hev-Hev, suggestive of the terrible Ereshkigal. But instead of a total sacrifice of identity, the Malekulan initiate must keep his wits about him in order to pass the remarkable test which Le-Hev-Hev sets for him at the entrance to the cave where life meets death.

She has drawn with her finger, in the sand, a geometric figure, and she sits beside it, waiting for the dead man† to come. He sees her from a distance. He is confused at the sight of her, and loses his way. When he regains his path and approaches the Devouring Ghost, she rubs out half the design. The dead man must know how to complete it. If he succeeds he passes through the lines of the geometric design into the Cave. If he does not succeed, he is devoured by this terrible ghost. Figure 5 is an illustration of the design she draws, which natives of these islands also draw sometimes in the sand; it is called "The Path," which might better be translated, "The Way." . . . Figure 6 is from a neighboring island. . . .

The significance of this ancient symbolism for a modern individual was borne out in the fact that my patient was suffering from a negative mother-complex[5]: Her approach to the unconscious presented her with the fear of being devoured or strangled by the snake and of having to pass a special sort of test similar to the Malekulan native's test for guessing the

* See p. 140.
† Symbolic of the initiate.

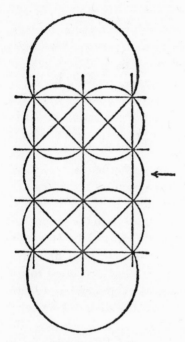

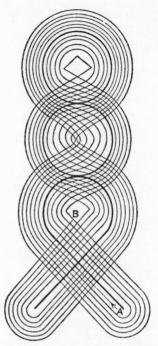

FIG. 5—"The Path" or "The Way." This is the design drawn in the sand by the Female Devouring Ghost. The figure consists of a single continuous line drawn around a framework of straight lines. As soon as the dead man approaches, the Devouring Ghost rubs out half the design, which the dead man must complete before he can pass through the middle of the sand-tracing in the direction indicated by the arrow. South West Bay, Malekula.

FIG. 6—"The Path" or "The Way." In this design, the dark line indicates the frame-work. The continuous line begins at *A* and ends at *B*. Oba Island.

other half of the labyrinthine design presented by Le-Hev-Hev. This dream came some time after she had very satisfactorily resolved her personal problems with her actual mother so it was clear that her crossing of this threshold had to do with an initiation into a region of the psyche hitherto unknown to her, having been masked by an overpersonal preoccupation with negative feelings toward her mother and mothers in general. Thus in the end, passing the initial test and finding "the Way" beyond the symbolic labyrinth brought her into a place of inner self-containment she had never been able to achieve previously. Instead, she had sought ways of proving herself in the heroic mode. This had led to a falsification of her feminine nature which therefore needed the correction of initiation to acquaint her with the deeper experience of her womanhood.

The experience of the labyrinth, whether as a pictorial design, a dance, a garden path, or a system of corridors in a temple, always has the same psychological effect. It temporarily disturbs rational conscious orientation to the point that, like the Malekulan "dead man" at the sight of Le-Hev-Hev, the initiate is "confused" and symbolically "loses his way." Yet in this descent to chaos the inner mind is opened to the awareness of a new cosmic dimension of a transcendent nature.

Just inside the west portal entering the nave of Ely Cathedral in England there is, set in the stone, a large mosaic designed as a maze. I myself once followed this maze, slowly walking through it in and out or following it with my eyes from beginning to end with the striking discovery that my mental threshold was lowered, not just through dizziness, but in such a way that when I emerged from out the maze I could respond more naturally, more genuinely to the beauty of the great church beyond. While this is but a reminiscence of the ancient patterns of death and rebirth enacted in the ritual dances of antiquity or in contemporary tribal societies, its message is still authentic when it comes with a sense of renewal from within.

In the dream of a modern businessman, accustomed to approaching life in a practical, highly rational manner,[6] a steam roller was describing an intricate design which the man later drew. He depicted a beautiful labyrinthine pattern ending in a central spiral describing four intricate curves at the four symmetrical corners. Here we see that a ponderous mechanical and highly limited rational function, symbolized by the steam roller, is being converted to provide this man with the visual and emotional conception of a different, much more flexible attitude to life. Far from being a chaos which was disturbing to consciousness, it provided a new sense of order and harmony.

Naturally such psychic events seldom take place spontaneously. It is significant that these two individuals so far mentioned were enabled to approach the experience of such a rite of passage because they were in relation to a therapist to whom they could entrust a part of the leadership and responsibility for traversing the dangerous threshold without undue peril. But it would be a great mistake to think that this would be solely due to the therapist's personal influence, no matter how skillful, if he did not receive a special kind of transference from his patient. The leader or guide is therefore the next figure in the symbolism of the initiation archetype which now concerns us. We met him also in the myth of Inanna's descent as Ninshubur, to whom she says,

"O, thou who are my constant support,
My messenger of favorable words,
My carrier of true words,
I am now descending . . . .
Fill heaven with complaints of me . . . ."

And at the end it is to Ninshubur that she gives greatest credit for her return, he who

"Rushed about for me in the house of the gods . . . .
He brought me to life."

This role which has been carried traditionally by the priest is today frequently bestowed upon the psychiatrist as analyst in the language of dreams. I have been represented as a chauffeur, the leader of an archaeological expedition, the conductor of an orchestra, and the one who formulates something, a lecturer or teacher all in the spirit of this "messenger of favorable words." As a dentist, doctor, medicine man, male nurse, or priest I may be represented in the role of healer implying that an ordeal to which the dreamer has submitted is brought to a climax in a healing ceremony whether of a practical secular nature or as an act of spiritual enlightenment. The reader will no doubt be able to supply from literature and drama many more examples of this figure acting as an intermediary between the suffering initiate and his experience of the death which may or may not lead to a rebirth; for example, the role of Thoth in the myth of Isis and Horus, Virgil in the *Divina Commedia* as the guide to Dante, Hermes as the guide of Aeneas in the *Aeneid,* Heracles as messenger to the underworld in the *Alcestis.* It was not unintentional that T. S. Eliot patterned Reilly, the psychiatrist in *The Cocktail Party,* upon this aspect of Heracles as a semiheroic, trickster-figure enabled by his mercurial nature to act as mediator between the two worlds, conscious and unconscious. As we trace him back to more primitive levels we find him represented as the tribal medicine man identified with the animal as totem, who is known, whether in animal or human garb, as Master of Initiation.

It is this figure who prepares the way for the initiate by explaining, or in some other way indicating to him the probable stages through which he must pass to accomplish his initiation. As Van Gennep has so clearly shown, the basic ceremonial pattern represents a complete cycle of change beginning with a "rite of separation," going on to a "rite of transition," and ending with a "rite of incorporation." We have already described a type of separation rite in which the Malekula native's experience of the labyrinth separates him as "dead man" or as initiate from his former life and we have discussed partially its psychological meaning. The separation rite as a threshold experience is frequently symbolized as the act of passing through a door. "Therefore to cross a threshold is to unite oneself with a new world. It is thus an important act in marriage, adoption, ordination, and funeral ceremonies."[7] Accordingly these rites are described as "preliminal." As such they are accompanied by acts of purification of which the famous prototype in our Christian culture is baptism for which the archetypal master of initiation is John the Baptist, whose ecclesiastical representative is the bishop, priest, or clergyman. In the North American Indian Plains Tribes we find this phase represented by the sweat bath and by fasting and abstaining from sexual intercourse. All this emphasizes the need to transfer attention from outside, that is, profane, matters to inward, sacred images which may then take on the character of therapeutic agents. Frequently these are represented as therapeutic agents of monumental proportions, sometimes frightening enough to have to be appeased, or at least honored. They are "guardians of the threshold" as in Egypt and Assyria, where they are represented by winged dragons and sphinxes or as the more beneficent yet fiery, lionlike dogs, the Kilins, of Chinese temple entrances or exits.

In the dreams of modern people we also see these phenomena represented in the symbolism of "sliding into" a body of water, in which there may lurk threatening fish or snakes, or in the depths of which there may be felt to lie some precious talisman, like Gilgamesh's plant of immortality. Or it may be represented simply by the life-giving water itself as symbolic of the longing for deliverance. This is a kind of healing power such as Gawain or Parsifal brought to the sufferings of the Fisher King and the whole order of nature reduced to sterility in the Waste Land. The role of master of initiation in the Grail myths is divided between the sibyl and the ferryman, much as Gilgamesh's approach to initiation is aided by Siduri, the divine bar-maid "who dwells by the edge of the sea," and who directs him to the boatman Urshanabi. Thus he was conducted to the place of initiation where he experienced an incubation sleep induced by an archetypal pair, Utnapishtim and his wife.

Thus we see that purification or lustration goes over into

the symbolism of initiatory death as a kind of ritualized drowning. So, as in the traversal of the labyrinth, there is brought about that particular loss of ego-consciousness necessary for any fundamental change to take place. The initiate who enters "the gates of sleep" may undergo "a sea-change." The change itself becomes a new and important test which ushers in the period of transition. The symbolism of a return to the prenatal condition, so abundantly suggested in the composite idea of the labyrinth (intestines, birth canal, umbilical cord, etc.) and water (water of death or water of life as amniotic fluid), vanishes from sight and the evidence of rebirth becomes apparent. This is dramatically represented in the initiation rites of primitive people where boys, after the rites of purification and the ordeal of ritual death (as circumcision or some other type of mutilation), are fed on milk as if they were babies, then given new clothes and names as befitting their reborn state. Gilgamesh, after his sleep, "washed his long hair clean as snow in water . . . threw off his pelts that the sea might carry them away . . . replaced the band around his head with a new one . . ." etc.

At this point, the characteristic initiate upon the simplest cultural level we know, i.e., of the food-gathering peoples, is answerable to no one but himself; a visionary animal or plant or other talisman replaces the master of initiation. This has been described as a tutelary or guardian spirit to be cherished and obeyed from thence forward; in return, the youth will be given super-normal powers, whether in running or in gambling or in hunting or in becoming just simply a man. Such primitive folk are without any Celestial Beings or any complex culture-pattern associated with property or prestige which must be guarded and fought over. It is enough that they should become men and live successfully within the modest opportunities for achievement open to them as individuals, in an otherwise totally communal, undifferentiated group. But the men of higher cultures associated with family life expect a great deal more of society and also more of themselves. Accordingly, they have an increasing fear of failure to maintain the original vision of their own uniqueness.

The dream of a young man reflects this series of initiatory events in modern terms as a need to emerge from dependence upon society and discover the animal guardian spirit as a symbol of his unique quality as an individual. He dreamed he was leaving "the king's yacht" where he had lived in a favored but wholly passive condition. This represented the protection of his family and more recently the projected idea of a similar security in relation to me as his therapist. The dream marked a need for him to become more assertive and directive in his treatment as in his life as a whole. The next scene of the dream showed him riding a spirited horse which he associated with the heroic attitude of youth to throw caution aside and risk himself in some kind of adventure. But the horse did not carry him to heroic adventures but into a strange wild landscape where he encountered an elephant. This was no ordinary elephant but a sacred animal possessing a secret wisdom the dreamer wished to learn. This pertained to some knowledge of transformation and healing. He felt no ambition for heroic achievement in relation to this creature such as he had felt in relation to his horse, but an experience of submission to a power greater than himself. This would, he felt, have the power of changing him from a dependent or self-seeking egotist to a mature man with an individual capacity to judge what should belong to group adaptation and what should belong to himself alone. His main concern upon waking from this dream was how to foster this image until it should be strong enough to become operative in his actual life. He also sensed that he might have to lose it many times before finding it in any final sense and that, like his primitive brothers, he would have to repeat this initiatory "rite of vision" to recover it.

We can see in this dream, abbreviated as it is from the point of view of mythical stories of the same kind, an example of the "rite of separation" (leaving "the king's yacht") followed by the "rite of transition" (riding the spirited horse) and ending in the "rite of incorporation" (the elephant whose power of transformation was to be acquired).

How these images of uniqueness are found and lost and found again is a favorite subject of myth and legend. If told from the shamanistic viewpoint associated especially with the hunting tribes, we get a story in which the tutelary spirit is a sacred animal; if from the viewpoint of the agricultural and pastoral tribes, we get such myths as the Grail, in which a talisman is a mysterious cup or stone considered to be a magical food-producing object.

A pathetic story of the failure of initiation, probably dating from the period of transition between the primitive food gatherers and the early hunting tribes with their aggressive ambitions, is told in the story of *O-pe-che, the Robin Redbreast.** In his overweening ambition to obtain a powerful guardian spirit for his son, this father defeated his son's effort to achieve his own visionary goal. Had he left the boy to his own devices, he either would or would not have felt motivated to experience the rite of vision to obtain a tutelary spirit. He could not in any case produce such an image to please his father's ambition. How often in modern psychiatric practice we see this sad young person who has had to escape into dreamland to get away from too much life with father.

The failure of initiation at the end of the great epic where Gilgamesh tries to keep the plant of immortality for his own personal rejuvenation is a variation of this theme.† Still too strongly the hero figure drunk with his glorious successes, but inconsolable for the loss of his introspective other half, the natural man Enkidu, he is ambitious to achieve immortality only in the outward physical sense. Utnapishtim, the wise old man, recognizes this danger and even in the incubation sleep is mistrustful of Gilgamesh's motive for undergoing initiation. "Deceitful is mankind, he will try to deceive thee," he says to his wife, and instructs her to bake a loaf of

* See p. 181.
† See p. 143.

bread for each night of Gilgamesh's sleep. There are seven loaves altogether, which we can now recognize as pertaining in some way to the seven stages of initiation *as an inner process.* Will he get the point? No, when he awoke,

> Gilgamesh said to him, to Utnapishtim the Distant:
> "Hardly did sleep spread over me
> When quickly thou didst touch me and rouse me."
> Utnapishtim said to him, to Gilgamesh:
> ". . . count the loaves of bread!
> The days which thou didst sleep may they be known
>   to thee. . . ."

His initiation sleep therefore had no content, no revealing image, no mystery for him. Yet those loaves of bread baked by the demigoddess, who with her husband had survived the great flood, must have contained something like the fecundity of Mother Nature as a much more nourishing symbol for the content of initiation than the plant of immortality which he later found only to lose again immediately before tasting. In a psychologically just peripeteia, the plant of immortality becomes too slippery for acquisitive fingers to grasp and falls back, swallowed by the snake, into the unconscious depths whence it came in the first place. Only at the very end does Gilgamesh seem to realize his mistake, his sin of *hubris,* and the corresponding deceit Utnapishtim suspected in him. The snake got the plant of immortality and thereby gained the secret he should have had of immortality as rebirth.

> . . . sloughing its skin on its return.
> Then Gilgamesh sat down and wept,
> His tears flowing over his cheeks . . .
> . . . .
> "For myself I have not obtained any boon.
> For the earth-lion have I obtained the boon . . ."

What is required of the true initiate is courage, humility, and purity of heart, all of these qualities together seeming to stand for the awareness of self as infinitely more valuable than the possessive demands of the ego. Yet it is not required, even would be quite wrong, for the initiate to achieve sainthood or any kind of divinity. Scorning inflation he thus remains true to his own human identity, however enlightened or successful he may be in his quest. For this reason we see in the true story of initiation a model for the process of individuation, since it combines in right measure the claims of the ego and the claims of the Self.

Throughout the many versions of this mythologem, therefore, we find the same conditions as in the story of *Nachiketas*,* showing a coward's rare quality of courage and humility in confronting Yama, the god of Death, wherefrom he received the mysterious knowledge of Self.

But after all this preparation, what then, we may well ask, is the mystery; can we penetrate its secret or see behind its inscrutable mask? Certainly all the great mystery-religions of antiquity do maintain that they contain a most meaningful content of "things seen" "things done" and "things said." But when we do catch a glimpse of these marvels, any central drama which would unite the separate elements vanishes behind the eternal injunction of the masters of initiation to conceal the mystery with a finger of silence placed firmly before the closed lips of those who know about them but will not tell.

In spite of this injunction certain images have come to light which, on closer examination, are not so mysterious as one might expect. The Grail legend tells of

a Castle or Temple, wherein dwells an equally mysterious King Priest, who is both *Dead and Alive* and who guards certain talismans or symbols—Lance, Cup, Sword and Dish (or Stone). The object of innumerable hero-questors is to find this Castle . . . (a) to pass an initiation test, to prove his fitness, (b) to restore the Dead King to health and life. A procession appears from the various side chambers of the Hall of Initiation, and slowly *passes to and fro and round and round* the table at which the King and guests are seated. The proces-

* See p. 191.

sion consists of young girls and young men. The hero is expected to ask their meaning. If he fails to ask, the test has failed; if he asks but falls asleep before asking what all the grail symbols are his quest is only partially successful and he must return to the Castle after having overcome many fresh obstacles. . . . As a rule the Questor does at last succeed in reaching the Castle once again and often he is successful this second time in passing the tests and in healing the King and in restoring the Waste Land. His reward is succession to the Grail Kingdom and the Grail King's daughter (really the Grail Messenger) as his bride.[8]

The inspired work of Jessie L. Weston and others during the first two decades of this century threw a flood of light upon the meaning of this symbolism, and to this has been added the work of the depth psychologists and analysts which has confirmed or modified the sense of this research in its application to modern spiritual problems. It is impossible to encompass in this brief study all the conclusions arrived at to date, but I shall summarize the essential mythical and psychological meanings as I see them. In doing so I shall not restrict myself to an interpretation of the mystery of the Grail, but use it as the prototype for the stage of "transition" found in all mystery religions the world over.

We have previously spoken of the rites of "separation" in connection with the Grail legend, beginning with the initiate's encounter with water as a symbol of purification and the appearance of two masters of initiation, the ferryman or fisher, and the grail messenger as a young woman. All through the story we find a more or less symmetrical balance between male and female figures which culminates in their symbolic union in the cup and the spear, which in some versions is seen to drip blood into the cup. The whole ritual takes place within a sacred precinct or *temenos*, here represented by the Initiation Hall in the Grail Castle. The King who is suffering from an incurable wound, and who is therefore said to be both "Dead and Alive," signifies the superior man as an image of the Self to be regenerated and who is going through the "transition" as an *agon*, or period of suffering, before the final *telos*, or attainment of immortality, is reached.

Paul Schmitt puts it as follows: "Symbolically, man enters the underworld, he 'dies' in a *dromenon*, or is 'wedded,' and he is always symbolically reborn . . . the uninitiate and hence inconsecrate remains 'in death'. . . . Only he who in a suitable state of readiness, cleansed of guilt, participates in the *dromenon*, the sacral mime, becomes 'blessed.' "⁹ From an anthropological viewpoint mysteries of this type are kept secret not through desire to exclude others but because those participating in them at any one time necessarily form a secret or magical society. The psychological reason for this is still simpler to grasp since, in my experience, the true initiate is one who by the very nature of his psychic unrest or suffering needs a period of containment during which he can be healed. This means that the nature of his inner experience is to be kept safe from the interference of *his own* attachment to the material world of collective values. The secrecy is intended to convince *him* that his experience is individual and not to be shared with every Tom, Dick, and Harry. And these latter fellows should even be protected from him, since "as the poet said, 'one man's wisdom is another man's folly.' "¹⁰

So far we have the rationale of the mystery as denoting a symbolic union of male and female elements; as something inwardly seen to have meaning for the individual initiate and implying that he is to achieve within himself some sort of union between his masculine and feminine components, as gender. But if this were all, he would be self-enlightened but at the same time uncomfortably set apart by this experience from others. This is the moment when, as it says in the Grail legend, the questor so frequently falls asleep, which means he cannot experience the full consciousness of Self (i.e., the recitation of the King) without danger of becoming isolated or inflated by his knowledge. This is profoundly true not only of the traditional novice of the ancient mysteries but of the modern psychological "patient" as initiate. We do not see people running through a series of coherent dreams or fantasies which acquaint them once for all with the nature of their spiritual quest; and we analysts are for a long time at great pains to convince them of the individual nature of the *dromenon* they have experienced no matter how profoundly they have been affected by it. Modern examples of this sort have to be re-experienced many times while the coherence of the initiation archetype is broken up or distorted by many other problems pressing in from the personal affairs of everyday life and the claims of that very collective world in which we necessarily must live. The dream symbols themselves are, so to speak, impregnated with personal associations so closely interwoven with the archetypal images that it may take many months to unravel the two meanings of the same symbol, one belonging to the personal ego and the other to the impersonal Self. But fortunately the symbolism of initiation itself usually comes to the rescue with a new symbolic content of such universality as to redeem the individual from auto-erotic isolation and lift his experience to another level of meaning where ego and Self, personal and impersonal again may come together in a spirit of cooperation. This is represented in tribal cultures, as Van Gennep tells us, by the "ceremonies of incorporation." It marks the final period of the initiation pattern and is known as its *post-liminal* phase.

In the Grail legends this symbolism of incorporation is expressed in the images of the sword and the plate or dish (sometimes stone). In the sword we are taught to recognize the organized band of initiated young men known since the early Cretan bronze-age culture as the Kouretes (their prototype is found all over the world corresponding to the cultural period which produced them). They are archetypally represented as young men in arms, dancing or leaping about a holy infant who represents the newly born Self to be initiated, that is, one about to be incorporated into the life of the tribe in the rite of the new-birth. The youth is separated from his personal mother and is given as a new mother tribal group-identity in a spirit of enthusiasm for the Father God. We see this in the myth of Dionysos*, where the youthful god as "son-of-the-mother" is reborn from the thigh of his father, becoming "all-for-the-father."[11] But in the end there is a return to the Mother, expressed in the myth where Dionysos "came to the Underworld in search of Semele . . ." the price for which was "complete female surrender. . . . He fulfilled his promise with the help of a phallus made of fig-wood. . . ." So justice is again ensured for the balance of the male and female principles, to be honored through the stage of incorporation no less than during the stage of transition.

Then we come, at last, to the prime symbol of incorporation, the dish (or stone) as the true Grail, a magical food-producing object. This contains a symbolism so rich in meaning, so widely distributed, that it can only be touched upon briefly here. Suffice it to say that this is the principle of universal love which was originally bestowed upon mankind from the nurturant Mother but whose original agricultural meaning has been transformed into a hundred different forms of ritual practice or visionary symbol. It is the perfect ear of wheat, *Iakkos*, miraculously produced following the symbolic union of god and goddess (or their representative priest and priestess) in the Eleusinian Mysteries. It is also the communal meal experienced in a state of complete communal identity, such as we find in primitive communities where the totem animal (or man in cannibalistic societies) is eaten ritualistically. Or we find it on the religious plane where the last supper of the Lord Jesus Christ becomes the prototype of spiritual communion in which He, as a kind of universal Mother, offers to His disciples and thence to all mankind "my body and blood which was shed for thee." In the ceremonies of incorporation we complete the eternal round of destruction and re-creation, of death and rebirth, in which the Great Goddess is redeemed upon the plane of Self-realization through becoming, as it were, at one with the Father.

* See p. 172.

And so it is that the spiritual need of modern man reiterates the original initiation pattern: "separation" is followed by "transition" which is followed by "incorporation." This is experienced no longer in the outer ceremonial of past times, but inwardly as a meaningful procession of images: from descent to a death as sacrifice, there is passage to a sacred marriage rite, thence to a symbol of new birth from this union and an ascent and re-emergence into a light of that consciousness which has the power to redeem and reunite those elements of ego or of Self which were originally unconscious (e.g., the symbolic elephant in my patient's dream). After having been quiescently at one with each other, ego and Self were subsequently set at variance, and the initiation archetype was inevitably activated as a panacea to relieve such suffering and resolve the conflict.

But for all our religious instruction, research, psychology, and natural understanding, the mystery remains in some essential way unexplained and the visionary miracle retains its eternal appeal, whether as the "divine power of Pluto, conferred by the 'two goddesses' of Eleusis in the mystery of their cult," or "the *ploutos tou Christou*, 'the unsearchable riches of Christ' in the *oikonomia tou mysteriou*—'the dispensation of the mystery which hath been hidden from eternity in God Who created all things.' "[12]

VI. INITIATION AS PSYCHIC LIBERATION: THE MAGIC FLIGHT

In the last section we caught a glimpse of the master of initiation as medicine man and conductor of of souls from Earth to Heaven or from Earth to the Underworld. The figure of this mercurial messenger or guide retains attributes which suggest he was once a bird or had a bird-like spirit. Thoth is ibis-headed; Hermes has in latter-day Greece the wings of his caduceus and hat and sandals with which to achieve superhuman feats of levitation. But all these figures were transitional, appearing when needed for the express purpose of effecting a rite of passage into the stage of separation, or from the stage of separation into the stage of transition of initiation. They disappeared when the initiate became fully engaged in the experience of transition. We saw this figure again at the end of the myth of Inanna's descent, where, as Ninshubur, the master of initiation becomes a kind of savior. But this too is a secondary role to that performed by the initiate proper.

There is, however, a more classically archetypal figure from which all these others have sprung, the aboriginal shaman who, as the master of his own initiation, then provides the only valid expression of the initiation archetype for the entire tribal group to which he belongs. His power lies in being answerable to no human power, no chieftain, or totem clan; he is alone with the Supernatural Beings who have claimed him as their instrument. The shamans are real men who receive their clairvoyant gifts "in three ways: by inheriting the profession, by call or election, by personal quest." "The important stages of a shamanic initiation are five: first, torture and violent dismemberment of the body; second, scraping away of flesh till the body is reduced to a skeleton; third, substitution of viscera and renewal of the blood; fourth, a period spent in Hell, during which the future shaman is taught by the souls of the dead shamans and by 'demons'; fifth, an ascent to Heaven to obtain consecration from the God of Heaven."[1]

This whole initiation is, however, distinguished from another, preliminary initiation, or legend about the initiation, which is virtually the same as that we have already described as the theme of the swallowing monster. But there is an important difference! The initiate fated to become a shaman is not in any way killed (that is, dismembered, reduced to an embryo, or otherwise overcome by trance-like oblivion) by the swallowing monster, and is able to remember his sojourn in its belly. His dismemberment is carried out by other medicine men or their ghosts so that his levitational experience is regarded as an absolute piece of reality and not a symbolic vision. During this operation, it is said that the candidate visits the sky, whether by his own power climbing a rope or a tree or by being carried by a snake or by actually becoming a bird. The essence of his initiation is therefore designed to fit him (or his soul) to make an ecstatic "magic flight" to Heaven, and with an equally magic ability to return to inhabit his body, now renewed and re-articulated in his absence. The full range of his levitational powers includes an ability to descend to the Underworld as he had ascended to Heaven via the same world axis which is usually represented by a sacred pole or tree. He therefore can be in continuous communication with three cosmic zones; the world below, this world, and a world above.

The contrast between this type of initiation and the experience of ritualized "mysteries" is very striking. One can accept almost any miracle if it is suitably veiled or clothed in some attractive form of symbolism, but shamanism makes no such concession to our rational feelings. Either we reject it as the most dangerous imaginable form of occult tricksterism or we have to give credence to its literal claims. Mircea Eliade, one of the greatest authorities on the subject, comes, fortunately, to our rescue with an explanation of at least the inner meaning of these phenomena, and this allows us to pass over what we can neither prove nor disprove in terms solely of shamanistic initiatory techniques. Eliade says: "Shamanism is not only a technique of ecstasy; its theology and its philosophy finally depend on the *spiritual value* that is accorded to ecstasy, . . ." with its expression of "a break with the universe of daily life. The two-fold purpose of this break is obvious: it is the transcendence and the freedom that are obtained, for example, through ascent, flight, invisibility, incombustibility of the body . . . and the break from plane to plane effected by flight or ascent similarly signifies an act of transcendence . . . to transmute man's corporal modality into the spirit's modality."[2] Here we find none of that blissful incubation sleep of the initiate who is watched over by beneficent Mother and Father Gods. The shaman is more like the suffering Job in relation to Yahweh, who yet looked forward to his deliverance:

O that thou wouldst hide me in the grave, that thou wouldst keep me secret, until thy wrath is past, that thou wouldst appoint me a set time and remember me!
  If a man die, shall he live again? . . .[3]

and then

For I know that my redeemer liveth, and that he shall stand at the latter day upon the earth:
  And though after my skin worms destroy this body, yet in my flesh shall I see God. . . .[4]

The same literal spirit permeates Christianity:

Now if Christ preached that he rose from the dead, how say some among you that there is no resurrection of the dead? . . . and if Christ be not risen, then is your preaching vain, and your faith is also vain. . . .*

Concerning this actuality of the resurrection of the body we find a whole series of religious stories based upon the shamanistic principle of healing, expressed as the ability of the spiritual man to revive the dead. In this way, we read the story of Elijah, who brought back to life the son of the woman in whose house he was staying, or of Christ's miracle of bringing Lazarus to life after four days of death. The actual resurrection of Christ and the Last Judgment to be carried out by Him as "firstborn from the dead"[5] brought to millions of people a message promising relief from the eternal repetition of the "mysteries" of death and rebirth. Here was one completely liberating mystery, open to all, "that was to be 'proclaimed upon the housetops.' "[6] A further parallel of Christian symbolism with the shamanistic tradition is represented by the Cross as "the tree that 'springing from the depths of the Earth, rose to Heaven and sanctifies the uttermost bounds of the universe.' "[7]

We should be careful, however, not to strain the analogy between shamanism and Christianity. While we find the therapeutic powers of the shaman in the Hebrew and Christian traditions, we do not find in him the finality with which Job proclaimed his belief in a future redeemer or with which "Jesus proclaimed that the last age (the *eschaton*) had begun."[8] The shaman remains humbly true to his vocation and does not ever plan to deliver a Last Judgment or be in any sense a universal savior. He sticks to the principle of renewal, and if he has a philosophy it is much more akin to the oriental conception of transmigration. He makes an equally good pro-

* See p. 211.

totype, therefore, for the Buddhist as for the Christian, better in the sense that he lives by the memory of past incarnations as well as by future opportunities for transformation. "The shaman is the man who *knows* and *remembers*. . . . He is not solely an ecstatic, but also a contemplative. . . ."⁹ This is the prototype for the master yogis of India and China, of whom Eliade provides some excellent examples to show their transition from shamanism.

In this meditation,

the novice imagines that he is being stripped of his flesh and finally sees himself as a 'huge, white, shining skeleton.' We have come upon this same initiatory theme in Siberian and Eskimo shamanism. But in the case of the Indo-Tibetan *tchoed,* we have a new valuation of the traditional theme . . . the novice submits himself to an initiatory ordeal by stimulating his imagination to conjure up a terrifying vision, which, however, he masters by the power of his thought. He knows that what is before him is the creation of his own mind, that the Goddess and the demons are as unreal as is his own body. . . . For the novice is a Mahayana Buddhist; he knows that the world is 'void,' in other words, ontologically unreal.¹⁰

The simple transition from death to resurrection is no longer important. When we reach the higher levels of initiation known as Yoga, the meditation cannot be directly compared to the shamanic initiation, according to Eliade, since ". . . by virtue of Yoga, the ascetic abolishes the human condition (in Indian terms, the unenlightened life, the existence doomed to suffering) and gains . . . deliverance, freedom, *moksha, mukti, nirvana* . . . a mode of being that is transcendent, unconditioned."¹¹

In spite of the vast difference between the goals of Christian resurrection and Buddhist liberation, the process of initiatory death and rebirth provides a common denominator which is also the characteristic of any universal religious archetype. Real and symbolic become themselves relative to each other as also are life and death. Although the Christian theology of the first three centuries A.D. insisted upon the resurrection of the body as the final goal of spiritual deliverance, this tenet became somewhat softened or diluted by transfusions of ritual or image from the Greek mysteries and the Greco-Roman philosophers. So the religion of love (*agape* or compassion) had a better chance to win an equal if not superior place with the religion of judgment. In a reverse direction, Buddhism, which had always emphasized the importance of compassion (personified in Kwan Yin or Avaloketeshvara), instead of banishing all spiritual life to some ultimate void cherished a "traditional theme . . . of the 'new body' in which the initiate is reborn. . . . and Hatha Yogis, Tantrics, and alchemists seek through their respective techniques, to obtain a 'divine body' . . . which is absolutely spiritual . . . or to change the natural body, which is raw, 'unripe,' . . . into a body that is perfect, 'ripe.' "[12] Thus in Eastern and Western traditions of initiation we find homologous concepts which imply that there is a psychic reality or soul image which is so real that it cannot merely be dismissed as illusory, yet so changing in its structure that it cannot be concretized once and for all. The concept of a "subtle" or "divine" body becomes therefore the object of an "opus" or psycho-philosophic work whereby the gross material of the body-soul complex is refined (as in alchemy) and transformed into a permanent thing. Whether we call it Nirvana or Resurrection or the Philosopher's Stone it does not seem to matter. We shall never see it face to face unless we become saints or master yogis, but we shall believe in it as firmly as if we could. Only thus can the spirit become as real a motive for existence as instinct. And, after all, who knows what comes after death; at least a certain preparation for something that may come has given the greatest minds of the greatest centuries much to think about.

VII. RESURRECTION AND REBIRTH IN THE PROCESS OF INDIVIDUATION

It must be apparent from what has been said that the experience of rebirth and the experience of resurrection, expressed psychologically, must spring from two different roots, although both draw their nourishment from a common source in the archetype of initiation. Van Gennep's schema for the pattern of initiation is certainly true for the rite of the new birth, in which the rite of separation is followed by the rite of transition and that in turn is followed by the rite of incorporation. Incorporation here refers to the reintegration of the initiate with what the Greeks called *physis,* the basic configuration of the social group from which he sprang and to which he must return. Incorporation through initiation provides him with a spirit of devotion to the task of continuing and/or adding to the cultural and spiritual life of this group, whether it be family, township, country, totem clan, secret society, or the spiritual brotherhood of mankind.

Joseph Campbell gives us a useful term to describe this result of initiation as the "function of reference or engagement" represented by the organism "of the Hieratic City State, which engages every member in a context of apparent significance, relating him, as a part, to a whole. . . . The significance of such a symbol is unquestioned. Like an excellent work of art, it is an end in itself, communicating to the mind beholding it a sense of felicity, and to the life engaged in it a sense of meaning."[1]

FIG. 7—The solar lion couch, with erect tail as phallic symbol, supports the god Osiris, who is in the position representing the resurrection of the sun at sunrise. Underneath the couch are three sons of Horus, guides and protectors of the soul, and behind is a sacred fan, the hieroglyph of which means shadow.

In contrast to incorporation, on the other hand, we have seen, in discussing the symbolism of the shaman's initiation, that the end result of the process is not just return to a safe and sane social group but the ability to maintain his essentially antisocial vocation as an "aboriginal man of high degree," independent of any human compulsion or agency. He is the one who keeps himself in readiness for the next "magic flight" beyond the sensuous plane of objects or images. Instead of incorporation, his initiation aims for release. Campbell describes this as the function of "disengagement, transport and metamorphosis." Quoting Dr. Jung's definition of the symbol as "the best possible designation or formula for something relatively unknown yet recognized to be present, or required," he goes on to say, "When the symbol is functioning for engagement the cognitive faculties are held, fascinated by and bound to the symbol itself, and are thus simultaneously informed by and protected from the unknown. But when the symbol is functioning for disengagement, transport, or metamorphosis, it becomes a catapult to be left behind. . . ."[2]

The shaman's "trance is the bird flight of the feathered arrow. His mind, disengaged from the protection of the symbol, is to meet directly the *mysterium tremendum* of the unknown."[3] In the higher religions connected with the spirit of shamanism we have seen that this function of disengagement even aspires to a transcendence beyond what we can even designate as unknown, something which lies "beyond even the highest . . . mystical, esoteric, 'spiritual,' or 'angelic,' vocabulary. . . . 'For then alone,' wrote Aquinas, 'then alone do we know God truly, when we believe that he is far above all that man can possibly think of God.' And we have heard the words of *Kena Upanisad:*

> It is other, indeed, than the unknown,
> And, moreover, above the unknown.[4]

When we explore the inner life of modern individuals in respect to these end points of initiation, the difference between the symbols of rebirth and resurrection is not so easily found as in the history of religious literature. We are often left with a sense of confusion as to whether functions of engagement or disengagement are uppermost. In some cases, the direction of psychic energy is of course crystal clear and we do not need dreams to show us that a young person is in need of becoming disengaged from his family or social group in order to find his own intrinsic nature and vocation. Also we can be quite certain that a somewhat older, but still young person, who has achieved his first initiation into life, vocationally and sexually, needs to become engaged, rooted, incorporated into a meaningful socio-religious context along with his peers. Again, we can see quite frequently in later life, after many years of meaningful engagement during which people have exercised their vocations and raised their families, that the spirit of shamanism asserts itself in an impulse for release. The individuating factor expresses itself, therefore, at either of the extremes of engagement or disengagement whether with the objects or people of the phenomenal world or the images of the dream world.

But the real crisis of individuation expresses itself in mature people who apparently need both these principles working together. The symbolism of the Self, at any rate, seems to combine these two principles as psychic impulses or directions which should meet and in some way intersect each other somewhat as a centered radial design might be intersected at right angles by a vertical design. The radial design, in which all parts are related to the whole in this sense, would correspond to the symbol of incorporation or engagement, while the vertical design would correspond to the symbol of an *axis mundi* at the center of the known universe with its rope-like or tree-like extension down into the Underworld or up to Heaven as a dynamic extrasensory path of disengagement from all that is organized, related and at rest.

The complex, devious ways in which this symbolism can be observed in the modern unconscious are outside the scope of this study,* but occasionally an example of the ambiguity of the individuation process is simple and clear enough to be, I think, quite understandable to those who have no technical acquaintance with the intricacies of modern depth psychology. A reasonably good example of this kind comes from a

---

* But a large number of examples will be found in the works of C. G. Jung, following and including his *Psychology and Alchemy* (New York: Bollingen Series XX, *The Collected Works of C. G. Jung*, Vol. 12, 1953). In these books the complex nature of this problem may be seen as well as the pioneering work that is being done today to understand the meaning of this symbolism.

woman patient of mine who produced an initiation dream in which are represented the two poles of our study and a hypothetical image of the way they may be joined. The rite of separation is expressed in the fact that the patient is at first accompanied by her mother, later her mother is replaced by her sister, and then separated from them she encounters a strange woman who personifies the leading actress of a play about to be enacted. This actress has been delayed because she has been suffering from an illness. There is a man who is to play the masculine role, which has to do with his "yearning" for this woman and with his "asking the question" which is presumably to ask for her hand in marriage.

We may guess from this opening part of the dream that the central theme here is the hierogomy or sacred marriage which gives this episode its character as an initiation in which male and female are to be brought together in an aspirational sense expressive of true love. It is suggestive of the mystery of the Grail, where we also found the motif of illness, the need to ask a question, and the symbolic union of male and female elements. At this point in the dream the mysterious woman becomes a kind of mistress of initiation. An excited stir takes place in the audience and several women, including the patient, go up to her to receive some special kind of blessing. Now the patient is again with her mother briefly. The symbolism here is most probably to be regarded as a fertility rite suggestive of the rite associated with Demeter and Persephone in the Eleusinian Mysteries; it is a woman's rite which acknowledges the primacy and importance of ensuring rebirth by learning in a new way to be on good terms with the Great Mother as an archetypal figure different from the personal mother. The rite of incorporation is suggested in the fact that the woman is experiencing the rite in association with a few other women, which implies she may form with the others a kind of archetypal sorority or female secret society. But any kind of implied organization of the tribal type is significantly absent. Each woman is treated individually, and the patient responds to this lady individually and with confidence as to one who, she says, "reacts well to my essential nature." Therefore we know we are not dealing here with a puberty rite or group initiation but with an initiation which is part of a process of individuation.

After a brief scene with the leading man, the dramatic ritual (*dromenon*) is finished and the patient is presented with a picture representing the meaning of all she has witnessed or experienced. She says:

> It was an impressive drawing showing the steps of man's aspiration, the different levels on which he can 'ask the question.' The drawing resembled an ancient temple or maybe just seven great steps hewn out of stone. The lowermost step represented the mating of man and woman. Then there were ascending levels of 'yearning,' and on the topmost step was 'God's Image,' which represented the uppermost level. . . . I was profoundly impressed with this, as if in some new way it made man's life meaningful and understandable.

In a rough diagram of steps leading from the union of man and woman to "God's Image," she represented the man and woman by the symbols, ♂, male, and ♀, female; there were seven steps, and God's Image was a characterless circular blob, by which she designated that which is by its very nature unknown and unknowable.

In connection with this dream picture, I was struck by the number *seven* because of its many connections with initiation, here associated with an ascent leading to the idea of God. But it is also rooted in the symbolism of the *coniunctio* (symbolic sexual union) which we find in alchemy[5] and in the symbolism of the sacred *temenos* or temple, or in the center of many mantras from Tibet. What is especially striking here is how this woman describes the drawing as being in a way both temple, as symbol of engagement, and stairway which I would describe as a symbol of disengagement. God here is clearly not a personified godhead (i.e., Mother or Father) but a symbol of resurrection as release. Yet it is firmly connected to the symbol of containment as *coniunctio* so characteristic of the condition necessary for rebirth.

The full amplification from historical sources of this symbolism must be assumed for lack of space, but I can mention a few relevant parallels. There was the important part which the Stairway of the Seven Planets played in Apuleius' *Golden Ass,* which is an account of a symbolic initiation. Jung tells us:

> The initiations of late classical syncretism, already saturated with alchemy (cf. visions of Zosimos) were particularly concerned with the theme of ascent, i.e., sublimation. The ascent was often represented by a ladder; hence the burial gift in Egypt of a small ladder for the *Ka* of the dead. The idea of an ascent through the seven spheres or planets symbolizes the return of the soul to the sun-god from whom it originated. . . . Thus the Mystery of Isis described by Apuleius culminated in what medieval alchemy, going back to Alexandrian culture as transmitted by Arab tradition, called the *solificatio,* where the initiand was crowned Helios.[6]

Here the number seven stands for the highest stage of illumination associated with a sun symbolism. Yet we previously found that seven stages associated with moon symbolism were a characteristic of Inanna's descent to the Land of No-Return. There the psychological attitude was one of submission to a deep unknown Goddess of Death, from which sprang a vital impulse for rebirth as symbol of reengagement in the cycle of nature. We also saw how Gilgamesh clung to his demand for the immortality of ego-consciousness, and, failing to understand or assimilate the meaning of the seven loaves, thereby failed his initiation in this respect.

How then can we reconcile these two opposing uses of the seven stages of initiation, one a descent, one an ascent, one a submission, the other a transcendent release from engagement? Is one older than the other so that one is merely a secondary elaboration through transference of the other? This is a question which can only be answered objectively by the historian of religion, but the psychologist, in the interpretation of a contemporary dream content, can answer the subjective part, and this may influence the objective meaning as an evaluation.

The dream I have cited seems to me to say that the opposite tendencies for engagement or release may be held together by the archetypal knowledge of initiation as a process of death and rebirth, symbolized by the number seven. Any question of the primacy of one over the other is irrelevant. The very heart of the mystery lies in the paradox that in order to live an individual life instead of a collectively oriented, ego-centered life, there must be a reconciliation of opposites on the plane of image and the plane of experience. Only a great novelist or poet can create the impression that the paltry affairs of personal life are worthy to be seen in the light of such a universal symbolism. Yet it is so, and the mystery of initiation weaves its eternal thread through our lives and on into the shadows of death.

MYTHS OF DEATH, REBIRTH, AND RESURRECTION

A Note on the Myths

I have tried to localize the different myths and assign them their places in history. On the other hand, the reader must bear in mind that the very nature of mythology is its capacity for spontaneously regenerating its themes irrespective of time, place, and external causality.

The history of mythology might be compared to a vast river that gradually grew and spread out over the earth. From its wellspring, the fathomless human psyche, this river has carried its archetypal motifs throughout the world and the development of man.

Students of mythology do not agree as to whether the archetypal motifs of myths rose from a common source or from many sources that sprang into existence in different parts of the world simultaneously.

They both may be right. For we now know that apart from the main stream of mythology, there are also primary streams or brooks. These have risen locally and independently and have contributed their own unique mythology. Where and when these divergent waters met and mixed, and what emerged from the contact is of increasing interest to the mythologists.

MAUD OAKES

DEATH AND REBIRTH
AS COSMIC PATTERN:*
THE MYTHS

The archetypal images of death and rebirth are mirrored in a type of myth which is expressed as a cosmic occurrence. Although the cosmic patterns frequently are personified, the actors in the drama provide a picture of destruction and creation affecting the visible earth, the stars—even the whole universe. But we are brought back again and again through these stories to their source in the imaginative capacity of human beings for observing themselves and for changing their inner lives in accordance with a basic pattern of psychic transformation. The cosmic imagery of these myths merely calls attention to the universality of the archetypal image as a form of truth accessible to all. Modern psychology has called this type of universality the COLLECTIVE UNCONSCIOUS.

The student of mythology may take several different avenues to learn more about the origin of such myths and their function in the cultural life of the people. One of these approaches is provided by the theory of a ritual origin for mythology elaborated by Jessie L. Weston in FROM RITUAL TO ROMANCE.[1] A second is expressed by the religious historian Mircea Eliade in THE MYTH OF THE ETERNAL RETURN,[2] who sees in mythology a statement of religious faith or philosophic conviction. Another approach is given by Joseph Campbell in THE MASKS OF GOD.[3] He provides a clear history of the significant recent findings of archeologists and anthropologists and, to some extent, of biologists and psychol-

---

* See Introduction, pp. 8 to 14.

*ogists, in an attempt to correlate these findings in the great myth-
ologies of the world.*

J.L.H.

THE DANCE OF SHIVA
(Hindu, 1500 B.C.—1000 B.C.)[4]

*The god Shiva is known as the Destroyer. But because Hinduism views
death as the passing into a new life rather than into nonexistence, Shiva
becomes a creator as well. He represents the energy of the universe in
producing and destroying forms.*

Amongst the greatest of the names of Shiva is Nataraja, Lord of
Dancers, or King of Actors (*Plate* 2). The cosmos is His theatre,
there are many different steps in His repertory, He Himself is
actor and audience. . . . Shiva is the Eros Protogonas of Lucian,
when he wrote:
"It would seem that dancing came into being at the beginning
of all things, and was brought to light together with Eros, that
ancient one, for we see this primeval dancing clearly set forth in
the choral dance of the constellations, and in the planets and fixed
stars, their interweaving and interchange and orderly harmony."
I do not mean to say that the most profound interpretation
of Shiva's dance was present in the minds of those who first danced
in frantic, and perhaps intoxicated energy, in honour of the pre-
Aryan hill god, afterwards merged in Shiva. A great motif in
religion or art, any great symbol, becomes all things to all men;
age after age it yields to men such treasure as they find in their
own hearts. Whatever the origin of Shiva's dance, it became in
time the clearest image of the *activity* of God which any art or
religion can boast of . . . .
The *Nadanta* dance of *Nataraja* before the assembly in the
golden hall of Chidambaram . . . the center of the Universe, first
revealed to gods and rishis after the submission of the latter in
the forest of Taragam, as related in the *Koyil Puranam*. . . .

In the forest of Taragam dwelt multitudes of heretical rishis. . . . Thither proceeded Shiva to confute them, accompanied by Vishnu disguised as a beautiful woman, and Ati-Sheshan. The rishis were at first led to violent dispute amongst themselves, but their anger was soon directed against Shiva, and they endeavoured to destroy Him by means of incantations. A fierce tiger was created in sacrificial fires, and rushed upon Him; but smiling gently, He seized it, and with the nail of His little finger, stripped off its skin, and wrapped it about Himself like a silken cloth. Undiscouraged by failure, the sages renewed their offerings, and produced a monstrous serpent, which however, Shiva seized and wreathed about His neck like a garland. Then He began to dance; but there rushed upon Him a last monster in the shape of a malignant dwarf, Muyalaka.* Upon him the God pressed the tip of His foot, and broke the creature's back, so that it writhed upon the ground; and so, His last foe prostrate, Shiva resumed the dance, witnessed by gods and rishis. . . .

What then is the meaning of Shiva's Nadanta dance, as understood by Shaivas? Its essential significance is given in texts such as the following:

"Our Lord is the Dancer, who, like the heat latent in firewood, diffuses His power in mind and matter, and makes them dance in their turn." (*Plate* 1.)

The dance, in fact, represents His five activities (*Pancakritya*), viz: *Shrishti* (overlooking, creation, evolution), *Sthiti* (preservation, support), *Samhara* (destruction, evolution), *Tirobhava* (veiling, embodiment, illusion, and also, giving rest), *Anugraha* (release, salvation, grace). These separately considered, are the activities of the deities Brahma, Vishnu, Rudra, Maheshvara, and Sadashiva. This cosmic activity is the central motif of the dance. . . .

Unmai Vilakkam, verse 36, tells us: "Creation arises from the drum: protection proceeds from the hand of hope: from the fire proceeds destruction: the foot held aloft gives release." It will be observed that the fourth hand points to this lifted foot, the refuge of the soul.

---

* "Who represents ignorance, the destruction of which brings enlightenment, true wisdom, and release from the bondage of existences."

Art of Indian Asia, Zimmer.[5]

We have also the following from *Chidambara Mummani Kovai:*

"O my Lord, Thy hand holding the sacred drum has made and ordered the heavens and earth and other worlds and innumerable souls. Thy lifted hand protects both the conscious and unconscious order of Thy creation. All these worlds are transformed by Thy hand bearing fire. Thy sacred foot, planted on the ground, gives an abode to the tired soul struggling in the toils of causality. It is Thy lifted foot that grants eternal bliss to those that approach Thee. These Five-Actions are indeed Thy Handiwork."

The following verses from the *Tirukuttu Darshana* (Vision of the Sacred Dance), forming the ninth tantra of Tirumular's *Tirumantram,* expand the central motif further:

"His form is everywhere: all-pervading in His Shiva-Shakti:
Chidambaram is everywhere, everywhere His dance:
As Shiva is all and omnipresent,
Everywhere is Shiva's gracious dance made manifest.
His five-fold dances are temporal and timeless.
His five-fold dances are His Five Activities.
By His grace He performs the five acts,
This is the sacred dance of Uma-Sahaya.
He dances with Water, Fire, Wind and Ether,
Thus our Lord dances ever in the court."

Visible to those who pass over Maya and Mahamaya (illusion super-illusion)

"Our Lord dances His eternal dance.
The form of the Shakti is all delight—
This united delight is Uma's body:
This form of Shakti arising in time
And uniting the twain is the dance.
His body is Akash, the dark cloud therein is Muyalaka,
The eight quarters are His eight arms,
The three lights are His three eyes,
Thus becoming, He dances in *our* body as the congregation."

This is His dance. Its deepest significance is felt when it is realized that it takes place within the heart and the self. Everywhere is God: that Everywhere is the heart. Thus also we find another verse:

"The dancing foot, the sound of the tinkling bells,
The songs that are sung and the varying steps,
The form assumed by our Dancing Gurupara—
Find out these within yourself, then shall your fetters fall away."

. . . Shiva is a destroyer and loves the burning ground. But what does He destroy? Not merely the heavens and earth at the close of a world-cycle, but the fetters that bind each separate soul. Where and what is the burning ground? It is not the place where our earthly bodies are cremated, but the hearts of His lovers, laid waste and desolate. The place where the ego is destroyed signifies the state where illusion and deeds are burnt away: that is the crematorium, the burning ground where Shri Nataraja dances, and whence He is named Sudalaiyadi, Dancer of the burning ground. In this simile, we recognize the historical connection between Shiva's gracious dance at Nataraja, and His wild dance as the demon of the cemetery. . . .

The conception of the world process as the Lord's pastime or amusement (*lila*) is also prominent in the Shaiva scriptures. Thus Tirumular writes, "The perpetual dance is His play." This spontaneity of Shiva's dance is so clearly expressed in Skryabin's *Poem of Ecstasy* that the extracts following will serve to explain it better than any more formal exposition—what Skryabin wrote is precisely what the Hindu imager moulded:

The Spirit (purusha) *playing,*
The Spirit longing,
The Spirit with fancy (yoga-maya) *creating all,*
Surrenders himself to the bliss (ananda) *of love . . .*
Amid the flowers of His creation (prakriti), *He lingers in a kiss. . . .*
Blinded by their beauty, He rushes, He frolics, He dances, He
  whirls. . . .
He is all rapture, all bliss, in this play (lila)
Free, divine, in this love struggle.
In the marvellous grandeur of sheer aimlessness,
And in the union of counter-aspirations
In consciousness alone, in love alone,

The Spirit learns the nature (svabhava) of His divine being. . . .
"O, my world, my life, my blossoming, my ecstasy!
Your every moment I create
By negation of all forms previously lived through:
I am eternal negation (neti, neti). . . ."
Enjoying this dance, choking in this whirlwind,
Into the domain of ecstasy, He takes swift flight.
In this unceasing change (samsara, nitya, bhava), *in this flight, aimless,*
   divine,
The Spirit comprehends Himself,
In the power of will, alone, free,
Ever-creating, all-irradiating, all-vivifying,
Divinely playing in the multiplicity of forms, He comprehends Him-
   self. . . .
"I already dwell in thee, O, my world,
Thy dream of me—'twas I coming into existence. . . .
And thou art all—one wave of freedom and bliss. . . ."
By a general conflagration (maha-pralaya) *the universe* (samsara) *is*
   embraced,
The Spirit is at the height of being, and He feels the tide unending
Of the divine power (shakti) *of free will. He is all-daring:*
What menaced, now is excitement,
What terrified, is now delight. . . .
And the universe resounds with the joyful cry I am.

. . . The Essential Significance of Shiva's Dance is threefold:
First, it is the image of his Rhythmic Play as the Source of all
Movement within the Cosmos, which is Represented by the Arch:
Secondly, the Purpose of his Dance is to Release the Countless
souls of men from the Snare of Illusion: Thirdly, the Place of the
Dance, Chidambaram, the Centre of the Universe, is within the
Heart. . . .

In the night of Brahma, Nature is inert, and cannot dance
till Shiva wills it: He rises from His rapture, and dancing sends
through inert matter pulsing waves of awakening sounds, and lo!
matter also dances appearing as a glory round about Him.
Dancing, He sustains its manifold phenomena. In the fulness of
time, still dancing, he destroys all forms and names by fire and
gives new rest. This is poetry; but none the less, science.

DEATH AND REBIRTH OF THE
UNIVERSE (Hindu)[6]

The cosmic unit of time, according to Hindu mythical astronomy, is the Kalpa, or a day of Brahma the creator. Brahma creates in the morning, and at night the three worlds, . . . Earth, Heaven and Hell, are reduced to chaos, every being that has not obtained liberation retaining its essence which takes form according to its Karma, when Brahma wakes up in the morning. Thus the eventful days and nights pass on, till Brahma reaches the hundredth year of his life when "not only the three worlds but all planes and all beings, Brahma himself, Devas, Rishis, Asuras, men, creatures and matter" are all resolved into Mahapralaya (the great cataclysm). After a hundred years of chaos, another Brahma is born. . . . A Kalpa or day of Brahma is equivalent to 4,320,000,000 earth years. . . .

The manner of destruction of the world at the end of the Kaliyuga* is differently described in the Puranas. In one account it is related that Vishnu will appear as Kalki, "an armed warrior, mounted on a white horse, furnished with wings and adorned with jewels, waving over his head with one hand the sword of destruction and holding in the other a disc.

The horse is represented as holding up the right fore-leg; and when he stamps on the earth with that, the tortoise supporting the serpent Shesha on whose hood the world rests, shall fall into the deep, and so rid himself of the load; and by that means all the wicked inhabitants of the world will be destroyed."

In the Bhagbata we are told that the "age of destruction is so horrible that during it the clouds never fall on the earth as drops of rain for one hundred years. The people then find no food to eat . . . and are compelled to eat one another. Being thus overpowered by what is wrought by time, the men gradually lead themselves to utter destruction."

Elsewhere the universal cataclysm is predicted in vivid de-

---

* The day of Brahma is divided into 1,000 Mahayugas (great ages) of equal length, each consisting of four Yugas; namely, Krita, Threta, Dwapara, and Kali. Kalijuga is the present age of degeneration [and consists of 432,000 years].

tail. "After a drought lasting many years, seven blazing suns will appear in the firmament; they will drink up all the waters. Then the wind-driven fire will sweep over the earth, consuming all things; penetrating to the netherworld it will destroy what is there in a moment; it will burn up the universe. Afterwards many coloured and brilliant clouds will collect in the sky looking like herds of elephants decked with wreaths of lightning. Suddenly they will burst asunder, and rain will fall incessantly for twelve years until the whole world . . . is covered with water. The clouds will vanish. Then the self-created lord, the first cause of everything, will absorb the winds and go to sleep. The universe will become one dread expanse of water."

THE PARADE OF ANTS (Hindu)[7]

During the period of the supremacy of the dragon, the majestic mansions of the lofty city of the gods had cracked and crumbled. The first act of Indra was to rebuild them. All the divinities of the heavens were acclaiming him their savior. Greatly elated in his triumph [over the dragon] and in the knowledge of his strength, he summoned Vishvakarman, the god of arts and crafts, and commanded him to erect such a palace as should befit the unequaled splendor of the king of the gods.

The miraculous genius, Vishvakarman, succeeded in constructing in a single year a shining residence, marvelous with palaces and gardens, lakes and towers. But as the work progressed, the demands of Indra became even more exacting and his unfolding visions vaster. He required additional terraces and pavilions, more ponds, groves, and pleasure grounds. Whenever Indra arrived to appraise the work, he developed vision beyond vision of marvels remaining to be contrived. Presently the divine craftsman, brought to despair, decided to seek succor from above. He would turn to the demiurgic creator, Brahma, the pristine embodiment of the Universal Spirit, who abides far above the troubled Olympian sphere of ambition, strife, and glory.

When Vishvakarman secretly resorted to the higher throne and presented his case, Brahma comforted the petitioner. "You will soon be relieved of your burden," he said. "Go home in peace." Then, while Vishvakarman was hurrying down again to the city of Indra, Brahma himself ascended to a still higher sphere. He came before Vishnu, the Supreme Being, of whom he himself, the Creator, was but an agent. In beatific silence Vishnu gave ear, and by a mere nod of the head let it be known that the request of Vishvakarman would be fulfilled.

Early next morning a brahmin boy, carrying the staff of a pilgrim, made his appearance at the gate of Indra, bidding the porter announce his visit to the king. The gate-man hurried to the master, and the master hastened to the entrance to welcome in person the auspicious guest. The boy was slender, some ten years old, radiant with the luster of wisdom. Indra discovered him amidst a cluster of enraptured, staring children. The boy greeted the host with a gentle glance of his dark and brilliant eyes. The king bowed to the holy child and the boy cheerfully gave his blessing. The two retired to the hall of Indra, where the god ceremoniously proffered welcome to his guest with oblations of honey, milk, and fruits, then said: "O Venerable Boy, tell me of the purpose of your coming."

The beautiful child replied with a voice that was as deep and soft as the slow thundering of auspicious rain clouds. "O King of Gods, I have heard of the mighty palace you are building, and have come to refer to you the questions in my mind. How many years will it require to complete this rich and extensive residence? What further feats of engineering will Vishvakarman be expected to accomplish? O Highest of Gods,"—the boy's luminous features moved with a gentle, scarcely perceptible smile—"no Indra before you has ever succeeded in completing such a palace as yours is to be."

Full of the wine of triumph, the king of the gods was entertained by this mere boy's pretension to a knowledge of Indras earlier than himself. With a fatherly smile he put the question: "Tell me, Child! Are they then so very many, the Indras and Vishvakarmans whom you have seen—or at least whom you have heard of?"

The wonderful guest calmly nodded. "Yes, indeed, many have I seen." The voice was as warm and sweet as milk fresh from the cow, but the words sent a slow chill through Indra's veins. "My dear child," the boy continued, "I knew your father, Kashyapa, the Old Tortoise Man, lord and progenitor of all the creatures of the earth. And I knew your grandfather, Marichi, Beam of Celestial Light, who was the son of Brahma. Marichi was begotten of the god Brahma's pure spirit; his only wealth and glory were his sanctity and devotion. Also, I know Brahma, brought forth by Vishnu from the lotus calix growing from Vishnu's navel. And Vishnu himself—the Supreme Being, supporting Brahma in his creative endeavor—him too I know."

"O King of Gods, I have known the dreadful dissolution of the universe. I have seen all perish, again and again, at the end of every cycle. At that terrible time, every single atom dissolves into the primal, pure waters of eternity, whence originally all arose. Everything then goes back into the fathomless, wild infinity of the ocean, which is covered with utter darkness and is empty of every sign of animate being. Ah, who will count the universes that have passed away, or the creations that have risen afresh, again and again, from the formless abyss of the vast waters? Who will number the passing ages of the world, as they follow each other endlessly? And who will search through the wide infinities of space to count the universes side by side, each containing its Brahma, its Vishnu, and its Shiva? Who will count the Indras in them all—those Indras side by side, who reign at once in all the innumerable worlds; those others who passed away before them; or even the Indras who succeed each other in any given line, ascending to godly kingship, one by one, and, one by one, passing away? King of Gods, there are among your servants certain who maintain that it may be possible to number the grains of sand on earth and the drops of rain that fall from the sky, but no one will ever number all those Indras. This is what the Knowers know.

"The life and kingship of an Indra endure seventy-one eons, and when twenty-eight Indras have expired, one Day and Night of Brahma has elapsed. But the existence of one Brahma, measured in such Brahma Days and Nights, is only one hundred and eight years. Brahma follows Brahma; one sinks, the next arises; the endless series cannot be told. There is no end to the number of those Brahmas—to say nothing of Indras.

"But the universes side by side at any given moment, each harboring a Brahma and an Indra: who will estimate the number of these? Beyond the farthest vision, crowding outer space, the universes come and go, an innumerable host. Like delicate boats they float on the fathomless, pure waters that form the body of Vishnu. Out of every hair-pore of that body a universe bubbles and breaks. Will you presume to count them? Will you number the gods in all those worlds—the worlds present and the worlds past?"

A procession of ants had made its appearance in the hall during the discourse of the boy. In military array, in a column four yards wide, the tribe paraded across the floor. The boy noted them, paused, and stared, then suddenly laughed with an astonishing peal, but immediately subsided into a profoundly indrawn and thoughtful silence.

"Why do you laugh?" stammered Indra. "Who are you, mysterious being, under this deceiving guise of a boy?" The proud king's throat and lips had gone dry, and his voice continually broke. "Who are you, Ocean of Virtues, enshrouded in deluding mist?"

The magnificent boy resumed: "I laughed because of the ants. The reason is not to be told. Do not ask me to disclose it. The seed of woe and the fruit of wisdom are enclosed within this secret. It is the secret that smites with an ax the tree of worldly vanity, hews away its roots, and scatters its crown. This secret is a lamp to those groping in ignorance. This secret lies buried in the wisdom of the ages, and is rarely revealed even to saints. This secret is the living air of those ascetics who renounce and transcend mortal existence; but worldlings, deluded by desire and pride, it destroys."

The boy smiled and sank into silence. Indra regarded him, unable to move. "O Son of a brahmin," the king pleaded presently, with a new and visible humility, "I do not know who you are. You would seem to be Wisdom Incarnate. Reveal to me this secret of the ages, this light that dispels the dark."

Thus requested to teach, the boy opened to the god the hidden wisdom. "I saw the ants, O Indra, filing in long parade. Each was once an Indra. Like you, each by virtue of pious deeds once ascended to the rank of a king of gods. But now, through many rebirths, each has become again an ant. This army is an army of former Indras."

"Piety and high deeds elevate the inhabitants of the world to the glorious realm of the celestial mansions, or to the higher domains of Brahma and Shiva and to the highest sphere of Vishnu; but wicked acts sink them into the worlds beneath, into pits of pain and sorrow, involving reincarnation among birds and vermin, or out of the wombs of pigs and animals of the wild, or among trees, or among insects. It is by deeds that one merits happiness or anguish, and becomes a master or a serf. It is by deeds that one attains to the rank of a king or brahmin, or of some god, or of an Indra or a Brahma. And through deeds again, one contracts disease, acquires beauty and deformity, or is reborn in the condition of a monster.

"This is the whole substance of the secret. This wisdom is the ferry to beatitude across the ocean of hell.

"Life in the cycle of the countless rebirths is like a vision in a dream. The gods on high, the mute trees and the stones, are alike apparitions in this phantasy. But Death administers the law of time. Ordained by time, Death is the master of all. Perishable as bubbles are the good and evil of the beings of the dream. In unending cycles the good and evil alternate. Hence, the wise are attached to neither, neither the evil nor the good. The wise are not attached to anything at all."

The boy concluded the appalling lesson and quietly regarded his host. The king of gods, for all his celestial splendor, had been reduced in his own regard to insignificance. . . . [Then] the brahmin boy, who had been Vishnu, disappeared. . . . The king was alone, baffled and amazed.

THE FIVE SUNS (Aztec)[8]

The Aztec gods were givers of the laws of nature. In this tale, their struggles give rise to the death and rebirth of the universe. The well-known Aztec Calendar Stone called "Eagle Bowl" is an image of a cosmic cycle (Plate 3). On it are carved the symbols of the five suns.

The nocturnal Tezcatlipoca,* whose *nahual* or disguise is the jaguar, its spotted skin resembling the heavens with their myriad

* Tezcatlipoca . . . signified the nocturnal cycle and was connected with the moon and all stellar gods, hence he brought misfortune, death, and destruction, and war associated with witchcraft.

stars, was the first to become a sun, and with him began the first era of the world. The first men created by the gods were giants; they neither sowed grain nor tilled the soil, but lived by eating acorns and other fruits and wild roots. Tezcatlipoca was also the constellation of Ursa Major, whom the Aztecs pictured as a jaguar. While he was ruling the world as the sun, his enemy, Quetzalcoatl, struck him a blow with his staff. Tezcatlipoca fell into the water, changing into a jaguar. He devoured the giants, and the earth was depopulated and the universe was without a sun. This occurred on the day called "4 Jaguar."

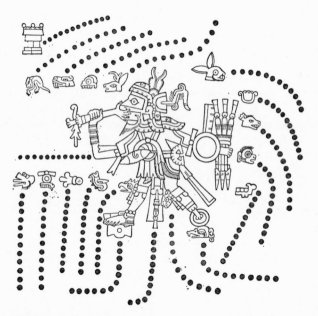

Fig. 8—The Wizard Tezcatlipoca and the twenty days of the Aztec calendar.

Then Quetzalcoatl became the sun, until the jaguar struck him down with a blow of his paw. Then a great wind arose, and all the trees were uprooted, and the greater part of mankind perished. Those men who survived were transformed into monkeys, that is, into subhuman creatures. This took place on the day "4 Wind." Men at that time ate only pine nuts or *acocentli*. The creator gods then chose Tlaloc, the god of rain and celestial fire, as the sun, but Quetzalcoatl made the fire rain down, and men either perished or were changed into birds. This happened on the day "4 Rain." The sustenance of men during this age was a seed called *acecentli*, or "water corn."

Then Quetzacoatl selected Tlaloc's sister as the sun. She was the goddess Chalchiuhtlicue, "the lady of the jade skirts," goddess of water. But no doubt it was Tezcatlipoca who caused it to rain so hard that the earth was flooded and men either perished or were transformed into fish. This occurred on the day called "4 Water." During this age men ate . . . *teocentli*, the ancestor of corn.*

Laurette Sejourne[9] believes that there were five suns. The face in the centre of the Calendar Stone is the face of Quetzalcoatl, our present sun.

That is why the Fifth Sun (five is the number of the centre), is the Sun of Movement [earthquake], . . . "The name of this Sun is Naollin (Four Movements), now is ours, by which today we live. . . . It was also the Sun of Quetzalcoatl. . . ."

This sun, whose emblem is a human face, not only represents the central region, but also what is above and what is below, that is, heaven and earth. The symbol of the world is thus brought together in a cross.

THE RAGNAROK
(Icelandic, 13TH Century)[10]

The Ragnarok, from the epic Prose Edda, is the Doom of the Gods in Icelandic mythology. In this last glorious battle, all the gods battle against the Fenris Wolf, the World Serpent and the helhound Garmr. Odin (father of all the gods), Thor (god of thunder), Loki (Mischief Maker and father of lies), and the other gods are all slain, and in turn destroy the three monsters. This destruction precedes a re-creation of the world—when the earth shall rise from the sea and men shall live in love.

The details of the Ragnarok are many and terrible,[11] and first that the Winter shall come which is called the Monstrous Winter,

---

* Another legend reverses the order of the Suns.

when blizzards shall drive from every quarter, frosts shall be iron-hard and winds sharp, nor shall the sun afford respite. These winters shall come three in a row with no summer between. But to work up to that there shall be three other winters in which the whole world shall be embroiled in war. For sordid greed, brother shall slay brother; neither father nor son shall show each other mercy in slaughter and fornication. . . . Then comes that to pass which is awesome news: the Wolf swallows the Sun. Men shall think that a mighty disaster. The other Wolf shall take the Moon at one bite, an irreparable loss; while the stars shall turn from their steadings in heaven. The next news is that the earth and the mountains shake, woods are torn up by the roots, crags crack from top to bottom and all fetters and bonds are smashed and split. Thereupon, the Wolf Fenris breaks loose, and a great bore of waters inundates the land as, in a gigantic fury, the World Serpent buckles and boils up out of the sea! Then it comes to pass that the vessel called Naglfar slips her moorings. That ship is built of the nails of dead men. . . . The Fenris Wolf gallops with his jaws agape, his lower fangs raking the earth, his upper scraping heaven, and wider yet would he yawn were there room enough: flames are sprouting from his eyes and nostrils. The World Serpent blows such clouds of poison that he sprinkles all the earth and sky: he would make your blood run cold as he comes on the other side of the Wolf.

At the height of the clangour the heavens split asunder and through the rift ride Múspell's Sons. Surtr rides first, flinging fire before him and after him both, in his fist the supreme sword more dazzling than the sun. And when they gallop up over Bifröst, the bridge crumbles behind them as was foretold. All the hosts of Múspell plough steadily on the plain called Vígrídr to meet with Fenris the Wolf and the World Serpent. There too came Loki and Hrymr who leads all the Frost Giants, while Loki's followers are the Sons of Hel; and the Children of Múspell form an army on their own—a blazing host! The Valley Vígrídr is a hundred leagues wide and a hundred leagues broad.

When this comes to pass, Heimdallr stands forth and blows lustily on Gjallarhorn to turn out all the gods, who fall in together. Then Odin rides to Mímir's Well to seek advice for him-

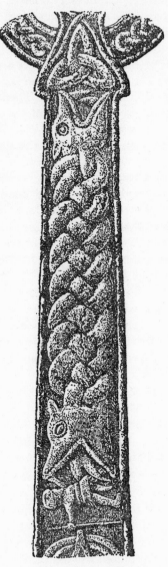

FIG. 9—Vídarr's fight with the Fenris-Wolf. Relief from a cross, Churchyard of Gosforth, Cumberland.

self and his people. Yggdrasill the World Ash begins to tremble; no corner of heaven or earth but is seized with terror. The gods and the Einherjar do on their battle harness and march to the field. Odin is riding at their head wearing his golden helmet and a sparkling war coat, and porting his spear called Gungir. He charges full tilt at Fenrir the Wolf with Thor by his side but unable to help him, for he has enough on his hands to fight with the Serpent of the World. Frey and Surtr attack each other, when a violent conflict ensues before Frey is slain: he had sealed his own death warrant when he gave his incomparable sword to his servant Skírnir.

Now the helhound Garmr, who was chained by the Bottomless Pit, at last breaks free, a fearsome monster. He savages Týr and each of them slays the other. Thor carries death to the Serpent of the World, but staggers away a mere nine steps: then he himself sinks down dead to the earth enveloped in the poison mist the Serpent blew upon him. The Wolf gorges Odin: That is how he dies, but at once Vídarr flies forward and plants one foot inside the Wolf's lower jaw. . . . In his fists he grips the Wolf's upper jaws and so rips asunder his maw: and that is how the Wolf dies. But at last Surtr pitches flame over the earth and burns up the whole of heaven.

. . . When Gylfi has heard the recital of the events of the Ragnarok he enquires,[12] "But what comes after? What happens when all Creation is burned up, when the gods are all dead as well as the Chosen Warriors and the Races of Men? . . . Will there be any gods alive, or will there be any earth or heaven?"

High replied, "Surely the earth shall rise up green and fair out of the sea, and plants shall grow there where none were ever sown. Vídarr and Váli shall live on as though neither the sea nor the fires of Surtr had impaired them, and they shall settle in Idavöllr where Asgard formerly was. There too shall come the sons of Thor, Modi and Magni bringing with them Thor's hammer. After them shall come Balder and Hodr from hel. They shall live in love and talk long together and revive all their old wisdom and shall put behind them all the ancient evils of the Serpent of the World and Fenriswulf. Then in the grass they shall stumble upon the golden chessmen owned by the gods before."

THE VOLUNTARY DEATH (Hindu)[13]

In the Hindu view of the cosmic pattern, the gods are alternately se-
duced and disenchanted by their feminine counterparts who symbolize
māyā, the world-illusion. In this version from the Puranas, *popular*
Hindu texts, the god Shiva takes the beautiful Satī to be his bride and
they live in bliss for thousands of years. In the end, Shiva is punished
for his absorption in the world-illusion represented by Satī, and she
leaves him, revealing her other side as Kali, the Terrible Mother.

Amid the thundering boom of the cloud-drums Shiva took his
leave of Vishnu. He lifted Satī, radiant with joy, upon the back
of his mighty bull, and while the whole assemblage of the gods,
demons, and created beings raised an immense uproar of jubila-
tion, the couple started on their way. Brahmā and his ten mind-
born sons, and the Lords of Creatures, and the gods, and the
heavenly musicians, together with the dancing girls, all accompanied them a short stretch of the road, before releasing the two
with a great farewell, and scattering to their innumerable habi-
tations. The whole of creation was jubilant, Shiva having finally
taken to himself his consort.

The couple arrived at Shiva's abiding place among the fast-
ness of the Himālayan peaks, and the god took his bride down
from the back of Nandī, the bull. Then he dismissed the bull and
also the tumultuous company of his host. "Leave the two of us
alone now. But when I take thought of you," said he, "be immediately at hand." And so, then, the god and goddess consum-
mated their festival in the secrecy of their solitude, and they
dwelt long in love with each other, night and day.

. . . The bridal couple had scarcely arrived in the Himālayas
when the God of Love came, in a gala mood, together with the
Spring and Desire. Majestic Spring worked magic: all the trees
and vines broke into blossom, the water surfaces were covered
with lotus chalices swarmed about by bees, . . . In bowers and by
the banks of high, torrential mountain streams, Shiva and Satī
tasted each other; and Satī's desire was so powerful that Shiva
was never without great delight in her. When she gave herself,
it was as though she was melting into his body, drowning in his

fire. He decked her whole person in chains of flowers and studied her; he joked and laughed and conversed with her; he lost himself in her, as a yogi in full self-collection submerges in the Self, there deliquescing totally. Shiva swallowed the nectar of her mouth, and, as though it were the divine liquor of immortality imbibed from the cup of the moon, his body became filled with unflagging desire and knew nothing of the exhaustion known to men. The scent of her lotus-countenance, her grace and her nuances of allure, linked him, like powerful cords around the ankles of a bull elephant, so that he could never break away from her. With such changing delights, the godly couple, in the remote mountain solitudes of Himālaya, went on for nineteen heavenly years and five (nine thousand two hundred and forty human years) among the bowers and in caves, knowing only the ravishment of love. . . .

The rainy season threatened and Satī . . . pleaded for a house. Shiva answered gaily, and his face was luminous with the light of the moon in his hair: "Where we are going, my beloved, to enjoy our love, there will not be any clouds. Clouds reach only to the hips of the great mountains; the mountain heads are zones of everlasting snow, untouched by seasonal rain. Which pinnacle do you choose?" . . .

Satī replied: "I should prefer Mount Himālaya." And they proceeded directly to its summit, whither no bird can fly, no clouds come, and where the wives of the blessed play. Shiva and Satī dwelt there for three thousand, six hundred years. . . . Shiva's heart was wholly held by Satī, and he was indefatigable in his offering of love. Day and night he knew no other joy, knew nothing now of the serene Essence of Being, never gathered consciousness to the ardent vivid point of self-submersion. For Satī's gaze held to his countenance, and his eyes, in turn, never left the loveliness of her features. The inexaustible fountain of their passion watered abundantly the roots of their tree of love, and the tree continually grew.

But now Daksha, Satī's father, began preparations for a prodigious sacrificial ceremony, which should redound to the well-being of all the worlds and creatures. . . .

Every living thing in all the reaches of space was invited to attend, gods and seers, men, birds, trees, and grasses. They

began to arrive—wild and domesticated animals, all the inhabitants of the upper regions, saints and sages, and all the denizens
of the depths, rich subterranean demons and magnificent serpent
kings and queens. Clouds and mountains were invited, rivers and
oceans; monkeys and all beings came to partake of their share of
the feast. The kings of the earth arrived in state with their sons,
and followed by their counselors and troops. All living existences
in all the regions of the universe, whether moving or fixed in
place, made their appearance; both the conscious creatures and
the unconscious were invited. And Daksha paid out everything
he owned in fees to the priests. Throughout all the vast, wide-
reaching, lofty and abysmal reaches of the world, there was only
one being whom Daksha did not invite, and that was Shiva, his
son-in-law, together with Satī, the daughter whom he loved. They
were not invited because they were judged to be ceremonially
impure. "He is a beggar ascetic and not fit to be present at the
sacrifice," said Daksha; "he meditates among corpses and carries
a skull for a begging bowl. Neither is Satī qualified; she is his
wife and contaminated by association."

Vijayā, the daughter of a sister of Satī, visited the mountain
retreat just when the creatures of all the worlds had begun to
stream from their far-flung places to all the precinct of the universal festival. She discovered Satī alone, Shiva having gone off
on his bull, Nandī, to perform his evening meditations on the
shore of Lake Manasa, upon the summit of Mount Kailāsa. "You
have come alone?" said Satī. "Where are your sisters?"

Vijayā made it known that all the women in the universe
were on their way to the great party being held by her grandfather, Daksha. "I have come to fetch you," she said. "Are not
you and Shiva coming?"

Dumbfounded amazement brought a glaze to Satī's eyes.

"Have you not been invited?" exclaimed Vijayā. "Why, all
the saints and seers are coming! The Moon and his wives! Everyone in all the worlds has been invited. Haven't you?"

Satī was struck, as by a bolt of lightning. Anger began to
burn in her, and her eyes hardened. She had understood immediately, and fury increased in her beyond bounds. "Because my
husband bears a skull in his hand for a begging bowl," she said,
"we have not been invited." She thought for a moment, in order
to decide whether to blast Daksha to ashes with a curse, but then

she suddenly remembered the words she had uttered to him, the time she had mercifully granted the great boon of becoming flesh in the earthly status of his daughter: "If, for even a single instant, you should lack for me proper reverence, I will quit my body immediately, whether happy in it or no." And with that, her own eternal form became visible to her spiritual eye, complete and incomparably terrible, the form out of which the universe is made. She submerged herself in the contemplation of this, her primary character, which is Māyā, known also as "The World-Creative Dream-Drunkenness of the Sustainer of the Cosmos," and she meditated: "The world period of the universal dissolution has not yet arrived; that is true; Shiva has not yet a son. The great wish that agitated all the gods became fulfilled for them: Shiva, caught in my spell, found his joy in woman. But what good did it do them? There is no other woman in all the worlds who could arouse and satisfy Shiva's passion; he will never marry another. That, however, is not going to stop me. I will quit this body, just as I declared I would. Some later day, I can reappear for the redemption of the world, here on Himālaya, where I have dwelt so long in happiness with Shiva. . . . I will marry Shiva again, dwell with him again, and complete the work that all the divinities have in mind." (*Plate* 15.)

Thus she meditated. Then her wrath overcame her. She closed the nine portals of her senses in yoga, stopped her respiration, and braced all her powers. The life breath ripped through the coronal suture of her skull, out of the tenth portal (the so-called Brahmā-fissure), and shot upward from her head. The body slumped inanimate to the ground.

When the gods above beheld the wind of her life, they lifted a universal shout of woe. Vijayā threw herself across the lifeless form and wept with agony. . . .

DEATH OF THE SKELETON
MOWER (Egyptian)[14]

This is the thirteenth card of the Tarot (Plate 5). There are 78 cards in all and they supposedly represent all the knowledge of the universe col-

*lected by the ancient Egyptians. They decided to transmit their knowl-
edge by covering tablets with symbols, concealing the doctrine. Then the
priests invented a gambling game with the tablets, to ensure their dis-
persion throughout the world.*

*"Present-day psychology has confirmed . . . that the Tarot cards
comprise an image (comparable to that encountered in dreams) of the
path of initiation. At the same time, Jung's view, coinciding with the
secular, intuitive approach to the Tarot enigmas, recognizes the por-
trayal of two different, but complementary struggles in the life of man:
(a) the struggle against others (the solar way) which he pursues through
his social position and calling; and (b) against himself (the lunar way),
involving the process of individuation. . . ."*—Dictionary of Symbols,
Cirlot.15

The Thirteenth Hebrew letter *(Mem)*. The hieroglyphic meaning of the *Mem* is a woman, the companion of man; it therefore
gives rise to ideas of fertility and formation. It is pre-eminently
the maternal and female . . . an image of eternal and passive
action. Employed at the end of words, this letter becomes a collective sign (final *Mem*). In this case, it develops the idea of
being in unlimited space.

Creation necessitates equal destruction in a contrary sense,
and therefore the *Mem* designates all the regenerations that have
sprung from previous destruction, all transformations, and con-
sequently death, regarded as the passage from one world to the
other . . .

[Description of the card:] A skeleton mows down heads in a
field, from which hands and feet spring up on all sides, as the
scythe pursues its work.

The works of the head (conception) become immortal as
soon as they are realized (hands and feet) . . .

DEATH AND REBIRTH
AS CYCLES OF NATURE:*
THE MYTHS

T HE *myths in this section all reflect, in their different ways, the archetype of death and rebirth as a
cycle of nature. In the seven stages of Inanna's descent, we find
a reference to the phases of the moon: through its waning (death)
and waxing (rebirth) it completes a cycle, which then recurs indefinitely. More direct references to the moon symbolism are
found in other stories.†*

In the myths of Adonis, Attis, *and* Persephone *we also find
a cycle, but here it is the cycle of the agricultural year; from
autumn and winter (death), to spring and summer (rebirth). In
the myth of* Isis *(where she exhorts Thoth to heal Horus from a
death wound inflicted by a serpent and bring him into a new
life), we find a reference to the pattern of death and rebirth associated with a sun cycle, the setting sun representing death and
the rising sun new life, i.e., rebirth.*

*Symbols of rebirth such as the snake†, the scarab, the phoe-
nix, and the bee‡ are found in these myths as a part of nature.
The sacred tree is perhaps the prime symbol for the cycle of death
and rebirth in nature, with the yearly shedding of its leaves in
autumn and its renewal in spring time. Sometimes its quality as
a symbol of immortality is expressed in the evergreen tree whose
leaves remain green throughout the winter as well as the re-*

* See Introduction, pp. 15 to 31.
† See *The Lady of the Moon,* etc.
‡ See *Lemminkainen,* pp. 121 to 127.

mainder of the year. From the topmost branches of the tree there emerge symbols of rebirth and immortality, such as the mistletoe, the sacred child, moon disc or sun disc, or bird or god in the moment of his apotheosis.

Another version of the death and rebirth cycle is found in the ritual sacrifice of a youth as a vegetation daimon to the sun, a beautiful example of which is told in Tezcatlipoca's Feast. *An analogous sacrifice of a maiden is told in* The Girl Who Was Sacrificed *by her Kin. The whole is a fertility rite which is intended to renew the creative forces of man or of nature.*

The wisdom of the feminine and the curious powers of renewal by an elixir derived from the moon, symbolizing immortality through rebirth, are occasionally rejected by the arrogance of masculine consciousness with tragic results. Another version of this theme in a negative vein is told in the fairy tale The Three Snake-Leaves. *Tales such as this are instructive, however, in showing the amoral interplay of good and evil forces as they emerge from the unconscious in folk art and literature. While justice is frequently done at the end of these myths, the essential point of the story lies in the expressive ambiguity of those same forces of destruction or creation we saw in the cosmic myths of creation.*

The chief difference between the cosmic cycle and the nature cycle is, very roughly, the difference between a masculine creative agency (e.g., Shiva) and a feminine creative agency (e.g., Inanna). This division of archetypal configurations seems basic to any understanding of mythology, while the interaction of the two provides one of the germinal points of psychological development of an individual nature. This can be seen in the symbolism of the unconscious of modern people as well as in the traditional myths.

J.L.H.

INANNA'S DESCENT TO THE NETHER WORLD (Sumerian)[1]

"The Sumerians were a non-Semitic, non-European people who flourished in southern Babylonia from the beginning of the fourth to the end

of the third millennium B.C. . . . 'They' represented the dominant cultural group of the entire Near East. . . .

"The Sumerians produced a vast and highly developed literature, largely poetic in character, consisting of epics and myths, hymns and lamentations, proverbs and 'words of wisdom.' These compositions are inscribed in cuneiform script on clay tablets which date largely from approximately 1750 B.C. . . . As literary products, these Sumerian compositions rank high among the creations of civilized man. . . .

"Their significance for a proper appraisal of the cultural and spiritual development of the Near East can hardly be overestimated. The Assyrians and Babylonians took them over almost in toto. The Hittites translated them into their own language. . . . The form and contents of the Hebrew literary creations and to a certain extent even those of the ancient Greek were profoundly influenced by them. . . ."—Sumerian Mythology, *Kramer.*[2]

"The Sumerian myth of 'Inanna's Descent to the Nether World' is highly significant for the light on the Sumero-Babylonian religious tenets, particularly those concerning death and the nether world. Moreover, as the predecessor and prototype of the Semitic myth 'Ishtar's Descent to the Nether World,' it provides us with an ancient and highly instructive example of literary borrowing and transformation."—Ancient Near Eastern Texts, *Pritchard.*[3]

> From the "great above" she set her mind toward the "great
>   below,"
> The goddess, from the "great above" she set her mind towards
>   the "great below,"
> Inanna* from the "great above," she set her mind towards
>   the "great below."
> My lady abandoned heaven, abandoned earth, to the nether
>   world she descended,
> Abandoned lordship, abandoned ladyship, to the nether
>   world she descended.
> In Erech she abandoned Eanna, to the nether world she
>   descended, . . .
> She arrayed herself in the seven ordinances,
> She gathered the ordinances, placed them in her hand,
> All the ordinances she set up at her waiting foot,
> The *Sugurra*, the crown of the plain, she put upon her head,

* Queen of Heaven, goddess of Light and Love. (*Plate* 7.)

The wig of her forehead she took
The measuring rod and line of lapis lazuli she gripped in
her hand,
Small lapis lazuli stones she tied about her neck,
Sparkling . . . stones she fastened to her breast,
A gold ring she put about her hand,
A breastplate which . . ., she tightened about her breast,
With a *pala*-garment, the garment of ladyship, she covered
her body,
Kohl which . . . , she daubed on her eyes.
Inanna walked towards the nether world.
Her messenger Ninshubur walked at her side,
The pure Inanna says to Ninshubur:
"O thou who are my constant support,
My messenger of favorable words,
My carrier of true words,
I am now descending to the nether world.
When I shall have come to the nether world,
Fill heaven with complaints for me,
In the assembly shrine cry out for me,
In the house of the gods rush about for me, . . .
To the Ekur, the house of Enlil,* all alone direct thy step.
Upon entering the Ekur, the house of Enlil,
Weep before Enlil:
'O Father Enlil, let not thy daughter be put to death in the
nether world,'
If Enlil stands not by thee in this matter, go to Ur, . . .
[The city of the moon-god Nanna.
If he refuses to help go to Eridu.]
Let not thy good metal be covered with the dust of the nether
world,
Let not thy good lapis lazuli be broken up into the stone of
the stoneworker,
Let not thy boxwood be cut up into the wood of the
woodworker,
Let not the maid Inanna be put to death in the nether world.
In Eridu, upon thy entering the house of Enki [god of water
and wisdom]

* God of air, chief divinity of the Sumerian pantheon.

PLATE 1. *Śiva, King of Dancers.*

PLATE 2. *Śiva Natarāja.*

PLATE 3. *Aztec Calendar Stone.*

PLATE 4. *Birth of Adonis.*

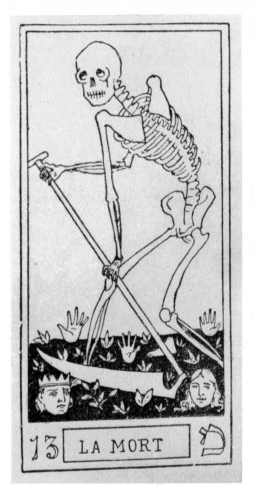

PLATE 5. *The Death Card.*

PLATE 6. *The Crucifixion*.

PLATE 7. *The Goddess Innina.*

Weep before Enki:
"O Father Enki, let not thy daughter be put to death in the
    nether world. . . ."

Father Enki, the lord of wisdom,
"Who knows the food of life, who knows the water of life,
He will surely bring me to life."
Inanna walked towards the nether world,
To her messenger Ninshubur she says:
"Go, Ninshubur,
The word which I have commanded thee do not neglect."
When Inanna arrived at the palace, the lapis lazuli mountain,
    of the nether world,
At the door of the nether world she acted evilly,*
In the palace of the nether world she spoke evilly:
"Open the house, gatekeeper, open the house,
Open the house, Neti, open the house, all alone I would
    enter."
Neti, the chief gatekeeper of the nether world,
Answers the pure Inanna:
"Who, pray, art thou?"
"I am Inanna of the place where the sun rises."
"If thou art Inanna of the place where the sun rises,
Why pray hast thou come to the land of No Return?
On the road whose traveler returns not, how hath thy heart
    led thee?"
The pure Inanna answers him,
"My elder sister Ereshkigal,
Because her husband, the lord Gugalanna, had been killed,
To witness his funeral rites,
. . . ; verily 'tis so."
Neti, the chief gatekeeper of the nether world,
Answers the pure Inanna;
"Stay, Inanna, to my queen let me speak,
To my queen Ereshkigal [Queen of the nether world] (*Plate*
    8) let me speak; . . . let me speak."
Neti, the chief gatekeeper of the nether world,

* More literally, "set up that which is evil."

Enters the house of his queen Ereshkigal and says to her:
*"Behold thy sister Ishtar (Inanna) is waiting at the gate,
  (*Plate* 9)
She who upholds the great festivals,
Who stirs up the deep before Ea, the king."
When Ereshkigal heard this,
Her face turned pale like a cut-down tamarisk,
While her lips turned dark like a bruised *kuninu*-reed.
"What drove her heart to me? What impelled her spirit
  hither?
Lo, should I drink water with the Anunnaki?
Should I eat clay for bread, drink muddied water for beer?
Should I bemoan the men who left their wives behind?
Should I bemoan the maidens who were wrenched from the
  laps of their lovers?
Or should I bemoan the tender little one who was sent off
  before his time?
Go, gatekeeper, open the gate for her,
Treat her in accordance with the ancient rules."
Forth went the gatekeeper to open the door for her:*
Neti, the chief gatekeeper of the nether world,
Heeded the word of his queen,
Of the seven gates of the nether world, he opened their locks,
Of the gate Ganzir, the face of the nether world he defined
  its rules.
To the pure Inanna he says:
"Come, Inanna, enter."
Upon her entering [the first gate],
The sugurra, the crown of the plain of her head was removed.
"What, pray, is this?"
"Be silent, Inanna, the ordinances of the nether world are
  perfect,
O Inanna do not question the rites of the nether world." . . .
[To pass through each gate Inanna removed one of the
  ordinances, and at the last gate—]
Upon her entering the seventh gate,
The *pala*-garment, the garment of ladyship of her body, was
  removed.

* . . . * Akkadian version of the Descent of Ishtar to the Nether World.
Lines 24-27. *Ancient Near Eastern Texts*, p. 107.

"What, pray, is this?"

"Be silent, Inanna, the ordinances of the nether world are
    perfect,

O Inanna, do not question the rites of the nether world."

Bowed low . . .

The pure Ereshkigal seated herself upon her throne,

The Anunnaki,* the seven judges, pronounced judgment
    before her,

They fastened their eyes upon her, the eyes of death,

At their word, the word which tortures the spirit, . . .

The sick "woman" was turned into a corpse,

The corpse was hung from a stake.

After three days and three nights had passed,

Her messenger Ninshubur, . . .

Her carrier of true words,

Fills the heaven with complaints for her,

Cried out for her in the assembly shrine,

Rushed about for her in the house of the gods, . . .

To the Ekur, the house of Enlil, all alone he directed his step.

Upon his entering the Ekur, the house of Enlil,

Before Enlil, he weeps,

"O, Father Enlil, let not thy daughter be put to death in the
    nether world, . . ."

Father Enlil answers Ninshubur:

"My daughter has asked for the 'great above,' has asked for
    the 'great below,' . . .

The ordinances of the nether world, the . . . ordinances, the
    ordinances—she has reached their place, . . ."

Father Enlil stood not by him in this matter, he went to
    Ur, . . .

[and Nana also refused aid].

In Eridu upon his entering the house of Enki,

Before Enki he weeps:

"O Father Enki, let not thy daughter be put to death in the
    nether world, . . .

---

* The Anunnaki, to judge from the available material, are the unnamed
"great gods" of the Sumerian pantheon who participated in the assemblies
called by the leading deities before making final decisions; they were conceived as begotten by the heaven-god Anu on the "mountain of heaven and
earth."

* Since Ishtar has gone down to the land of No Return,
The bull springs not upon the cow, the ass impregnates not
    the jenny,
In the streets the man impregnates not the maiden."*
"Let not the maid Inanna be put to death in the nether
    world."
Father Enki answers Ninshubur:
"What has happened to my daughter! I am troubled, . . .
What has happened to the queen of all the lands! I am
    troubled,
What has happened to the hierodule of heaven! I am
    troubled,"
From his fingernail he brought forth dirt and fashioned the
    kurgarru,
From his red-painted fingernail he brought forth dirt and
    fashioned the *kalaturru.*†
To the *kurgarru* he gave the food of life,
To the *kalaturru* he gave the water of life,
Father Enki says to the *kalaturru* and *kurgarru:*
" (Nineteen lines badly damaged)
Upon the corpse hung from a stake they directed the *pulhu*
    and the *melammu,*
Sixty times the food of life, sixty times the water of life,
    sprinkle upon it,
Surely Inanna will arise."
(break of approximately twenty lines)
. . . Upon the corpse hung from a stake they directed the
    pulhu and the *melammu,*
Sixty times the food of life, sixty times the water of life, they
    sprinkled upon it,
Inanna arose.
Inanna ascends from the nether world,
The Anunnaki fled,
Who now of the dwellers of the nether world will descend
    peacefully to the nether world!
When Inanna ascends from the nether world,

---

* Akkadian version. Lines 48-51. *Ancient Near Eastern Texts,* p. 108.
  † The kurgarru and the kalaturru, two sexless creatures, and (he) en-
trusts to them the "food of life" and the "water of life."

Verily the dead hasten ahead of her.
Inanna ascends from the nether world, . . .
They who accompanied Inanna,
Were beings who know not food, who know not water,
Who eat not sprinkled flour,
Who drink not libated water,
Who take away the wife from the loins of man,
Who take away the child from the . . . of the nursemaid.
Inanna ascends from the nether world,
Upon Inanna's ascending from the nether world,
Her messenger Ninshubur threw himself at her feet,
Sat in the dust, dressed in sackcloth.
The demons say to the pure Inanna:
'O Inanna, wait before thy city, let us carry him off."
The pure Inanna answers the demons:
"My messenger of favorable words,
My carrier of true words,
Who fails not my directions,
Neglected not my commanded word,
Fills the heaven with complaints for me,
Cried out for me in the assembly shrine,
Rushed about for me in the house of the gods, . . .
He brought me to life. . . ."*

THE DEATH AND REBIRTH OF HORUS
(Egyptian)[5]

*In this tale of ancient times, the death of Horus brings about darkness.
His rebirth, through the offices of the god Thoth (son of the great Ra),
is associated with the rise of the sun.*

I am Isis, pregnant with her child, bearing Horus divine, and I
gave birth to Horus, the son of Osiris, in the nest of Chemmis.
    I am very much rejoiced at that, for in him I saw the aven-

* [See Kramer's *Mythologies of the Ancient World*[4] for a newly discovered
ending to our present myth.]

ger of his father. I hid him and concealed him for fear of that
(evil) one. I wandered to Im (?) begging* all the while for fear
of the evil-doer. I longed for the child the whole day whilst taking
care of his needs. I returned to embrace Horus, but I found that
he, the beautiful Horus of gold, the innocent, fatherless child, had
moistened the banks with liquid of his eye and saliva of his lips.
His body was limp, his heart weak, and the veins of his body
did not beat.

I uttered a cry, saying: "It is I, it is I." But the child was too
weak to answer. My breasts were full, but his stomach was empty
and his mouth longed for its food; the well overflowed, but the
child was thirsty. I wanted to come and protect him; great was
the mischief: an innocent child, who still resisted the bottle and
had been left alone too long. I was afraid, because nobody came
on my voice. My father is in the nether world, my mother is in
the realm of the dead. My elder brother is in the sarcophagus,
the other is an enemy, obstinate in his malice towards me. My
younger sister is in his house. Whom among men shall I call?
Then their heart will care for me. . . .

Then a woman came to me, known in her town and a queen
in her home. She came to me bearing a life-sign whilst she had
every confidence in her knowledge: "Fear not, fear not, son
Horus; be not despondent . . . mother of the god. The child is
protected against the malice of his brother. The bush is hidden.
Death does not penetrate into it. It is the magic power of Atum,
father of the gods, who is in heaven, who has made my life-sign.
Seth does not penetrate into this home, he does not go about at
Chemmis. Horus is protected against the malice of his brother.
His followers do not injure him. Look for the reason this has hap-
pened, then Horus will live for his mother. Certainly, a scorpion
has stung him or an evil snake has bitten him."

Isis put her nose into his mouth to know the smell of it in
his skull. She examined the disease of the divine heir. She found
that he had been poisoned. She quickly embraced her son, jump-
ing about with him like fishes put on a coal-fire.

"Horus has been bitten, Horus has been bitten. O, Re, your
son has been bitten."

. . . Serket said: "What is the matter . . . whatever is the
matter with the child? Sister Isis, do call to heaven, then there

* Begging for food.

will be a stand-still with the crew of the boat,* and there will be
no favourable wind in the boat of Re, as long as the son Horus
lies on his side."

Isis uttered her cry to heaven, her lamentation to the boat
of millions. Aton stopped in front of her and did not move from
his place. Thoth came provided with magic power and with the
high command of justification: "What is the matter, . . . Isis
divine, skillful one, who knows her spell. Horus your son, is not
in mischief, I hope? His protection is the boat of Re. Today I
have come from the bark. Aton is in his place of yesterday. Darkness has come, the light has been driven away until Horus will
be healthy for his mother Isis, . . ."

Isis divine said: "Thoth, how self-confident you are, but how
slow are your plans! Have you really come provided with magic
power and with the high command of justification? Misery upon
misery, the number whereof is not known. Behold, Horus is in
distress on account of the poison. The mischief is the deed of his
brother, death is their complete destruction. Would that I were
with the eldest son of his mother. Then I would not have lived
to see this after him. From the beginning however I submitted to
it and I have waited to avenge him. Horus, Horus, remain on
the earth! Since the day I conceived him, I yearned to rehabili-
tate his father, the father of the child, who suffers from something."

"Fear not, . . . Isis divine. . . . [Thoth replied] I have come
from heaven with the breath of life to cure the child for his
mother. Horus, Horus, your heart be strong, be it not weak on account of the fire. The protection of Horus is he who is in his disk
and who illuminates the two lands with his two eyes. The protection of the patient likewise.

"The protection of Horus is the eldest in heaven, who rules
everything that exists. The protection of the patient likewise.

"The protection of Horus is that great dwarf who goes about
the Netherworld at twilight. . . .

". . . is the lion of the night who travels in the Western
Mountain. . . .

". . . is the great hidden Ba, who goes about in his two eyes. . . .

". . . is the great falcon who flies in the sky, on earth and in
the Netherworld. . . .

* The boat of the sun.

"... is the sacred beetle, the great ... beetle in the sky. ...

"... is the secret corpse whose mummy is sacred in its sarcophagus. ...

"... is the Netherworld, the lands where faces are reversed, secret of contents. ...

"... is the divine phoenix who sits in his eyes. ...

"... is his own body. The magic power of his mother Isis is his protection. ... (*Plate* 11)

"... are the names of his father, his images in his names. ...

". . . is the lamentation of his mother, the cries of his brothers. ...

". . . is his own name. The gods care for him, protecting him. ...

"Wake up, Horus, your protection is permanent. Comfort your mother's heart. The words of Horus will delight the hearts. He reassures the distressed one.

"Rejoice, you who are in heaven, for Horus avenges his father. Recede, poison. Behold you are conjured by the mouth of Re, the tongue of the great god averts you. The boat of Re stands still and does not sail. Aton is in his place of yesterday, until Horus will be healthy for his mother Isis. ...

"Come to the earth, then the boat will sail and the crew of heaven will sail. The foods are stopped up, the temples blocked, until Horus will be healthy for his mother Isis. ...

"The demon of the dark goes about, the seasons are not separated, the figures of the shadow are not seen, until Horus will be healthy for his mother Isis. ...

"The sources are blocked, the crops are withering, the food is taken from mankind until Horus will be healthy. ... Come to the earth, O, poison, then the hearts will rejoice and the light of the sun will go round. I am Thoth, the eldest, son of Re, with the command of Atum, the father of the gods, that Horus may be healthy for his mother Isis ... Horus, Horus, your Ka is your protection, your followers protect you. The poison is dead, its heat driven away from stinging the son of the lady. Depart to your homes for Horus lives for his mother. ...

"... Re in heaven vouches for him, his father watches over him, the magic power of his mother is his protection, while she makes love go about for him and brings fear of him among men.

"They are waiting for me to push off the evening-boat and to make the morning-boat sail. Horus belongs to you, assigned to life. . . . The poison is powerless.

"Rejoice, Re-Harachte, your son Horus has been assigned to life. All people and all animals which are poisoned will live likewise."

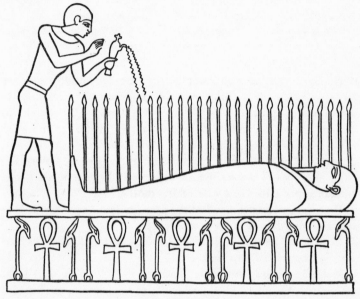

FIG. 10—Osiris as the personification of the earth to be regenerated. The ankh as symbol of generation and the Uas as a sceptre representing power are placed below the god. The priest is watering the grain (from which new life will arise) from a sacred urn. From bas-relief found in chamber dedicated to Osiris in Temple of Isis at Philae, Egypt. The inscription reads, "This is the form of him whom one may not name, Osiris of the mysteries, who sprang from the returning waters."

THE NEW YEAR'S FESTIVAL
(Babylonian)[6]

The ritual of the New Year at Babylon and as told in the Assur tablet, enact the basic solar pattern of the day and the year: Nature's cycle of

*death and rebirth—the death of the sun in the west and his re-emergence
at dawn in the east.*

"*. . . This daily pattern was seen also in the pattern of the year—
the shortening of the days after the summer solstice when the light of
the god was slowly 'eaten' by the evil ones in the West as he entered his
tomb of earth. In Egypt, [there was] the god's reawakening at midnight
as Sokaris, birth god of the necropolis, leading to his final rebirth out
of the earth at winter solstice and his . . . ultimate fulfilled glory at
mid-day when day and night were again equal.*"—*N. Rambova.*

*The following is a reconstruction of the New Year ritual based on
the Assur text from the first Babylonian Dynasty, 2225-1926 B.C.*

Bel is imprisoned in the lower world [the Mountain] and the
celebrants seek to bring him forth. A celebrant rides in haste to
some kind of sepulchre (?). That means Nebo, who hastens to
the lower world to comfort Bel, held captive in the lower world.

Celebrants hasten in the streets crying, "Where is Bel?" and
a priestess prays to the moon-god and the sun-god to restore Bel
to life. She goes to a gate, which represents Bel's sepulchre. She
probably represents Bel's wife or his mother.

Watchmen [twins] stand at the gate of Bel's temple, who represent the guardsmen of Bel's sepulchre.

Celebrants lament, because Bel was bound and slain, and because he descended into hell. . . .

A goddess (Bel's consort?) descends to hell to be with him;
some deity (Nebo?—Bel's son?) refuses to descend to Bel, for
Assur (-Bel) has declared that he should not be wounded, but he
stands guard over Bel's prison.

A head . . . is fastened to the door of the temple of Beltis,
Bel's consort. This means the malefactor who was slain with Bel,
and whose head was hung on the neck of the statue of Beltis.

Nebo returns to Barsippa, which means that, after the slaying of Bel, tumult and strife arose in the city.

Nebo comes again to Babylon to do homage to the dead Bel
and to behold the slain malefactor, who is symbolized by a swine.
The malefactor has gone to the lower world with Bel.

Celebrants go before Nebo; they symbolize the people who
weep for Bel.

A magus goes wailing before Beltis, who descends to hell

seeking Bel. The magus brings Bel's garments to Ishtar of Erech. These symbolize Bel's garments which were taken from him after his death. Beltis of Erech or Ishtar is here brought into the ritual from the parallel cult of Tammuz, in which Ishtar, mother of Tammuz, descends to the house of the dead seeking Tammuz. . . .

Milk before Ishtar of Nineveh is placed (?), which symbolizes his nursing by the mother goddess.

The Epic of Creation is sung before Bel, prayers are said, and the celebrant cries, "What was Bel's sin?" This describes Bel's unjust suffering and death.

A celebrant looks to heaven in prayer. This symbolizes Bel in the lower world, who implores the gods of heaven for life. . . .

A celebrant looks toward the lower world in prayer. This means that Bel, who has been laid in a sepulchre, will rise from the house of death.

Some deity (?) refuses to go with Bel to the house of sacrifice at the New Year festival of Nisan, which means that Bel bears the . . . (?) of the malefactor, who was bound and sits with him in the lower world.

Also Beltis, Bel's consort, goes not with him to the house of sacrifice at the New Year festival, and celebrants pray before Beltis, asking her to guard the temple during Bel's imprisonment. This means that Bel's wife rules the temple until his release.

Beltis puts on garments of mourning. This means that she cared for the wounded body of Bel.

On the eighth day of the New Year's festival a pig is slaughtered; this symbolizes the malefactor concerning whom they question Beltis, asking who was this malefactor slain with Bel.

. . . the water is stirred up, made muddy, and poured away; . . . the act refers to some phase of Bel's wounding and death.

The . . . garment (in which Bel was wrapped) again appears in the ritual in connection with water used in the ritual; these are said to symbolize Bel's suffering. The ritual introduces hymns on the divine origin of water. . . .

Celebrants run a race in the streets in frenzy. Here the ritual symbolizes a part of the myth of creation, having no relation at all to the death and resurrection of Bel. The race symbolizes

Ninurta (-Bel) (of the Semitic Babylonian myth) , sent to conquer the dragons, who returns to tell the gods of his victory. . . .

Psalmists participate in the race, carrying Bel's relics plundered (from the temple?) when he was slain. This is said to symbolize how the gods his fathers [permitted him to be bound and wounded?].

The messenger-god Nusku hastens past Esabad, temple of Gula. This means that the mother-goddess Gula sent Nusku (to tell the gods of Bel's death?) .

Bel's clothing and sandals are brought to Beltis, his consort. This means that Nusku (?) brought them to her, so that he cannot escape from the lower world.

A chariot and horses are sent out recklessly to the house of sacrifice, speeding headlong, without a driver. This signifies Bel's disappearance.

A goddess goes out of the city weeping, which symbolizes the women who wept at Bel's wounding.

The ritual now introduces a door slit with an aperture to let in the light. This symbolizes the door of Bel's sepulchre, where the gods imprisoned him. But the gods at last break down the door, battle (with the gods of the lower world?) and bring Bel back to life and the upper world. (*Plate* 10.)

The Colophon at the end of this tablet says that the explanations of the mystic meanings of these acts in the ritual are not to be read by those not lawfully initiated into the priesthood of this cult. . . .

THE TOMB OF EYE (Egyptian)[7]

In the tombs of King Akh-en-Aton and his nobles are inscriptions containing hymns of the Aton (sun disc) faith. This particular hymn of praise comes from the tomb of Eye.

"We do not find in Egyptian texts a description of Elysian fields or even of a plain of Asphodels, neither a Valhalla nor an island of the Blessed. This absence of definition of the hereafter is in keeping with the conception we have found to underlie the various images of life after death: there was no land of the dead to be described. The dead

lived in the great cosmic circuit of sun and stars. They lived in the sky but also below the horizon, in the netherworld; they descended in the West and rose in the East. They maintained at the same time some connection with their tomb, and through it, with life upon earth. But their lasting happiness lay beyond the earth and the tomb."—Ancient Egyptian Religion, *Frankfort*.[8]

Thou appearest beautifully on the horizon of heaven,
Thou living Aton, the beginning of life!
When thou art risen on the eastern horizon,
Thou hast filled every land with thy beauty.
Thou art gracious, great, glistening, and high over every land;
Thy rays encompass the lands to the limit of all that thou
     hast made.
Though thou art far away, thy rays are on earth;
Though thou art in their faces, no one knows thy going.

When thou settest in the western horizon,
The land is in darkness, in the manner of death.
They sleep in a room, with heads wrapped up.
Every lion is come forth from his den;
All creeping things, they sting.
Darkness is a shroud, and the earth is in stillness,
For he who made them rests in his horizon.
At daybreak, when thou arisest on the horizon,
When thou shinest as the Aton by day,
Thou drivest away the darkness and givest thy rays.
The Two Lands are in festivity every day,
Awake and standing upon their feet,
For thou hast raised them up.
Washing their bodies, taking their clothing,
Their arms are raised in praise at thy appearance.
All the world, they do their work.

How manifold it is, what thou hast made!
They are hidden from the face of man.
O sole god, like whom there is no other!
Thou didst create the world according to thy desire,
Whilst thou wert alone.

Thou settest every man in his place,
Thou suppliest their necessities:
Everyone has his food, and his time of life is reckoned.
Their tongues are separate in speech,
And their natures as well;
Their skins are distinguished,
As thou distinguishest the foreign peoples.

How effective they are, thy plans, O lord of eternity!
Thou makest the seasons in order to rear all that thou hast
   made,
The winter to cool them,
And the heat that they may taste thee.
Thou madest millions of forms of thyself alone.
Cities, towns, fields, road, and river—
Every eye beholds thee over against them,
For thou art the Aton of the day over the earth.
Thou art in my heart.

ATTIS (Greek)[9]

The Agdos rock—so the story runs—had assumed the shape of
the Great Mother. Zeus fell asleep upon it. As he slept, or as he
strove with the goddess, his semen fell upon the rock. In the tenth
month the Agdos rock bellowed and brought forth an untamable,
savage being, of twofold sex and twofold lust, named Agdistis.
With cruel joy Agdistis plundered, murdered, and destroyed whatever it chose, cared for neither gods nor men, and held nothing
mightier on earth or in heaven than itself. The gods often consulted together as to how this insolence could be tamed. When
they all hesitated, Dionysos took over the task. There was a certain spring to which Agdistis came to assuage its thirst when it
was overheated with sport and hunting. Dionysos turned the
spring-water into wine. Agdistis came running up, impelled by
thirst, greedily drank the strange liquor and fell perforce into
deepest sleep. Dionysos was on the watch. He adroitly made a cord

of hair, and with it bound Agdistis's male member to a tree. Awakened from its drunkenness, the monster sprang up and castrated itself by its own strength. The earth drank the flowing blood, and with it the torn-off parts. From these at once arose a fruit-bearing tree: an almond-tree or—according to another tale —a pomegranate tree. Nana, the daughter of the king or rivergod Sangarios (Nana is another name for the great goddess of Asia Minor), saw the beauty of the fruit, plucked it and hid it in her lap. The fruit vanished, and Nana conceived a child of it. Her father imprisoned her, as a woman deflowered, and condemned her to death by starvation. The Great Mother fed her on fruits and on the foods of the gods. She gave birth to a little boy. Sangarios had the child left out in the open to perish. A he-goat tended the suckling, who, when he was found, was fed upon a liquor called 'he-goat's milk.' He was named Attis, either because *attis* is Lydian for a handsome boy or because *attagus* was Phrygian for a he-goat.

Attis was a boy of marvellous beauty. The tale goes on that Agdistis fell in love with him. The savage deity took the grown lad out hunting, led him into the most inaccessible wilderness and gave him spoils of the chase. Midas, King of Pessinous, sought to separate Attis from Agdistis, and to this end gave the boy his own daughter to wife. Agdistis appeared at the wedding and drove the participants mad with the notes of a syrinx. Attis castrated himself beneath a pine-tree, crying out: "Unto thee, Agdistis!" And thus he died. From his blood sprang the violets. Agdistis was repentant and besought Zeus to bring Attis* back to life. All that Zeus, in accordance with Fate, could grant was that Attis' body should never putrefy, his hair should evermore continue to grow, and his smallest finger should remain alive and move of its own accord.

* "His worship, characterized by frenzied orgies, was carried to Rome after the worship of Cebele had been adopted by the Romans, in 204 B. C. Each year on March twenty-second a pine-tree was cut and brought to the sanctuary of Cebele where it was swathed in woolen bands and decked with violets; an effigy of . . . Attis was tied to it . . . [When] the ceremonies reached their peak there was blood-letting . . . to bespatter the altar and the sacred tree with their blood. Probably it was on this day that they . . . mutilated [themselves] which was an essential part of the cult. On the next day the resurrection of Attis was celebrated in the form of a licentious carnival." *Standard Dictionary of Folklore, Mythology and Legend,* Funk and Wagnalls.[10]

FIG. 11—The sacred tree of Attis (decked with votive objects and pine cones representing new life) and a sacrificial bull and ram. Relief from an altar to Cybele.

ADONIS (Greek)[11]

Myrrha, the daughter of Kinyras, having offended Aphrodite, was by her inspired with a passion for her own father. After a long struggle against it, she gratified it by the aid of her nurse, unknown to its object. When Kinyras found what he had unwittingly done, he pursued his daughter with his drawn sword, to efface her crime in her blood. He had nearly overtaken her, when she prayed to the gods to make her invisible, and they in pity changed her into a myrrh-tree. In ten months afterwards, the tree opened, and the young Adonis came to light (*Plate* 4). Aphrodite, delighted with his beauty, put him in a coffer, unknown to all the gods, and gave him to Persephone to keep. But the goddess of the underworld, as soon as she beheld him, refused to part with him; and the matter being referred to Zeus, he decreed that Adonis should have one third of the year to himself, another third with Aphrodite, and the remaining third with Persephone. Adonis gave his own portion to Aphrodite, and lived happily with her; till having offended Artemis, he was torn by a wild boar and died.

The ground where his blood fell was sprinkled with nectar by the mourning goddess, and . . . the anemone or wind-flower sprang up from it, . . . the rose also derived its present hue from this fatal event, for as the distracted goddess ran barefoot through the woods . . . to the aid of her lover, the thorns of the rose-briars tore her delicate skin, and their flowers were thenceforth tinged with red. . . .

Fig. 12—A Greek scene from a fertility rite in which a priestly figure prepares a youth for his ritual performance as vegetation daimon. He is decked with ribbons and leaves symbolic of rebirth and is crowned with a head-dress in the form of a hare, suggestive of the lunar cycle of change and transformation.

PERSEPHONE (Greek)[12]

Persephone, . . . was in the Nysian plain with the Ocean nymphs gathering flowers. She plucked the rose, the violet, . . . when she beheld a narcissus of surprising size and beauty, an object of amazement . . . for one hundred flowers grew from one root; unconscious of danger the maiden stretched forth her hand to seize the wondrous flower, when suddenly the wide earth gaped, Hades in his gold chariot rose, and catching the terrified goddess carried her off in it shrieking to her father for aid, unheard and unseen by gods or mortals, save only Hecate, . . . who heard her as she sat in her cave, and by king Helios, whose eye nothing on earth escapes.

So long as the goddess beheld the earth and starry heavens, the fishy sea and the beams of the sun, so long she hoped to see her mother and the tribes of the gods; and the tops of the mountains and the depth of the sea resounded with her divine voice. At length her mother heard: she tore her head-attire with grief, cast a dark robe around her, and like a bird hurried "over moist and dry." Of all she inquired tidings of her lost daughter, but neither gods nor men nor birds could give her intelligence. Nine days she wandered over the earth, with flaming torches in her hands; she tasted not of nectar or ambrosia, and never once entered the bath. On the tenth morning Hecate met her. . . . Together they proceed to Helios: . . . and Demeter entreats that he will say who the ravisher is. The god of the sun, . . . tells her that it was Hades, who by permission of her sire had carried her [Persephone] away to be his queen; . . . .

. . . the goddess, incensed at the conduct of Zeus, abandoned the society of the gods, and came down among men. But now she was heedless of her person, and no one recognized her. Under the disguise of an old woman, . . . she came to Eleusis, and sat . . . by a well, beneath the shade of an olive tree. . . .

The Princess Kallidike [who had come to the well to draw water] tells the goddess . . . to wait till she had consulted her mother, Metaneira, who had a young son in the cradle, of whom, if the stranger could obtain the nursing her fortune would be made; . . . [Metaneira] agreed to hire the nurse at large wages; . . . As she entered the house a divine splendor shone all around. . . . She undertook the rearing of the babe, . . . beneath her care "he throve like a god." . . .

It was the design of Demeter to make him immortal, but the curiosity and folly of Metaneira deprived him of the intended gift. . . . Demeter tells who she is, and directs that the people of Eleusis should raise an altar and temple to her . . . and the temple was speedily raised. The mourning goddess took up her abode in it, but a dismal year came upon mankind; the earth yielded no produce, . . . in vain was the seed of barley cast into the ground;

"well-garlanded Demeter" would suffer no increase. The whole race of man ran risk of perishing, the dwellers of Olympos of losing gifts and sacrifices, had not Zeus discerned the danger and thought on a remedy. He . . . invites Demeter back to Olympos, but the disconsolate goddess will not comply with the call. . . . she will not ascend to Olympos, or suffer the earth to bring forth, till she has seen her daughter. (*Plate* 14.)

. . . Zeus sends . . . [Hermes] to Erebos, to endeavor to prevail on Hades to suffer Persephone to return to the light. . . . he [Hermes] quickly reached the "secret places of earth," and found the king at home . . . with his wife, who was mourning for her mother. On making known to Hades the wish of Zeus, "the king of the Subterraneans smiled with his brows" and yielded compliances. He kindly addressed Persephone, granting her permission to return to her mother. The goddess instantly sprang up with joy, and heedlessly swallowed a grain of pomegranate which he presented to her.

Hermes conducted his fair charge safe to Eleusis . . . and Persephone sprang from the car to meet and embrace her mother. . . .

Demeter anxiously inquired if her daughter had tasted anything while below; . . . if but one morsel had passed her lips, nothing could have her from spending one-third of the year with her husband; she should however pass the other two with her and the gods.

Persephone ingenuously confesses the swallowing of the grain of pomegranate, and then relates to her mother the whole story. . . . Zeus sends Rhea to invite them back to heaven. Demeter now complies.

LEMMINKAINEN, HIS DESTRUCTION AND HIS RESTORATION TO LIFE
(Finnish)[13]

Into the forest went Lemminkainen. As he went he chanted his Magic Song, "O Tapio, Lord of the Forest, aid me: lead me where I may take my quarry! Nyyrikki, O thou son of the Forest's Lord, red-capped one, mighty hero, make a path for me through your father's domain; clear the ground for me and keep me on the proper roadway!" Lemminkainen, the handsome, the light-stepping one, chanted Magic Songs to win the forest divinities as he went seeking the Elk of Hiisi.

Another Magic Song he chanted: "O Mielikki, Mistress of the Forest, fair-faced, bountiful lady, send the game towards me; turn it into the pathway of the hunter; open the thickets; unlock Tapio's storehouse; make wide the door of his castle in the forest! Do this during this hunting-trip of mine!" Other Magic Songs Lemminkainen chanted as he went through the forest seeking the Elk of Hiisi. "If thou wilt not trouble thyself about me, Mistress of the Forest, charge thy little serving-girls to help me! And thou, Tapio's girl, little maiden of the forest, put the flute to your mouth of honey, whistle through thy pipe so that the Lady of the Forest may rouse herself and harken to my Magic Songs!"

So he went through the forest; but the quarry he sought was not turned towards him. Through the trackless forest he went, across the marshes, over the heaths. At last he went up a mountain; he climbed a knoll; he turned his eyes to the north-west; he turned his eyes to the north; there, across the marshes, he saw Tapio's mansions with their doors and windows all golden.

Then once more the quick-moving, light-stepping Lemminkainen went onward. He dashed through all that lay across his path. Under the very windows of the mansions of the Lord of the Forest he came. Through the windows he saw those whose business it was to dispense the game to the hunters. They were resting; they were lolling; their worst wear they had on them. Under the windows Lemminkainen chanted his Magic Songs:

"Mistress of the Forest, wherefore do you sit here and do you let the others sit here in such shabbiness? You are loathsome to behold! Yet when I went through the forest I saw three castles— one a wooden one, one a bone one, one a stone one; they had six windows, all bright, all golden; they who were within had rustling, golden garments on! Re-array as before thyself and thy household! Put away now your birch-bark shoes, your old garments, your disgusting shabbiness! Mistress of the Forest, put on thy garments of good fortune! Put thy golden bracelets on thy wrists, thy golden rings on thy fingers, a headdress of gold put on! Put gold coins in thy hair, gold rings in thine ears, gold beads around thy neck! Long and wearily have I wandered hereabouts; I wander for nothing; the quarry I seek is not to be seen by me!

"Greybeard with the pine-leaf hat," he chanted, "with the cloak of moss! Re-array the woods; give the aspens their greyness, give the alders a robe of beauty, clothe the pine-trees in silver, adorn the fir-trees with gold, and the birch-trees with golden blossoms. Make it as in the former years when days were better, when the waste-places flowed with honey. O Daughter of Tapio, Tuulikki, gracious virgin, drive the game this way! Take a switch; strike the game on their haunches; drive the game toward the one who seeks for it and waits for it! Master of Tapio's mansions, mistress of Tapio's mansions, make wide the doors, send forth the game that has been shut in!"

So Lemminkainen chanted; for a week he ranged through the forest. His Magic Songs appeased the Lord of the Forest, delighted the Mistress of the Forest, and made glad the hearts of all the Forest Maidens. To where the Elk of Hiisi had his lair they went; they drove forth the Elk; they turned it in the direction of the one who waited for it.

Over the Elk Lemminkainen threw his lasso. And when he held the Elk he chanted his Magic Song once more, "Lord of the Forest, Tapio; Mistress of the Forest, Mielikki, come now and take your reward for the good you have done me! Come now and take the gold and silver I scatter on the ground of the forest!" So he chanted; then to the north, to Pohjola, he journeyed with the Elk he had captured. "I have caught the Elk of Hiisi! Come forth now, ancient one of Pohjola; give me your daughter; give me the bride I have come for!"

Louhi, the Mistress of Pohjola, came out of her dwelling, and she looked upon Lemminkainen and the Elk he had captured. "I will give you my daughter, I will give you the bride you have come for, when you capture the Steed of Hiisi, and bring it to me here."

Then Lemminkainen took a golden bridle and a halter of silver; he went through the green and open meadows; he went out upon the plains. No sign he saw of the Steed of Hiisi. He called upon Ukko, the God of the Sky, and he chanted a Magic Song:

"Open the clefts of the Heavens; cast the hail upon the back

of Hiisi's Steed; fling ice-blocks upon him that he may race from
where he is, that he may come to where I am!" Ukko rent the
air; he scattered ice-blocks; they were smaller than a horse's head,
but they were bigger than a man's head. They struck the back of
Hiisi's Steed. It raced forward. Then Lemminkainen chanted,
"Steed of Hiisi, stretch forth thy silver head; push it into this
golden bridle! I will never drive thee harshly; with a rope's end
I will never smite thee. No, with silver cords I will lead thee, and
with a piece of cloth I will drive thee!" So he chanted, and the
Steed of Hiisi put forward his head; the golden bridle with the
bit of silver went across his head and into his mouth.

Then to the north went Lemminkainen bringing the chest-
nut steed with the foam-flecked mane. He called to the Mistress
of Pohjola, "I have captured the Steed of Hiisi and the Elk of
Hiisi. Now give thy daughter to me, give me the bride that I have
come for."

But Louhi, the Mistress of Pohjola, answered him, "I will
give thee my daughter, I will give thee the bride thou hast come
for when thou hast shot with an arrow, and using one arrow only,
the white Swan on Tuonela's dark water." Then Lemminkainen
took his bow. He went down into Manala's abysses. He went to
where Tuoni's murky river flowed. He went to where the waters
made a dread whirlpool.

There the cowherd Märkähattu lurked; there the blind man
waited for Lemminkainen. When Lemminkainen had come first
to Pohjola he had chanted his Magic Songs; he had chanted them
against the swordsmen and the young heroes who were there,
and he had driven them all away, banning them with his Magic
Songs. One old man he had not banned—Märkähattu the cowherd who sat there, his eyes closed in blindness. Lemminkainen
had scorned him. "I have not banned thee," he cried, "because
thou art so wretched a creature. The worst of cowherds, thou hast
destroyed thy mother's children, thou hast disgraced thy sister,
thou hast crippled all the horses, thou hast wearied to death the
foals." Märkähattu, greatly angered, left the place where Lemminkainen had scorned him; ever since he had waited by the
whirlpool for the coming of Lemminkainen.

The white Swan was on the dark river of Tuonela. Lemminkainen drew his bow. As he did, Märkähattu grasped a water-snake; he hurled it; he pierced Lemminkainen with the serpent. Lemminkainen knew no Magic Songs to relieve himself from the wounds made by water-snakes. He sank into the murky river; he was tossed about in the worst of whirlpools; he was dashed down the cataract; the stream brought him into Tuonela.

There Tuoni's bloodstained son, drawing his sword, hewed him into pieces. He hewed him into eight pieces and he flung the pieces into the dark river. "Be tossed about for ever with thy bow and thy arrows, thou who camest to shoot the sacred Swan upon our sacred River!"

Only through his mother could help come to Lemminkainen. She had bided at home, troubled by his long delay in returning. One day she looked up the comb and the hair-brush he had left behind: she saw blood trickling from the comb, blood dripping from the hair-brush. She knew that blood was coming from the body of her son. She gathered up her skirt and she went off to find him.

Valleys were lifted up as Lemminkainen's mother went on; hills were levelled; the high ground sank before her and the low ground was lifted up. She hastened to Pohjola. She came to the door and she questioned the Mistress of Pohjola.

"Whither hast thou sent my son, Lemminkainen?" "I know no tidings of your son. I yoked a steed for him; I fixed a sledge for him, and he started off from my dwelling; perhaps in driving over a frozen lake he sank into it." "Shameless are the lies thou tellst me. Tell me whither thou hast sent him or I will break down the doors of Pohjola." "I fed him; I gave him meat and drink, and I placed him in his boat; he went to shoot the rapids, but what has befallen him I do not know." "Shameless are the lies thou tellst. Tell me whither thou has sent him or this instant death will come to thee." "Now I will tell thee, now I will tell thee truly. Lemminkainen went to shoot the sacred bird, the Swan on Tuonela's River."

Then his mother went in quest of him; she questioned the trees, she questioned the pathway, she questioned the golden moon in the sky. But the trees, the pathway, the golden moon in the sky, all had their own troubles, and they would take no trouble for any woman's son. She questioned the sun in the heavens, and the sun told her that her son was in Tuonela's River.

Then to the smith Ilmarinen went Lemminkainen's mother. For her Ilmarinen fashioned a rake, a rake with a copper handle and with teeth of steel—a hundred fathoms was the length of the teeth, five hundred fathoms was the length of the handle. To Tuonela's River she went: there she chanted a Magic Song.

She prayed the sun to shine with such strength that the watchers in Manala would sleep and that the the powers of Tuonela would be worn out. And the sun stooped upon a crooked birch-tree and shone in his strength so that the watchers of Manala were worn out—the young men slept upon their sword-hilts; the old men slept resting upon their staffs; the middle-aged men, the spearmen, slept resting upon the hafts of their spears. Then Lemminkainen's mother took her rake; she raked the river against the current; once she raked it, and she raked it again. The third time she raked the river she brought up the hat and stockings of her son Lemminkainen. She went into the river, and she waded in its deepest water. She drew up the body with her rake of iron.

Many fragments were wanting to make up the body of Lemminkainen—half of his head, a hand, many little fragments. Life was wanting in the body. But still his mother would not cast it back into the river. Once again she raked Tuonela's deep river, first along it and then across it; his hand she found, half of his head she found, fragments of his backbone she found, and pieces of his ribs.

She pieced all together; the bones fitted, the joints went together. She chanted a Magic Song, praying that Suonetar would weave the veins together, and stitch with her finest needle and her most silken thread the flesh and the sinews that were broken. She sang a Magic Song, praying that Jumala would fix together the bones. Then the veins were knit together, the bones were fastened together, but still the man remained lifeless and speechless.

Then Lemminkainen's mother sang a Magic Song. She bade the bee go forth and find the honey-salve that would give final healing. The bee flew across the moon in the heavens; he flew past the borders of Orion; he flew across the Great Bear's shoulders, and into the dwelling of Jumala the Creator. In pots of silver, in golden kettles was the salve that would give final healing. The bee gathered it and brought it back to Lemminkainen's mother.

With the salve she rubbed him. She called upon her son to rise out of his slumbers, to awaken out of his dreams of evil. Up he rose; out of his dreams he wakened, and speech came back to him. Even then he would have slain the Swan so that he might win a bride in Pohjola. But his mother persuaded him, and his mother drew him back with her to his home. There the bride awaited him whom he had won in another place and on another day, Kyllikki, the Flower of Saari.

THE RETIREMENT AND EMERGENCE OF THE SUN GODDESS (Japanese)[14]

From his contact with death and the defiled nether land, Izanagi proceeds to purify himself. This he does in a small river in Tsukushi (i.e., Kyushu). As he throws his clothing on the ground some twelve deities are born of the individual garments and jewelry. Avoiding the water of the upper river as being too fast and that of the lower river as being too sluggish, he bathes himself in the middle course, and from the maculations on his body are born other divinities—some fourteen in all. At last, from his left eye is born the sun goddess, Amaterasu, the "Heaven Shining" and from his right eye, the moon god. From his nose is born Susanowo, the "Impetuous Male." Of these three divinities, Amaterasu and Susanowo are to occupy henceforth the central place in the legend; the moon god fades rapidly from the account.

Amaterasu is resplendent and shining; Izanagi places under her domination the Plain of High Heaven and bestows upon her a necklace of jewels. Susanowo is impetuous and dark, and to him is given the rule of the Sea Plain. But the Impetuous Male is disconsolate; he weeps and laments loudly without ceasing until the mountains wither and the seas dry up. All the gods are baffled and distracted. At last, Izanagi questions him on his clamorous despair, to which, indeed, he seems more devoted than to his duties as ruler of the Sea Plain. Susanowo answers that he is lamenting because he wishes to visit his mother (Izanami) in the Land of Darkness, and that such is the cause of his distress. Izanagi is furious at such impertinence and as punishment banishes him from the land.

Susanowo resolves then to take leave of his sister the sun goddess and sets off for her realm in the heavens. But so boisterous is his approach that the sun goddess is frightened lest his arrival mean a coming encroachment on her own domains. So she prepares herself for meeting him. She slings a thousand-arrow quiver on her back, and another holding five hundred, and, grasping her bow, she takes her stance with such vigor that her legs sink to the thighs in the ground, and her appearance is that of a mighty warrior. Face to face with this formidable amazon, Susanowo assures her he has come only to take his leave, that he arrives with no "strange intentions." In order that she may know the sincerity of his motives, he suggests they take an oath together and produce children, which they do. She accepts the ten-grasp sword he gives her and, breaking it into three pieces, puts them in her mouth and chews them. He does the same with the jewels she has presented to him. And as they spew out the bits, numerous divinities come into being.

In spite of all his assurances, the Impetuous Male does not give up his rude ways. In fact, in certain respects his behavior worsens. He breaks down the divisions in the rice fields, which had been laid out by Amaterasu, fills the irrigation ditches, defiles her dwelling place with excrement. Curiously enough, she at first excuses him, blaming his actions on drunkenness. But when he flays a piebald colt with a backward flaying and flings it into the weaving hall where she is working with her attendants so that they are fatally wounded in their private parts by the flying shuttles; she is profoundly annoyed. To underline her displeasure, she retires into a rock cave and makes the entrance fast.

With the retirement of the sun goddess, light leaves the world, and the alternation of day and night ceases. The myriads of divinities are deeply perturbed at this turn of events and gather in the river bed of heaven to consult among themselves as how best to entice the goddess from her hiding place. They place long-singing night birds (i.e., roosters?) near the entrance of the cave and cause them to crow; they suspend from a tree a string of curved jewels, a mirror, and offerings of white cloth, and they all recite official liturgies (*norito*). But what is to prove finally efficacious is a lascivious madcap dance performed by the goddess Ama no uzume, who, stamping loudly on the ground, pulling the nipples of her breasts, and lowering her skirts, so delights the assembled gods that they break out into raucous and appreciative laughter. Piqued with understandable curiosity, the sun goddess peers out of the cave, whereupon the mirror is pushed to the door and the goddess, intrigued with her own image, gradually steps out. A rope is passed in back of her, beyond which she is forbidden to return. With the appearance of the sun, light returns once again to the world, and the alternation of night and day recommences.

TEZCATLIPOCA'S FEAST (Aztec)[15]

Tezcatlipoca (Smoking Mirror) was one of the most important Aztec gods (mentioned in another myth, The Five Suns*). He symbolized many opposites; he was a creator god and a destroyer; he was god of divine providence and god of ruin; god of purity and yet protector of sin. He symbolized the night sky; hence his connection with the stars, the moon, evil, sorcery, and death. Huitzilpochtli, the god of the day sky and the sun, was so closely identified with Tezcatlipoca that they are thought to be two aspects of one god. Tezcatlipoca was the brother of the great god Quetzalcoatl and yet his mortal enemy. The smoking mirror, Tezcatlipoca's symbol, is found on his head near the temple, or in place of his foot which the earth monster bit off.*

"Tezcatlipoca's feast: 'which was like Easter and fell close to the Feast of Resurrection . . .' was the most important of all and took place halfway through the fifth month, when the sun first passes through the zenith after the winter solstice. On this occasion, Tezcatlipoca, sacrificed in the person of a prisoner, was reborn immediately into the body of another youth, who represented him until he in his turn died at the feast the following year.

"The rituals accompanying these cermonies were particularly moving, because the anonymous horde of sacrificed slaves was here replaced

by one solitary individual, whose fate stands out against the cosmic
drama in which he had become involved."—Burning Water, *Sejourne.*[16]
    This story is taken from a study of the Aztec natives made by a six-
teenth-century Spanish friar.

In the month of Toxcatl, the great feast of Tezcatlipoca was held.
At that time died his impersonator, who for one year had lived as
Tezcatlipoca. (*Plate* 12a.)
    And at that time once more was offered to the people his new
impersonator, who would again live for one year. . . .
    For he who was chosen was of fair countenance, of good un-
derstanding and quick, of clean body—slender like a reed; long
and thin like a stout cane; well-built; not of overfed body, not
corpulent, and neither very small nor exceedingly tall. . . .
    He who was thus, without flaw, who had no bodily defects, . . .
they then looked well that he be taught to blow the flute; that he
might pipe and play his flute well; and that with it he hold his
flowers and his smoking tube and blow and suck upon it, and
smell the flowers.
    Thus he went bearing his flute, his flowers, and his smoking
tube together as he walked through the streets.
    And while yet he lived and was cared for in the house of the
guardian, before he appeared before the people, care was taken
that he might be prudent in his discourse, that he might talk gra-
ciously, converse well, and greet people agreeably on the road, if
he met anyone.
    For he was much honored when he appeared as the imper-
sonator; because he was the likeness of [Tezcatlipoca]; he was ac-
knowledged as our lord, treated like a lord; one begged favors,
with sighs; before him the common people bowed in reverence
and kissed the earth. . . .
    And for one year he thus lived; at the feast of Toxcatl, he ap-
peared before the people. And when the man died who had been
impersonator for one year, he who had led the way, he who had
cast the spear for one year, who had given commands for one year,
forthwith was one chosen to be set in his place, from all whom the
temple guardians had saved and cared for at the time . . .
    Thereupon he began his office; he went about playing his
flute. By day and by night he followed whatever way he wished.

His eight young men went following him. . . .

And four warriors, who instructed youths in the art of war, . . .

Then Montezuma adorned the impersonator well and arrayed him in varied garb; . . . he adorned him in great pomp with all costly articles, which he caused to be placed upon him; for verily he took him to be his beloved god. His face was anointed with black; it was said: "He fasteth with blackened face." A thick layer of black was smeared on his cheeks. White feathers were placed upon his head—the soft down of eagles. They placed it on his hair, which fell to his loins.

And when he was attired, he went about with sweet-smelling flowers upon his head, a crown of flowers. And these same were hung over both shoulders, as far down as his armpits. This was called "the flowery garment."

And from both ears hung curved, gold, shell pendants. And they fitted his ears with ear plugs made of a mosaic of turquoise. And he wore a shell necklace. Moreover, his breast ornament was of white sea shells. . . .

Then they placed golden bracelets on both upper arms, and on both wrists they put carved bracelets with precious stones, covering almost all the forearm. And he put on his net cape like a fish-net of wide mesh with a fringe of brown cotton thread. And his costly breech clout reached to the calves of his legs.

And then they placed his bells on both legs, all golden bells, called *oioalli*. These, as he ran, went jingling and ringing. Thus they resounded. And he had princely sandals with ocelot skin ears. Thus was he arrayed who died after one year.

When the feast of Toxcatl was drawing near, when it was approaching him, when it was coming to him, first they married him to four women whom they sought out for him. . . .

And he left off, scattered in various places, and abandoned the ornaments he had had, in which he had walked about fasting, painted black. His hair was shorn; he was given a tuft of hair tied upon his forehead, like that of a war captain. Thus they bound his hair, knotting it with brown cotton thread called *tochiacatl*; and they tied to his long hair his forked heron feather ornament with single quetzal feathers attached.

Only twenty days he lived, lying with and married to the

women. Four women* he lived with, who also were cared for, for one year, in the guardian's house. . . .

And still on the eve of the feast of Toxcatl, still five days from . . . the feast day of Toxcatl . . . they began to sing and dance.

Now, during this time, Montezuma came not forth; those who had been the impersonator's companions provided the people with food and favors. . . .

They sang and danced [for four days]. . . .

After they had sung and danced, then he embarked in a canoe. The women went traveling with him; they went consoling him and keeping him merry. Then the canoe arrived; then it touched the shore; then it was beached. . . .

For here he was abandoned, a little distance from Tlapit-zauhcan. The women then returned; and only they who had freely become his pages accompanied him while he yet lived.

So, it was said, when he arrived where he was to die, where a small temple stood, called Tlacochcalco, he ascended by himself, of his free will, to the place where he was to die. When he climbed the first step, he passed one step, he there broke, shattered, his flute, his whistle, etc.

And when he had mounted all the steps, when he had reached the summit, then the priests fell upon him; they threw him on his back upon the sacrificial stone. Then one cut open his breast, seized his heart, and raised it as an offering to the sun.†
(*Plate* 12b.)

For in this manner were all these captives offered up. But his body they did not roll down; rather, they lowered it. Four men carried it.

And his severed head they strung on the skull-rack. Thus he ended in the adornment in which he died. Thus he there ended his life, there he terminated his life, when he went to die. . . .‡

---

* Incarnations of the wives of the god of providence.

† The Aztecs believed that the Sun would die unless fed with human blood.

‡ "We do not need to make any detailed analysis to see that this is a dramatization of the annual cycle, and that the unblemished youth plays the part of the Sun. It may be that the twenty days preceding his sacrifice symbolize the winter solstice, during which the Sun, sojourning . . . in the subterranean world, begins to fear for his freedom . . . If the winter solstice reproduces on a larger scale the daily drama of light imprisoned by darkness, the prisoner's death must signify his liberation. . . ." *Burning Water*, Sejourne.[17]

THE GIRL WHO WAS SACRIFICED
BY HER KIN (African)[18]

The sun was very hot and there was no rain, so the crops died and hunger was great. This happened one year; and it happened again a second, and even a third year, that the rain failed. The people all gathered together on the great open space on the hilltop, where they were wont to dance, and they said to each other, "Why does the rain delay in coming?" And they went to the Medicine-Man and they said to him, "Tell us why there is no rain, for our crops have died, and we shall die of hunger."

And he took his gourd and poured out its contents. This he did many times; and at last he said, "There is a maiden here who must be bought if rain is to fall, and the maiden is named Wanjiru. The day after tomorrow let all of you return to this place, and every one of you from the eldest to the youngest bring with him a goat for the purchase of the maiden."

On the day after the morrow, old men and young men all gathered together, and each brought in his hand a goat. Now they all stood in a circle, and the relations of Wanjiru stood together, and she herself stood in the middle. As they stood there, the feet of Wanjiru began to sink into the ground, and she sank in to her knees and cried aloud, "I am lost!"

Her father and mother also cried and exclaimed, "We are lost!"

Those who looked on pressed close and placed goats in the keeping of Wanjiru's father and mother. Wanjiru sank lower to her waist, and again she cried aloud, "I am lost, but much rain will come!"

She sank to her breast; but the rain did not come. Then she said again, "Much rain will come."

Now she sank in to her neck, and then the rain came in great drops. Her people would have rushed forward to save her, but those who stood around pressed upon them more goats, and they desisted.

Then Wanjiru said, "My people have undone me," and she sank down to her eyes. As one after another of her family stepped forward to save her, someone in the crowd would give to him or her a goat, and he would fall back. And Wanjiru cried aloud for the last time, "I am undone, and my own people have done this thing." Then she vanished from sight; the earth closed over her, and the rain poured down, not in showers, as it sometimes does, but in a great deluge, and all the people hastened to their own homes.

Now there was a young warrior who loved Wanjiru, and he lamented continually, saying, "Wanjiru is lost, and her own people have done this thing." And he said, "Where has Wanjiru gone? I will go to the same place." So he took his shield and spear. And he wandered over the country day and night until, at last, as the dusk fell, he came to the spot where Wanjiru had vanished. Then he stood where she had stood and, as he stood, his feet began to sink as hers had sunk; and he sank lower and lower until the ground closed over him, and he went by a long road under the earth as Wanjiru had gone and, at length, he saw the maiden. But, indeed, he pitied her sorely, for her state was miserable, and her raiment had perished. He said to her, "You were sacrificed to bring the rain; now the rain has come, and I shall take you back." So he took Wanjiru on his back as if she had been a child and brought her to the road he had traversed, and they rose together to the open air, and their feet stood once more on the ground.

Then the warrior said, "You shall not return to the house of your people, for they have treated you shamefully." And he bade her wait until nightfall. When it was dark he took her to the house of his mother and he asked his mother to leave, saying that he had business, and he allowed no one to enter.

But his mother said, "Why do you hide this thing from me, seeing I am your mother who bore you?" So he suffered his mother to know, but he said, "Tell no one that Wanjiru has returned."

So she abode in the house of his mother. He and his mother slew goats, and Wanjiru ate the fat and grew strong. Then of the skins they made garments for her, so that she was attired most beautifully.

It came to pass that the next day there was a great dance, and her lover went with the throng. But his mother and the girl waited until everyone had assembled at the dance, and all the road was

PLATE 8. *Lilith, Goddess of the Underworld.*

PLATE 9. *Ishtar-Venus.*

PLATE 10. *Assyrian Vegetation God.*

PLATE 11. *Isis.*

PLATE 12a. *Impersonator of Tezcatlipoca.*

PLATE 12b. *Sacrifice of impersonator of Tezcatlipoca.*

PLATE 13. *The Great Mother.*

PLATE 14. *Demeter and Kore.*

PLATE 15. *Pārvatī, the Thunder Goddess.*

empty. Then they came out of the house and mingled with the crowd. When the relations saw Wanjiru, they said, "Surely that is Wanjiru whom we had lost."

And they pressed to greet her, but her lover beat them off, for he said, "You sold Wanjiru shamefully."

Then she returned to his mother's house. But on the fourth day her family again came and the warrior repented, for he said, "Surely they are her father and her mother and her brothers."

So he paid them the purchase price, and he wedded Wanjiru who had been lost.

THE THREE SNAKE-LEAVES
(European)[19]

There was once on a time a poor man, who could no longer support his only son. Then said the son: "Dear father, things go so badly with us that I am a burden to you. I would rather go away and see how I can earn my bread." So the father gave him his blessing and with great sorrow took leave of him. At this time the King of a mighty empire was at war, and the youth took service with him, and went out to fight. And when he came before the enemy, there was a battle, and great danger, and it rained shot until his comrades fell on all sides, . . . those left were about to take flight, but the youth stepped forth, spoke boldly to them, and cried: "We will not let our fatherland be ruined!" Then the others followed him, and he pressed on and conquered the enemy. When the King heard that he owed the victory to him alone, he raised him above all the others, . . . and made him the first in the kingdom.

The King had a daughter who was very beautiful, but she was also very strange. She had made a vow to take no one as her lord and husband who did not promise to let himself be buried alive with her if she died first. "If he loves me with all his heart," said she, "of what use will life be to him afterwards?" On her side she would do the same, and if he died first, would go down to the grave with him. This strange oath had up to this time frightened away all wooers, but the youth became so charmed with her beauty that he cared for nothing, but asked her father for her. "But do you know what you must promise?" said the King. "I must be buried with her," he replied, "if I outlive her, but my love is so great that I do not mind the danger." Then the King consented, and the wedding was solemnized with great splendor.

They lived now for a while happy and contented with each other, and then it befell that the young Queen was attacked by a severe illness, and no physician could save her. And as she lay there dead, the young King remembered what he had been obliged to promise, and was horrified at having to lie down alive in the grave, but there was no escape. The King had placed sentries at all the gates, and it was not possible to avoid his fate. As the day came when the corpse was to be buried, he was taken down with it into the royal vault and then the door was shut and bolted.

Near the coffin stood a table on which were four candles, four loaves of bread, and four bottles of wine. . . . And now he sat there full of pain and grief, ate every day only a little piece of bread, drank only a mouthful of wine, and nevertheless saw death daily drawing nearer. Whilst he thus gazed before him, he saw a snake creep out of a corner of the vault and approach the dead body. And as he thought it came to gnaw at it, he drew his sword and said: "As long as I live, you shall not touch her," and hewed the snake in three pieces. After a time a second snake crept out of the hole, and when it saw the other lying dead and cut in pieces, it went back, but soon came again with three green leaves in its mouth. Then it took the three pieces of the snake, laid them together, as they fitted, and placed one of the leaves on each wound. Immediately the severed parts joined themselves together, the snake moved, and became alive again, and both of them hastened away together. The leaves were left lying on the ground, and a desire came into the mind of the unhappy man . . . to know if the wondrous power of the leaves which had brought the snake to life again, could not likewise be of service to a human being. So he picked up the leaves and laid one of them on the mouth of his dead wife, and the two others on her eyes. And hardly had he done this than the blood stirred in her veins, rose into her pale face, and colored it again. Then she drew breath, opened her eyes, and said, "Ah, God, where am I?" "You are with me, dear wife," he answered, and told her how everything had happened, and how he had brought her back to life. Then he gave her some wine and bread, and when she had regained her strength, he raised her up and they went to the door and knocked, and called so loudly that the sentries heard it, and told the King. The King came down himself and opened the door, and there he found both strong and well, and rejoiced with them that now all sorrow was over. The young King, however, took the three snake-leaves with him, gave them to a servant and said: "Keep them for me carefully, and carry them constantly about you; who knows in what trouble they may yet be of service to us!"

But a change had taken place in his wife; after she had been restored to life, it seemed as if all love for her husband had gone out of her heart. After some time, when he wanted to make a voyage over the sea, to visit his old father, and they had gone on board a ship, she forgot the great love and fidelity which he had shown her, . . . and conceived a wicked inclination for the skipper. And once when the young King lay there asleep, she called in the skipper and seized the sleeper by the head, and the skipper took him by the feet, and thus they threw him down into the sea. When the shameful deed was done, she said: "Now let us return home, and say that he died on the way. I will extol and praise you so to my father that he will marry me to you, and make you the heir to his crown." But the faithful servant who had seen all that they did, unseen by them, unfastened a little boat from the ship, got into it, sailed after his master, . . . He fished up the dead body, and by the help of the three snake-leaves which he carried about with him, and laid on the eyes and mouth, he fortunately brought the young King back to life.

They both rowed with all their strength day and night, and their little boat sailed so swiftly that they reached the old King before the others. He was astonished when he saw them come alone, and asked what had happened to them. When he learnt the wickedness of his daughter he said: "I cannot believe that she has behaved so ill, but the truth will soon come to light," and bade both go into a secret chamber and keep themselves hidden from everyone. Soon afterwards the great ship came sailing in, and the godless woman appeared before her father with a troubled countenance. He said: "Why do you come back alone? Where is your husband?" "Ah, dear father," she replied, "I come home again in great grief; during the voyage, my husband became suddenly ill and died, and if the good skipper had not given me his help, it would have gone ill with me. He was present at his death, and can tell you all." The King said: "I will make the dead alive again," and opened the chamber, and bade the two come out. When the woman saw her husband, she was thunderstruck, and fell on her knees and begged for mercy. The King said: "There is no mercy. He was ready to die with you and restored you to life again, but you have murdered him in his sleep, and shall receive the reward that you deserve." Then she was placed with her accomplice in a ship which had been pierced with holes, and sent out to sea, where they soon sank amid the waves.

INITIATION AS A
SPIRITUAL EDUCATION:*
THE MYTHS

An account of the Malekulan Journey of the Dead
*shows the basic pattern of initiation as beginning
with a rite of separation from the Mother as goddess, or from the
mother-world of childhood. If the latter, it is expressed as fear
of life; if the former, it is fear of death, both of which are to be
entered by rites of sacrifice and propitiation. These are called
rites of passage, associated with crossing a sacred threshold. To
accomplish this passage, a rite of death and rebirth is felt to be
central, and the primitive mind does not distinguish any difference between rites for entering and rites for leaving a particular
phase of life.*

*Following or coexistent with threshold rites are the cere-
monies of purification of which the prime ritual is baptism, expressed here as the early Christian Baptism celebrated between
Good Friday and Easter. The symbolism implies a cleansing by
water and a fertilization by fire (The Paschal Taper) reminiscent
of the water and fire initiation rites of Isis described in Apuleius'*
Golden Ass *and in other traditions.*

In The Quest of Gilgamesh *we find an account of Gilgamesh's
journey to achieve immortality expressed as an attempt at initiation with its threshold experience, baptismal experience, initiation
sleep,† and a return journey with a master of initiation. The*

* See Introduction, pp. 41 to 59.
† This is also emphasized in *The Hymn of the Robe of Glory*, pp. 153
to 160.

content of the initiation seems not to have been realized though the semidivine pair, Utnapishtim and his wife, would represent the motif of marriage or conjunction of opposites necessary to consummate the transitional period of initiation. This is an example of a favorite literary theme of the failure of initiation.

In contrast to this hero figure there is an account of Dionysos, the nature god who represents the true spirit of initiation as a surrender to the unconscious in a death, sometimes by dismemberment, for the sake of rebirth. As son of a divine mother, Persephone or Semele, Dionysos experiences initiation on the boyhood level, but as son of a divine father he is twice-born from the thigh of Zeus. From this vantage point he overcomes the typical male fear of the feminine. He is the prototype of all initiates in the experience of a sacred marriage as the central rite of initiation, thereby achieving unity or wholeness, along with productiveness expressed as fertility.

The fidelity of a relationship in the discipline of courtly love refers to the theme of the sacred marriage in medieval times as told in the tale of Tristan and Iseult. *Also in this tradition is a fine example of the theme of incorporation in the account of the* Procession of the Holy Grail.

Initiation in which a girl or the feminine spirit in man learns through many difficulties and tests of endurance to submit to the fertilizing power of the masculine is reflected in Prince Lindworm *which is a variant to the tale of* Beauty and The Beast. *Finally, myths derived from the primitive rites of initiation, in which tribal rites intermingle with solitary rites in the search for a mythical guardian spirit, are told with variations in* The Thunder Rite, Boshkwadosh, *and* O-Pe-Che.

J.L.H.

THE MALEKULAN JOURNEY OF
THE DEAD (Melanesian)[1]

Stone monuments in the form of dolmens or monoliths are to be found in various parts of the village. . . . The most important rite for which they are erected is [a great public rite related to the journey of the dead called] . . . Maki, a ritual cycle extending over a period of from fifteen to thirty years. . . . It has to do both with society and with the individual's aspiration toward a future life, which is its basic function, and one of its main features is the sacrifice of numerous tusked boars in order to propitiate and thereby circumvent the destructive power of a cannibalistic Female Devouring Ghost, whose object is to "eat" or annihilate the spirits of the dead and thus prevent them from accomplishing the long journey to the Land of the Dead. . . .

On Vao the most important sacrificial monument is a large dolmen. This dolmen represents, first, a stone tomb; secondly, the Cave said to be inhabited by the Female Devouring Ghost through which the dead man is supposed to pass on his journey to the Land of the Dead; and thirdly the womb through which the living achieve rebirth by means of sacrifice. A wooden image is set up in front of the dolmen, representing all those ancestors who have previously performed the rite (*Plate* 17) . . . . The sacrifice is performed on a stone platform which is set up directly behind the shrines. The sacrificer mounts the platform, sacrifices a tusked boar,* kindles a new fire, and assumes a new name to symbolize the fact that he has entered upon a new life. . . . In the first part of the rite the maternal uncles of the sacrificer bar his way to the dolmen, just as the Devouring Ghost . . . bars his way into the Cave of the Dead; both . . . have to be propitiated by an offering of tusked boars. In the second part of the rite, the fire which the sacrificer lights on the stone platform parallels the belief that the ghosts of the dead of high Maki rank, after having . . . passed through the Cave of the Dead, proceed to a final Home of the Dead on an active volcano on the neighboring island of Ambrym. . . .

Thus the central act of the whole Maki is the self-sacrifice of a man who symbolically immolates part of himself in the form of his tusked boars, these . . . precious possessions . . . with which he ritually identifies himself. . . .

A man gains the possibility of a future life by sacrificing

* . . . Although these animals are eaten after the sacrifice, they are raised primarily . . . for their tusks. [The tusks are trained] to form a complete spiral . . . [or several spirals]. Without a tusked boar to propitiate the Devouring Ghost, no man can be reborn or attain to the Land of the Dead. *Malekulan Journey of the Dead*, p. 121.

the tusked boars, so also during his lifetime he must have . . . a special boar for his relative to sacrifice at his death, in order that his spirit may be protected against the Devouring Ghost. . . .

[When] . . . the ghost of the dead man is sped on his way; . . . his body is buried in his paternal village, while certain [personal] objects . . . are sent back . . . to his mother's village, to which, in one level of belief, his spirit is also said to return. . . . The body wrapped in a fine mat, is lowered into the grave; many pigs are then sacrificed, including the "death pig," which is thrown alive into the grave for the dead man to use as ransom to redeem his spirit from the Devouring Ghost, which will otherwise destroy it. . . .

The "dead man" or "ghost" [spirit] makes his way to the long, black sand beach called Orap, situated on the Malekulan mainland. . . . Here he enters a cave called . . . "Cave of the Dead." As he goes in, his way is blocked by the Devouring Ghost Le-hev-hev,* whose sex is there not known.

As the dead man's ghost tries to enter the Cave, Le-hev-hev pulls him back . . . another mythical ghostly being, . . . an aspect of the benevolent creator-god Ta-ghar, who intercedes for the newcomer, and says to Le-hev-hev: "Leave him alone. Let him come and join all his friends. . . ." Le-hev-hev then releases the dead man's spirit, which at the same time presents her with the ghost of the pig sacrificed at his burial. If he had not such a pig, Le-hev-hev would devour him. The newcomer . . . then goes inside the Cave "to join his dead friends who are gathered there."

He does not stay, but continues . . . for some forty miles down the coast until he comes at sundown to a promontory . . . where he lights a great fire to attract the attention of the ghostly ferryman on Ambrym; (where the volcano is). The ferryman paddles over . . . and takes the newcomer back with him to Ambrym, where he is escorted up to the big volcano called . . . "Source of Fire."

The dead on the volcano† dance all night and sleep all day.

---

* [See the design drawn by the Female Devouring Ghost in South West Bay (fig. 5). These are a feature of the Journey of the Dead recorded on a larger island opposite the Malekulan mainland. Also see Introduction, page 44, for description of the tests given by the Female Devouring Ghost.]

† ". . . , being inside the volcano means beatitude, since to the native, fire means power and life, and the attainment of life after death in the volcano is the positive goal toward which every native strives."

THE QUEST OF GILGAMESH
(Akkadian) [2]

TABLET I
Two-thirds of him is god and one-third of him is man.
The form of his body none can match.

TABLET IX
Gilgamesh for Enkidu, his friend,
Weeps bitterly and roams over the desert.
"When I die, shall I not be like unto Enkidu?
Sorrow has entered my heart.
I am afraid of death and roam over the desert.
To Utnapishtim,* the son of Ubara-Tutu,
I have therefore taken the road and shall speedily go there. . . ."
[Gilgamesh arrives at a mountain range.]
The name of the mountain is Mashu.
As he arrives at the mountain of Mashu,
Which every day keeps watch over the rising and setting of the
	sun,
Whose peaks reach as high as the "banks of heaven,"
And whose breast reaches down to the underworld,
The scorpion-people keep watch at its gate,
Those whose radiance is terrifying and whose look is death,
Whose frightful splendor overwhelms mountains,
Who at the rising and setting of sun keep watch over the sun.
When Gilgamesh saw them,
His face became gloomy with fear and dismay.
But he took courage and approached them.
The scorpion-man calls to his wife:
"He who has come to us, his body is the flesh of gods!"
The wife of the scorpion-man answers him:
"Two-thirds of him is god, one-third of him is man."
The scorpion-man calls the man,
Speaking these words to the offspring of the gods:
"Why hast thou traveled such a long journey?

* The Babylonian Noah.

Why hast thou come all the way to me,
Crossing seas whose crossings are difficult?
The purpose of thy coming I should like to learn." . . .

"For the sake of Utnapishtim, my father, have I come,
Who entered into the assembly of the gods. . . .
Concerning life and death I would ask him."
The scorpion-man opened his mouth and said,
Speaking to Gilgamesh:
"There has not yet been anyone, Gilgamesh, who has been able
   to do that.
No one has yet traveled the paths of the mountains.
*For twelve leagues extends its interior.
Dense is the darkness and light there is none.
To the rising of the sun . . .;
To the setting of the sun. . . ."* . . .

"Though it be in sorrow and in pain,
In cold and heat,
In sighing and weeping, I will go!
Open now the gate of the mountains."
The scorpion-man opened his mouth and said
To Gilgamesh . . . :
"Go, Gilgamesh, . . .
The mountains of Mashu I permit thee to cross;
The mountains and mountain ranges thou mayest traverse.
Safely may thy feet carry thee back.
The gate of the mountains is open to thee."
When Gilgamesh heard this,
He followed the word of the scorpion-man.
Along the road of the sun he went. . . .

Dense is the darkness and there is no light;
Neither what lies ahead of him nor what lies behind him does
   it permit him to see. . . .
After he has traveled eleven double-hours, the dawn breaks.
After he has traveled twelve double-hours, it is light.

   * . . . * *Ancient Near Eastern Texts,* Pritchard.[3]

Before him stand shrubs of precious stones; upon seeing them,
   he went there directly.
The carnelian bears its fruit;
Vines hang from it, good to look at.
The lapis lazuli bears foliage;
Also fruit it bears, pleasant to behold. . . .

TABLET X

*Gilgamesh is addressing Siduri, the divine barmaid [who dwells by the
edge of the sea].*

"He who went with me through all hardships,
Enkidu, whom I loved so dearly,
Who went with me through all hardships,
He has gone to the common lot of mankind.
Day and night I have wept over him.
For burial I did not want to give him up, thinking:
'My friend will rise after all at my lamentation!'
Seven days and seven nights, until the worm fell upon his face.
Since he is gone, I find no life.
I have roamed about like a hunter in the midst of the steppe.
And now, O barmaid, that I see thy face,
May I not see death, which I dread!"
The barmaid said to him, to Gilgamesh:
"Gilgamesh, whither runnest thou?
The life which thou seekest thou wilt not find;
For when the gods created mankind,
They allotted death to mankind,
But life they retained in their keeping.
Thou, O Gilgamesh, let thy belly be full;
Day and night be thou merry; . . ."

Gilgamesh said to her, to the barmaid:
"I am Gilgamesh; I seized and killed the bull which came down
   out of heaven;
I killed the watchman of the forest;
I overthrew Humbaba, who dwelt in the cedar forest;
In the mountain passes I killed the lions."
The barmaid said to him, to Gilgamesh:

"If thou art Gilgamesh, . . .
Why is thy heart so sad, and why are thy features so distorted?
Why is there woe in thy heart,
And why is thy face like unto that of one who has made a far
journey? . . ."

Gilgamesh said to her, to the barmaid:
"Enkidu, my friend, whom I loved so dearly, who went with
me through all hardships,
Him the fate of mankind has overtaken!
Six days and seven nights I wept over him,

"I became afraid of death, so that I now roam over the steppe.
The matter of my friend rests heavy upon me.
. . . . Enkidu, my friend, whom I loved, has turned to clay.
And I, shall I not like unto him lie down
And not rise forever?"
Gilgamesh furthermore said to her, to the barmaid:
"Now, barmaid, which is the way to Utnapishtim?
What are the directions? Give me, oh, give me the directions! . . ."
"Gilgamesh, there never has been a crossing;
And whoever from the days of old has come thus far has not been
able to cross the sea. . . .

"Difficult is the place of crossing and too difficult its passage;
And deep are the waters of death, which bar its approaches.
Where, Gilgamesh, wilt thou cross the sea?
And when thou arrivest at the waters of death, what wilt thou do?
Gilgamesh, there is Urshanabi, the boatman of Utnapishtim.
With him are the stone images,* in the woods he picks. . . .
Him let thy face behold.
If it is possible, cross over with him; if it is not possible, turn
back home."
When Gilgamesh heard this,
He took his hatchet in his hand;
He drew the dagger from his belt, slipped into the woods, and

---

* These images may perhaps have been idols of an apotropaic character
enabling Urshanabi to cross the waters of death.

went down to them [the stone images]. . . .
Like an arrow he fell among them. . . .

Gilgamesh furthermore said to him, to Urshanabi:
"Now, Urshanabi, which is the road to Utnapishtim?
What are the directions? Give me, O give me the directions!
If it is possible, even the sea will I cross; but if it is not possible,
I will roam over the steppe."
Urshanabi said to him, to Gilgamesh:
"Thy hands, O Gilgamesh, have prevented thy crossing the sea;
For thou hast destroyed the stone images. . . .
The stone images are destroyed. . . .
Take the hatchet in thy hand, O Gilgamesh.
Go down to the forest and cut one hundred and twenty punting-
poles, each sixty cubits in length.
. . . . bring them to me."
When Gilgamesh heard this,
He took the hatchet in his hand, he drew the sword from his belt,
He went down to the forest and cut . . . punting-poles. . . .

Gilgamesh and Urshanabi then boarded the ship.
They launched the ship on the billows and glided along.
On the third day their voyage was the same as an ordinary one of
a month and fifteen days.
Thus Urshanabi arrived at the waters of death.
Urshanabi said to him, to Gilgamesh:
"Press on, Gilgamesh! Take a pole for thrusting. . . .
Let not thy hand touch the waters of death. . . .
Gilgamesh, take thou a second, a third, and a fourth pole; . . ."

With one hundred and twenty thrusts Gilgamesh had used up
the poles.
He ungirded his loins. . . .
Gilgamesh pulled off his clothes. . . .
With his hands he raised the mast.
Utnapishtim looks into the distance; he says to his heart and
speaks these words,
As he takes counsel with himself:
"Why are the stone images of the ship destroyed?

And why does one who is not its master ride upon it?
The man who is coming there is none of mine. . . ."

(Gilgamesh meets Utnapishtim and is asked the same questions that were addressed to him by the barmaid and the boatman. Gilgamesh answers Utnapishtim in exactly the same words.)

Gilgamesh furthermore said to him, to Utnapishtim:
"That now I might come to see Utnapishtim, whom they call 'the
     Distant,'
I went roaming around over all the lands,
I crossed many difficult mountains,
I crossed all the seas; . . ."

Utnapishtim said to him, to Gilgamesh: . . .

"Only the dragon-fly sheds his cocoon,
Only its face will see again the face of the sun.
From the days of old there is no permanence.
The sleeping and the dead, how alike they are!
Do they not both draw the picture of death?
Whether he was a servant or a master, who can tell it after they
     have reached their destiny?
The Anunnaki, the great gods, gather together;
Mammetum, the creatress of destiny, decrees with them the
     destinies.
Life and death they allot;
The days of death they do not reveal."

TABLET XI

Gilgamesh said to him, to Utnapishtim the Distant:
"I look upon thee, Utnapishtim,
Thine appearance is not different; thou are like unto me.
Yea, thou art not different; thou are like unto me.
My heart had pictured thee as one perfect for the doing of battle;
But thou liest idly on thy back.
Tell me, how didst thou enter into the company of the gods and
     obtain life everlasting?"
Utnapishtim said to him, to Gilgamesh:

"Gilgamesh, I will reveal unto thee a hidden thing,
Namely, a secret of the gods will I tell thee.
Shurippak—a city which thou knowest,
And which is situated on the bank of the river Euphrates—
That city was already old, and the gods were in its midst.
Now their heart prompted the great gods to bring a deluge. . . ."

[Ea the god of the waters said:]
"Man of Shurippak [Utnapishtim], son of Ubara-Tutu!
Tear down thy house, build a ship!
Abandon thy possessions, seek to save life!
Disregard thy goods, and save thy life!
Cause to go up into the ship the seed of all living creatures." . . .
[A long account of the preparation for the flood, and the flood
    itself.]
"When the seventh day arrived, the tempest, the flood,
Which had fought like an army, subsided in its onslaught.
The sea grew quiet, the storm abated, the flood ceased.
I opened a window, and light fell upon my face. . . ," [said
    Utnapishtim.]

"I bowed, sat down, and wept,
My tears running down over my face. . . ."

[He sent forth a dove and then a swallow. As there was no resting
    place they returned.]

"Then I sent forth a raven and let her go.
The raven went away, and when she saw that the waters had
    abated,
She ate, she flew about, she cawed, and did not return.
Then I sent forth everything to the four winds and offered a
    sacrifice.
I poured out a libation on the peak of the mountain.
Seven and yet seven kettles I set up.
Under them I heaped up sweet cane, cedar and myrtle.
The gods smelled the savor,
The gods smelled the sweet savor.
The gods gathered like flies over the sacrificer. . . ."

Ea opened his mouth and said, speaking to warrior Enlil:
'O warrior, thou wisest among the gods!
How, O how couldst thou without reflection bring on this deluge?
On the sinner lay his sin; on the transgressor lay his transgression!
Let loose, that he shall not be cut off; pull tight, that he may not
    get too loose. . . .

"Moreover, it was not I who revealed the secret of the great gods;
But to (Utnapishtim) I showed a dream, and so he learned the
    secret of the gods.
And now take counsel concerning him.'
Then Enlil went up into the ship." [said Utnapishtim.]
"He took my hand and caused me to go aboard.
He caused my wife to go aboard and to kneel down at my side.
Standing between us, he touched our foreheads and blessed us:
'Hitherto Utnapishtim has been but a man;
But now Utnapishtim and his wife shall be like unto us gods.
In the distance, at the mouth of the rivers, Utnapishtim shall
    dwell!'
So they took me and caused me to dwell in the distance, at the
    mouth of the rivers.
But now as for thee, who will assemble the gods unto thee,
That thou mayest find the life which thou seekest?
Come, do not sleep for six days and seven nights." . . .

Utnapishtim says to her, to his wife:
"Look at the strong man who wants life everlasting.
Sleep like a fog blows upon him."
His wife says to him, to Utnapishtim the Distant:
"Touch him that the man may awake,
That he may return in peace on the road by which he came,
That through the gate through which he came he may return to
    his land."
Utnapishtim says to her, to his wife:
"Deceitful is mankind, he will try to deceive thee.
Pray, therefore, bake loaves of bread for him and place them at
    his head.
And the days that he has slept mark on the wall!"

She baked loaves of bread for him and placed them at his head;
And the days that he slept she noted on the wall. . . .

The seventh was still over the glowing coals when he touched him
    and the man awoke.
Gilgamesh said to him, to Utnapishtim the Distant:
"Hardly did sleep spread over me,
When quickly thou didst touch me and rouse me."
Utnapishtim said to him, to Gilgamesh:
". . . . Gilgamesh, count thy loaves of bread!
The days which thou didst sleep may they be known to thee. . . .

The seventh was still over the glowing coals when I touched thee
    and thou didst awake."
Gilgamesh said to him, to Utnapishtim the Distant:
"Oh, what shall I do, Utnapishtim, or where shall I go,
As the robber* has already taken hold of my members?
Death is dwelling in my bedchamber;
And wherever I set my feet there is death!"
Utnapishtim said to him, to Urshanabi, the boatman:
"Take him, Urshanabi, and bring him to the place of washing;"

Urshanabi took him and brought him to the place of washing.
He washed his long hair clean as snow in water.
He threw off his pelts, that the sea might carry them away,
And that his fair body appeared.
He replaced the band around his head with a new one.
He clothed him with a garment, as clothing for his nakedness.
Until he would come to his city,
Until he would finish his journey,
His garment should not show any sign of age but should still be
    quite new.
Gilgamesh and Urshanabi boarded the ship;
They launched the ship on the billows and glided along. . . .

Then he, Gilgamesh, took a pole
And brought the ship near to the shore.
Utnapishtim said to him, to Gilgamesh:

* I.e., death?

"Gilgamesh, thou hast come hither, thou hast become weary, thou
    hast exerted thyself;
What shall I give thee wherewith thou mayst return to thy land?
Gilgamesh, I will reveal unto thee a hidden thing,
Namely, a secret of the gods will I tell thee:
There is a plant like a thorn. . . .
Like a rose its thorns will prick thy hands.
If thy hands will obtain that plant, thou wilt find new life."
When Gilgamesh heard that, . . .
He tied heavy stones to his feet;
They pulled him down into the deep, and he saw the plant.
    (*Plate* 18.)
He took the plant, though it pricked his hands.
He cut the heavy stones from his feet, . . .
Gilgamesh said to him, to Urshanabi, the boatman:
"Urshanabi, this plant is a wondrous plant,
Whereby a man may obtain his former strength. . . .

"Its name is 'The old man becomes young as the man in his
    prime.'
I myself will eat it that I may return to my youth." . . .

Gilgamesh saw a pool with cold water;
He descended into it and bathed in the water.
A serpent perceived the fragrance of the plant;
It came up from the water and snatched the plant,
Sloughing its skin on its return.*
Then Gilgamesh sat down and wept,
His tears flowing over his cheeks. . . .
"For whom, Urshanabi, have my hands become weary?
For whom is the blood of my heart being spent?
For myself I have not obtained any boon.
For the 'earth lion' [the serpent] have I obtained the boon. . . .

I have found something that has been set for a sign unto me; I
    will withdraw
And will leave the ship at the shore." . . .

* By eating this magic plant, the serpent gained the power to shed its
old skin and thereby to renew its life. . . .

THE HYMN OF THE ROBE OF GLORY
(Syrian)[4]

When, a quite little child, I was dwelling
In the House of my Father's Kingdom,

And in the wealth and the glories
Of my Up-bringers I was delighting,

From the East, our Home, my Parents
Forth-sent me with journey-provision.

Indeed from the wealth of our Treasure,
They bound up for me a load.

Large was it, yet was it so light
That all alone I could bear it.

Gold from the Land of Gīlān,
Silver from Ganzāk the Great,

Chalcedonies of India,
Iris-hued Opals from Ќushān.

They girt me with Adamant also
That hath power to cut even iron.

My Glorious Robe they took off me
Which in their love they had wrought me,

And my Purple Mantle also
Which was woven to match with my stature.

And with me they then made a compact;
In my heart wrote it, not to forget it:

"If thou goest down into Egypt,
And thence thou bring'st the one Pearl—

"The Pearl that lies in the Sea,
Hard by the loud-breathing Serpent,—

"Then shalt thou put on thy Robe
And thy Mantle that goeth upon it,

"And with thy Brother, Our Second,
Shalt thou be Heir in our Kingdom."

I left the East and went down
With two Couriers with me;

For the way was hard and dangerous,
For I was young to tread it.

I traversed the borders of Maishān,
The mart of the Eastern merchants,

And I reached the Land of Bābel,
And entered the walls of Sarbūg.

Down further I went into Egypt;
And from me parted my escorts.

Straightway I went to the Serpent;
Near to his lodging I settled,

To take away my Pearl
While he should sleep and should slumber.

Lone was I there, yea, all lonely;
To my fellow-lodgers a stranger.

However I saw there a noble,
From out of the Dawn-land my kinsman,

A young man fair and well favored,
Son of Grandees; he came and he joined me.

I made him my chosen companion,
A comrade, for sharing my wares with.

He warned me against the Egyptians,
'Gainst mixing with the unclean ones.

For I had clothed me as they were,
That they might not guess I had come

From afar to take off the Pearl,
And so rouse the Serpent against me.

But from some occasion or other
They learned I was not of their country.

With their wiles they made my acquaintance;
Yea, they gave me their victuals to eat.

I forgot that I was a King's son,
And became a slave to their king.

I forgot all concerning the Pearl
For which my Parents had sent me;

And from the weight of their victuals
I sank down into a deep sleep.

All this that now was befalling,
My Parents perceived and were anxious.

It was then proclaimed in our Kingdom,
That all should speed to our Gate—

Kings and Chieftains of Parthia,
And of the East all the Princes.

And this is the counsel they came to:
I should not be left down in Egypt.

And for me they wrote out a Letter;
And to it each Noble his Name set:

"From Us—King of Kings, thy Father,
And thy Mother, Queen of the Dawn-land,

"And from Our Second, thy Brother—
To thee, Son, down in Egypt,
Our Greeting!

"Up and arise from thy sleep,
Give ear to the words of Our Letter!

"Remember that thou art a King's son;
See whom thou hast served in thy slavedom.

"Bethink thyself of the Pearl
For which thou didst journey to Egypt.

"Remember thy Glorious Robe,
The Splendid Mantle remember,

"To put on and wear as adornment,
When thy Name may be read in
the Book of the Heroes,

"And with Our Successor, thy Brother,
Thou mayest be Heir in Our Kingdom."

My Letter was surely a Letter
The King had sealed up with His
Right Hand,

'Gainst the Children of Bābel, the wicked,
The tyrannical Daimons of Sarbūg,

It flew in the form of the Eagle,
Of all the winged tribes the king-bird;

It flew and alighted beside me,
And turned into speech altogether.

At its voice and the sound of its winging,
I waked and arose from my deep sleep.

Unto me I took it and kissed it;
I loosed its seal and I read it.

E'en as it stood in my heart writ,
The words of my Letter were written.

I remembered that I was a King's son,
And my rank did long for its nature.

I bethought me again of the Pearl,
For which I was sent down to Egypt.

And I began then to charm him,
The terrible loud-breathing Serpent.

I lulled him to sleep and to slumber,
Chanting o'er him the Name of my Father,

The Name of our Second, my Brother,
And Name of my Mother, the East-Queen.

And thereon I snatched up the Pearl,
And turned to the House of my Father.

Their filthy and unclean garments
I stripped off and left in their country.

To the way that I came I betook me,
To the Light of our Home, to the Dawn-land.

On the road I found there before me
My Letter that had aroused me—

As with its voice it had roused me,
So now with its light it did lead me—

On fabric of silk, in letters of red,
With shining appearance before me,

Encouraging me with its guidance,
With its love it was drawing me onward.

I went forth; through Sarbūg I passed;
I left Bābel-land on my left hand;

And I reached unto Maishān the Great,
The meeting-place of the merchants,

That lieth hard by the Sea-shore.

My Glorious Robe that I'd stripped off,
And my Mantle with which it was covered,

Down from the Heights of Hyrcānia,
Thither my Parents did send me,

By the hands of their Treasure-dispensers
Who trustworthy were with it trusted.

Without my recalling its fashion,—

In the House of my Father my childhood
had left it,—

At once, as soon as I saw it,
The Glory looked like my own self.

I saw it all in all of me,
And saw me all in all of it,—

That we were twain in distinction,
And yet again one in one likeness.

I saw, too, the Treasurers also,
Who unto me had down-brought it,

Were twain and yet of one likeness;
For one Sign of the King was upon them—

Who through them restored me the Glory,
The Pledge of my Kingship.

The Glorious Robe all-bespangled
With sparkling splendour of colours:

With Gold and also with Beryls,
Chalcedonies, iris-hued Opals,

With Sards of varying colours.
To match its grandeur, moreover,
it had been completed:

With adamantine jewels
All of its seams were off-fastened.

Moreover the King of King's Image
Was depicted entirely all o'er it;

And as with Sapphires above
Was it wrought in a motley of colour.

I saw that moreover all o'er it
The motions of Gnosis abounding;

I saw it further was making
Ready as though for to speak.

I heard the sound of its Music
Which it whispered as it descended:

"Behold him the active in deeds!
For whom I was reared with my Father;

"I too have felt in myself
How that with his works waxed my stature."

And now with its Kingly motions
Was it pouring itself out towards me,

And made haste in the hands of its Givers,
That I might take and receive it.

And me, too, my love urged forward
To run for to meet it, to take it.

And I stretched myself forth to receive it;
With its beauty of color I decked me,

And my Mantle of sparkling colors
I wrapped entirely all o'er me.

I clothed me therewith, and ascended
To the Gate of Greeting and Homage.

I bowed my head and did homage
To the Glory of Him who had sent it,

Whose commands I now had accomplished,
And who, had, too, done what He'd promised.

And there at the Gate of His house-sons
I mingled myself with His Princes;

For He had received me with gladness,
And I was with Him in His Kingdom;

To whom the whole of His Servants
With sweet-sounding voices sing praises. . . .

He had promised that with him to the Court
Of the King of Kings I should speed,

And taking with me my Pearl
Should with him be seen by our King.

BAPTISM (Christian)[5]

The Paschal Taper is taken down from its stand and carried in procession to the Baptismal Font as the choir sings:

Like as the hart panteth after the fountains of water so longeth my soul after thee, O God. My soul hath thirsted for the living God: when shall I come and appear before the face of God!

Arrived at the Font, the priest or bishop proceeds to the solemn consecration of the baptismal waters, singing an invocation similar in both form and chant to the Praeconium:

O God, whose Spirit in the very beginning of the world moved over the waters, that even the nature of water might receive the virtue of sanctification. O God, who by water didst wash away the crimes of the evil world, and in the overflowing of the Flood didst give a figure of regeneration: that one and the same element might, in a mystery, be the end of vice and the origin of virtue. . . . (*Plate 22.*)

As God with his "compass" divided the waters of Chaos in the beginning of time, the priest now with his hand divides the water of the Font in the form of a cross, singing:

Who makes this water fruitful for the regeneration of men by the arcane admixture of his Divine Power, to the end that those who have been conceived in sanctity, in the immaculate womb of this divine Font, may be born a new creature, and come forth a heavenly offspring*: and that all who are distinguished either in sex or in body, or by age in time, may be born into one infancy by grace, their mother.

After an exorcism of the water from the secret artifices of the powers of darkness, the priest utters the blessing itself:

* Baptism, as the Sacrament of Initiation, identifies the Christian with Christ—conceived by the "arcane admixture" of the divine power of the Holy Spirit with the humanity of the Immaculate Mother, and born as the first-fruit of the New Creation.

Wherefore I bless thee, O creature of water, by God ✠ the living, God ✠ the true, God ✠ the holy, by that God who in the beginning separated thee by his Word from the dry land; whose Spirit moved over thee.

Dividing the waters again with his hand, he scatters some of it towards each of the four quarters of the world, singing:

Who made thee to flow forth from the fountain of Paradise, and commanded thee to water the whole earth in four rivers. Who, changing thy bitterness in the desert to sweetness, made thee fit to drink, and produced thee out of the Rock to quench the thirst of the people. I bless ✠ thee also by Jesus Christ his only Son, our Lord, who in Cana of Galilee, in a wonderful figure, changed thee by his power into wine. . . . Who made thee to flow together with blood out of his side.*

As the blessing proceeds, he stoops to breathe thrice upon the water as God in the beginning breathed upon it with his Spirit.

Do thou with thy mouth bless these clear (simplices) waters that besides their natural virtue of cleansing the body, they may also be effectual for the purification of minds.

And then he takes the Paschal Taper and plunges it thrice into the Font, singing each time on a higher note:

May the power of the Holy Spirit descend into the fullness of this Font.

And breathing thrice upon it once more, he goes on:

And make the whole substance of this water fruitful for the effecting of regeneration.

And the Taper is finally lifted out of the water.
The chant continues:

Here may the stains of all sins be washed out: here may human nature, created in thine image, and reformed to the honor of its Principle, be

* Water and wine are symbols of the human and the divine, the union of the two being signified in the mixture or transformation of the one into the other.

cleansed from the entire squalor of the old man: that every one who enters into this sacrament of regeneration may be reborn into the new childhood of true innocence. Through our Lord Jesus Christ thy Son: who shall come to judge the living and the dead and the world by fire. Amen.

When the consecrated water has been sprinkled over the congregation, the priest takes vessels of the two holy oils called the Oil of Catechumens and the Oil of Chrism—one for the anointing of catechumens and the other for conferring the power of the Holy Spirit—oil being a symbol of healing and mercy. These he pours into the Font in the form of a cross, and finally spreads the oil over the whole surface of the water.

All is now ready for the initiation of the catechumens, for whom the whole liturgy has thus far been a kind of final instruction in the arcana of the Faith. The rite of the Blessing of the Font has sufficiently explained the mystery of Baptism. . . .

THE DISAPPEARANCE OF
QUETZALCOATL (Azetc) [6]

Quetzalcoatl, the "Plumed Serpent" was the god of wind, life, the morning, and the planet Venus. He was a priest-king, and teacher of astronomy and the calendar. He lived the life of a saint until his evil brother, Tezcatlipoca, led him into sin. Quetzalcoatl then fled his city, Tula.

Third Chapter, which telleth—in which is related—[the story of] Quetzalcoatl, who was a great wizard, and of the place where he ruled, and of what he did when he went [away].

This Quetzalcoatl they considered as a god. They all adored him as a god. He was prayed to in olden times there at Tula.

And there was his temple, [which was] very tall and high; lofty and towering. Very many [were its] steps, extending in a multitude, and not wide; but each one, in truth, was very narrow. On each step, the sole of one's foot could not be extended.

There, it is said, he lay; he lay covered; and he lay with only his face covered. And, it is said, he was monstrous.

His face [was] like a huge, battered stone, a great fallen rock;

it [was] not made like that of men. And his beard was very long—exceedingly long. He was heavily bearded.

And the Toltecs, his vassals, were highly skilled. Nothing that they did was difficult [for them]. They cut green stone, and they cast gold, and they made other works of the craftsman and the feather worker. Very skilled were they. These started and proceeded from Quetzalcoatl—all craft works and wisdom.

And there stood his green stone house, and his golden house, and his coral house, and his shell house, and his house of beams, his turquoise house, and his house of precious feathers. . . .

And these Toltecs enjoyed great wealth; they were rich; never were they poor. Nothing did they lack in their homes. Never was there want. And the small ears of maize were of no use to them; they only [burned them to] heat the sweat baths.

And this Quetzalcoatl also did penances. He bled the calf of his leg to stain thorns with blood. And he bathed at midnight. . . . Him the fire priests imitated, and the [other] priests. And the priests took their manner of conduct from the life of Quetzalcoatl. By it they ordained the law of Tula. Thus were customs established here in Mexico. . . .

Fourth Chapter, . . . And at this time, Quetzalcoatl and all the Toltecs became slothful. And there approached and came, as evil sorcerers, three demons—Uitzilopochtli, Titlacauan, and Tezcatlipoca. All three practised sorcery that they might bring ruin to Tula.

This Titlacauan began casting the spell. It is told that he turned himself into a little old man. He counterfeited and took the form of one who was much bent and whose hair was very white, very silvery. Thereupon he went to the home of Quetzalcoatl.

When he had gone there, he then said [to the retainers]: "I wish to see the chief, Quetzalcoatl." . . .

And thereupon they informed Quetzalcoatl. They said to him: "My prince, an old man hath come to speak with thee, one who seemeth like a net, like a trap for thee. We would turn him away, but he wisheth not to go. He saith only: 'I will see the chief for myself.' "

Then said Quetzalcoatl: "Let him come; let him enter. For I have awaited him for some little time."

Then they brought him in to Quetzalcoatl.

Thereupon the old man came and said to him: "My grandson, my chief, how is thy health? Here is a potion which I have brought for thee. Drink it."

And then Quetzalcoatl said: "Come here, O old one. Thou art spent; thou hast tired thyself. For some time I have awaited thee."

And then the old man replied to him: "My grandson, how, in sooth, is thy health?"

Then Quetzalcoatl said to him: "Verily, much do I ail in all parts. Nowhere am I well—my hands, my feet. In truth, my body is tired, as if it were undone."

And then the old one said to him: "Here is the potion, good, soothing, and intoxicating. If thou shalt drink of it, it will relieve and heal thy body. And thou shalt weep; thy heart shall become troubled. Thou shalt think upon thy death. And also thou shalt think upon where thou shalt go."

Then Quetzalcoatl said: "Where am I to go, old one?"

Then the old man said to him: "Yea, thou shalt go there to Tollan-Tlapallan. A man there standeth guard, one already aged. Ye shall consult with each other. And when thou shalt return here, thou shalt again have been made a child."

On this, Quetzalcoatl was [much] moved. And the old man once more said: "Be of good cheer. Drink the potion." . . .

And Quetzalcoatl then tasted a little, and afterwards drank heartily of it. . . .

And as soon as he had once more drunk of it—all,—then he became sotted.* Thereupon he wept, and greatly was he moved. Thus, at this time, was Quetzalcoatl aroused; his heart was quickened. No longer could he forget what had happened, but went on reflecting, realizing [that] indeed the devil had tricked him.

And the potion which [the old man] had offered him . . . was made of the sap of the *maguey*. . . .

Twelfth Chapter, . . . And still many more acts of sorcery were done to the Toltecs in order to destroy Tula.

And when these things happened, Quetzalcoatl was now troubled and saddened, and thereupon was minded that he should go—that he should abandon his city of Tula.

* In other versions, Quetzalcoatl gets drunk and sleeps with the beautiful Quetzalpetatl.

Thereupon he made ready. It is said that he had everything burned—his house of gold, his house of coral; and still other works of art, the marvelous and costly things, all [of these] he buried, he hid there in treacherous places: either within the mountains or in the canyons. . . .

Then he came to arrive at a place. A very thick tree arose [there], and very tall. He stood by it. Then he called for his mirror. Thereupon he looked at himself; he saw himself in the glass and said: "Verily, now I am an old man." . . . And then he cast and hurled stones at the tree. And as he stoned it, [the stones] remained firmly encrusted and affixed to the great tree. Always thus have they been visible. Thus are they seen; beginning at the foot, they rise there to its top.

And as Quetzalcoatl followed the road, they went blowing flutes for him.

Once more he came to rest at another place. Upon a stone [Quetzalcoatl] rested himself. He supported himself [on it] with his hands. Thereupon he looked toward Tula, and then wept; as one sobbing he wept. Now he shed two hail stones as tears over his face; they rolled over his face. Thus fell [tear] drops [which] verily pierced holes in the stone. . . .

Thirteenth Chapter, . . . And as he supported himself by his hands on the rock, he left deep imprints, as if [it were] on mud [that] he had planted the palms of his hands. . . .

And then when he arose he came to reach a place [where] there was water. A river burst forth [which] was very wide and long. [Quetzalcoatl] laid stones and made there a bridge. Then he crossed over on it. . . .

And thereupon he moved on and came to reach another point, a place named Cochtocan. And there a demon then came forth to meet him.

He said to him: "Whither goest thou?"

Then [Quetzalcoatl] said: "It is there to Tlapallan that I go, to learn [my fate]."

Then the demon said to him: "It is well. Drink this, the wine which I have brought here."

Quetzalcoatl said: "Nay, it may not be that I drink, even though it might be but little that I taste."

Then once more the devil said to him: "Verily, it may not be that thou shalt not drink nor taste of it. For no one do I give leave, or permit, to depart whom I give no wine and [not] make drunk and besotted. So do [as I bid thee]; be of good cheer and drink it."

Quetzalcoatl then drank the wine with a drinking tube. And when he had drunk, he quickly fell asleep in the road. He lay thundering as he slept, resounding a great distance as he snored. And when he awoke, thereupon he looked to one side and the other. He looked at himself, and arranged his hair. Then he named the place Cochtocan. . . .

Fourteenth Chapter, . . . Then once again he set forth and came to climb between Popocatepetl and Iztac tepetl. He led all the dwarfs and hunchbacks, his servants. It snowed upon them, and there they froze; they died of the cold.

And Quetzalcoatl thereupon was greatly moved and wept to himself. And he sang much to himself [as] he wept and sighed. . . .

And elsewhere he planted in the ground *maguey* fibers. At another place he built a ball court, all of stone. And in the middle of it, where the line was, the earth lay open, reaching deep; for it was thus pierced. And elsewhere he shot, as an arrow, a *bombax ceiba* tree, [shooting it] likewise into the midst of [another] *bombax ceiba* [so that one] rested piercing [the other]. And elsewhere he built a house all underground at a place named Mictlan.

And there were many more things which he did in all the villages. And it is said that he named all the mountains. And in all places he gave all the names here.

And when he had done these things, then he went to reach the seacoast. Thereupon he fashioned a raft of serpents. When he had arranged [the raft], there he placed himself, as if it were his boat. Then he set off going across the sea. No one knows how he came to arrive there at Tlapallan.

*. . . It is said that . . . having reached the celestial shore of the divine water (the seacoast), he [Quetzalcoatl] stopped, cried, seized his garments, and put on his insignia of feathers and his green mask. . . . Then when he was adorned he set fire to himself and burned. . . . It is said that when he burned, his ashes were at once raised up and that all the rare birds appeared when Quetzalcoatl died, for which reason they call him Lord of Dawn. They say that when he died dawn did not appear for four days,

PLATE 16. *Wheel of Mother Nature.*

PLATE 17. *Ancestor image.*

PLATE 18. *Gilgamesh.*

PLATE 19. *Coffin of Amenapet.*

PLATE 20. *Tomb of Rameses IX.*

PLATE 21. *Baptism of King Seti I.*

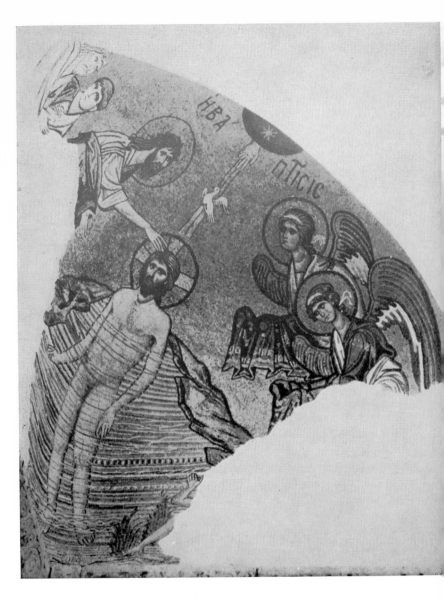

PLATE 22. *Le Baptême.*

PLATE 23. *Birth of Dionysus.*

PLATE 24. *The Moon Boat.*

FIG. 13—The God, Quetzalcoatl, sometimes known as the feathered serpent. He is seated upon a stool of snakes, suggesting the rafts of serpents which transported him to the state of rebirth.

because he had gone to dwell among the dead; and that in four days, he provided himself with arrows; for which reason in eight days there appeared the great star called Quetzalcoatl [Venus], and they add that he was enthroned as Lord.*

PRINCE LINDWORM (European)[8]

Once upon a time, there was a fine young *King* who was married to the loveliest of Queens. They were exceedingly happy, all but for one thing—they had no children. And this often made them both sad, because the *Queen* wanted a dear little child to play with, and the *King* wanted an heir to the kingdom.

One day the *Queen* went out for a walk by herself, and she met an ugly old woman. The old woman was just like a witch: but she was a nice kind of a witch, not the cantankerous sort. She said, "Why do you look so doleful, pretty lady?" "It's no use my telling you," answered the *Queen*, "nobody in the world can help me." "Oh, you never know," said the old woman. "Just you let

* . . . * *Annals of Cuauhtitlan.* See *Burning Water,* Sejourne.[7]

me hear what your trouble is, and maybe I can put things right."
"My dear woman, how can you?" said the *Queen:* and she
told her, "The *King* and I have no children: that's why I am so
distressed." "Well you needn't be," said the old witch. "I can
set that right in a twinkling, if only you will do exactly as I tell
you. Listen. Tonight, at sunset, take a little drinking-cup with
two ears" (that is, handles), "and put it bottom upwards on the
ground in the north-west corner of your garden. Then go and lift
it up to-morrow morning at sunrise, and you will find two roses
underneath it, one red and one white. If you eat the red rose, a
little boy will be born to you: if you eat the white rose, a little
girl will be sent. But, whatever you do, you mustn't eat *both* the
roses, or you'll be sorry—that I warn you! Only one: remember
that!" "Thank you a thousand times," said the *Queen,* "This is
good news indeed!" And she wanted to give the old woman her
gold ring; but the old woman wouldn't take it.

So the *Queen* went home and did as she had been told: and
the next morning at sunrise she stole out into the garden and
lifted up the little drinking-cup. She *was* surprised, for indeed
she had hardly expected to see anything. But there were two roses
underneath it, one red and one white. And now she was dreadfully
puzzled, for she did not know which to choose. . . .

However, at last she decided on the white rose, and she ate it.
And it tasted so sweet, that she took and ate the red one too:
without ever remembering the old woman's solemn warning.

Some time after this, the *King* went away to the wars: and
while he was still away, the *Queen* became the mother of twins.
One was a lovely baby-boy, and the other was a *Lindworm,* or
Serpent. She was terribly frightened when she saw the *Lindworm,*
but he wriggled away out of the room, and nobody seemed to
have seen him but herself: so that she thought it must have been
a dream. The baby *Prince* was so beautiful and so healthy, the
Queen was full of joy: and likewise, as you may suppose, was the
King when he came home and found his son and heir. Not a word
was said by anyone about the *Lindworm*: only the *Queen* thought
about it now and then.

Many days and years passed by, and the baby grew up into a
handsome young *Prince,* and it was time he got married. The
King sent him off to visit foreign kingdoms, in the royal coach,

with six white horses, to look for a *Princess* grand enough to be his wife. But at the very first cross-roads, the way was stopped by an enormous *Lindworm,* enough to frighten the bravest. He lay in the middle of the road with a great wide open mouth, and cried, "A bride for me before a bride for you!" Then the *Prince* made the coach turn round and try another road: but it was all no use. For, at the first cross-ways, there lay the *Lindworm* again, crying out, "A bride for me before a bride for you!" So the *Prince* had to turn back home again to the Castle, and give up his visits to the foreign kingdoms. And his mother, the *Queen* had to confess that what the *Lindworm* said was true. For he was really the eldest of her twins: and so he ought to have a wedding first.

There seemed nothing for it but to find a bride for the *Lindworm,* if his younger brother, the *Prince,* were to be married at all. So the *King* wrote to a distant country, and asked for a *Princess* to marry his son (but, of course, he didn't say which son), and presently a *Princess* arrived. But she wasn't allowed to see her bridegroom until he stood by her side in the great hall and was married to her, and then, of course, it was too late for her to say she wouldn't have him. But next morning the *Princess* had disappeared. The *Lindworm* lay sleeping all alone: and it was quite plain that he had eaten her.

A little while after, the *Prince* decided that he might now go journeying again in search of a *Princess.* . . . But at the first cross-ways, there lay the *Lindworm,* crying with his great wide open mouth, "A bride for me before a bride for you!" So the carriage tried another road, and the same thing happened, and they had to turn back again. . . . And the *King* wrote to several foreign countries, to know if anyone would marry his son. At last another *Princess* arrived. . . . And, of course, she was not allowed to see her future husband before the wedding took place,—and then, lo and behold! It was the *Lindworm* who stood at her side. And next morning the *Princess* had disappeared: and the *Lindworm* lay sleeping all alone; and it was quite clear that he had eaten her.

By and by the *Prince* started on his quest for the third time: and at the first cross-roads . . . lay the *Lindworm* . . ., demanding a bride as before. And the *Prince* went straight back to the Castle, and told the *King*: "You must find another bride for my elder brother."

"I don't know where I am to find her," said the *King,* "I have already made enemies of two great Kings who sent their daughters here as brides: and I have no notion how I can obtain a third lady. People are beginning to say strange things, and I am sure no *Princess* will dare to come."

Now, down in a little cottage near a wood, there lived the *King's* shepherd, an old man with his only daughter. And the *King* came one day and said to him, "Will you give me your daughter to marry my son the *Lindworm?* And I will make you rich for the rest of your life."—"No, sire," said the shepherd, "that I cannot do. . . . Besides, if the *Lindworm* would not spare two beautiful Princesses, he won't spare her either. He will just gobble her up: and she is much too good for such a fate."

But the *King* wouldn't take "No" for an answer: and at last the old man had to give in.

Well, when the old shepherd told his daughter that she was to be *Prince Lindworm's* bride, she was utterly in despair. She went out into the woods, crying and wringing her hands. . . . And while she wandered to and fro, an old witch-woman suddenly appeared out of a big hollow oak-tree, and asked her, "Why do you look so doleful, pretty lass?" The shepherd-girl said, "It's no use my telling you, for nobody in the world can help me."— "Oh, you never know," said the old woman. "Just you let me hear what your trouble is, and maybe I can put things right."— "Ah, how can you?" said the girl, "for I am to be married to the *King's* eldest son, who is a *Lindworm.* He has already married two beautiful Princesses, and devoured them: and he will eat me too! No wonder I am distressed."

"Well, you needn't be," said the witch-woman. "All that can be set right in a twinkling: If only you will do exactly as I tell you." So the girl said she would.

"Listen, then," said the old woman. "After the marriage ceremony is over, and when it is time for you to retire to rest, you must ask to be dressed in ten snow-white shifts. And you must then ask for a tub full of lye (that is, washing water prepared with wood-ashes) and a tub full of fresh milk, and as many whips as a boy can carry in his arms, and have all these brought into your bed-chamber. Then, when the *Lindworm* tells you to shed a shift, do you bid him slough a skin. And when all his skins are off, you must dip the whips in the lye and whip him; next, you must wash him in the fresh milk; and, lastly, you must take him and hold him in your arms, if it's only for one moment."

"The last is the worst notion—ugh!" said the shepherd's daughter, and she shuddered at the thought of holding the cold, slimy, scaly *Lindworm.*

"Do just as I have said, and all will go well," said the old woman. Then she disappeared again in the oak-tree.

When the wedding-day arrived, the girl was fetched in the royal chariot with the six white horses, and taken to the castle to be decked as a bride. And she asked for ten snow-white shifts to be brought her, and the tub of lye, and the tub of milk, and as many whips as a boy could carry in his arms. The ladies and courtiers in the castle thought, of course, that this was some bit of peasant superstition, all rubbish and nonsense. But the *King* said, "Let her have whatever she asks for." She was then arrayed in the most wonderful robes and looked the loveliest of brides. She was led to the hall where the wedding ceremony was to take place, and she saw the *Lindworm* for the first time as he came in and stood by her side. So they were married, and a great wedding-feast was held, a banquet fit for the son of a king.

When the feast was over, the bridegroom and bride were conducted to their apartment, with music, and torches, and a great procession. As soon as the door was shut, the *Lindworm* turned to her and said, "Fair maiden, shed a shift!" The shepherd's daughter answered him, *"Prince Lindworm, slough a skin!"* "No one has ever dared tell me to do that before!" said he.—"But I command you to do it now!" said she. Then he began to moan and wriggle: and in a few minutes a long snake-skin lay upon the floor beside him. The girl drew off her first shift, and spread it on top of the skin.

The *Lindworm* said again to her, "Fair maiden, shed a shift." The shepherd's daughter answered him, *"Prince Lindworm, slough a skin."*

"No one has ever dared tell me to do that before," said he and his little eyes rolled furiously. "But I command you to do it now," said she. Then with groans and moans he cast off the second skin: and she covered it with her second shift. . . . But the girl was not afraid, and once more she commanded him to do as she bade.

And so this went on until nine *Lindworm* skins were lying on the floor, each of them covered with a snow-white shift. And there was nothing left of the *Lindworm*, but a huge thick mass, most horrible to see. Then the girl seized the whips, dipped them in the lye, and whipped him as hard as ever she could. Next, she bathed him all over in the fresh milk. Lastly, she dragged him on the bed and put her arms round him. And she fell fast asleep that very moment.

Next morning very early, the *King* and the courtiers came and peeped in through the keyhole. They wanted to know what had become of the girl, but none of them dared enter the room. However, in the end, growing bolder, they opened the door a tiny bit. And there they saw the girl, all fresh and rosy, and beside her lay—no *Lindworm*, but the handsomest prince that anyone could wish to see.

The *King* ran out and fetched the *Queen*: and after that, there were such rejoicings in the castle as never were known before or since. The wedding took place all over again, much finer than the first, with festivals and banquets and merrymakings for days and weeks. No bride was ever so beloved by a *King* and *Queen* as this peasant maid from the shepherd's cottage. There was no end to their love and their kindness towards her: she had saved their son, *Prince Lindworm*.

DIONYSOS (Greek)[9]

Demeter came from Crete to Sicily, where, near the springs of Kayane, she discovered a cave. There she hid her daughter Persephone, and set as guardians over her two serpents that at other times were harnessed to her chariot. In the cave the maiden worked in wool—the customary occupation for maidens under the protection of Pallas Athene, in her sacred citadel at Athens. Persephone began weaving a great web, a robe for her father or her mother, which was a picture of the whole world. While she was engaged in this work Zeus came to her in the shape of a serpent, and he begat by his daughter that god [Dionysos] who, in the Orphic stories, was to be his successor, the fifth ruler of the world. . . . The birth of the son and successor to the throne actually took place in the maternal cave. A late ivory relief shows the bed in the cave: the bed in which the horned child—the horns signify that he is the son of Persephone—had just been born to the goddess.

. . . The Orphic story also named the toys of the new ruler of the world: toys that became symbols of those rites of initiation which were first undergone by the divine boy, the first Dionysos: dice, ball, top, golden apples, bull-roarer and wool. The last two played a part in the ceremony of initiation, . . .

It was told that the [Titans] surprised the child-god as he was playing with the toys. Jealous Hera had instigated them to this: . . . The Titans had whitened their faces with chalk. They came like spirits of the dead from the Underworld, to which Zeus had banished them. They attacked the playing boy, tore him into seven pieces and threw these into a cauldron standing on a tripod. When the flesh was boiled, they began roasting it over the fire on seven spits.

. . . When Zeus smote the Titans with his lightning they had already eaten the flesh of Dionysos. They must have been hurled back into the Underworld, since . . . they are invoked as the subterranean ancestors of mankind. . . .

The boiled limbs of the god were burnt—with the exception of a single limb—and we may presume that the vine arose from the ashes.* [The limb] was devoured neither by the Titans nor by the fire nor by the earth. . . . A goddess was present at the meal—in later tales, the goddess Pallas Athene—and she hid the limb in a covered basket. Zeus took charge of it. It was said to have been Dionysos's heart. This statement contains a pun: for it was also said that Zeus entrusted the *kradiaios Dionysos* to the goddess Hipta [or great mother Rhea], so that she might carry it on her head . . . *kradiaios* is a word of double meaning: it can be derived both from *kradia*, "heart", and from *krade*, "fig-tree", in which latter derivation it means an object made of fig-wood. The basket

* Dionysos's gift to man was wine.

on Hipta's head was a *liknon*: a winnowing-fan, such as was carried on the head at festal processions, and contained a phallus hidden under a pile of fruit—Dionysos himself having made the phallus of fig-wood. . . .

. . . our mythology also told of a second Dionysos, the son of Semele. . . . It was told that when Zeus came to Semele, this was not a divine mating. He had prepared a potion from the heart of Dionysos, and this he gave Semele to drink. The potion made the girl pregnant. When Hera heard of this, she tried to prevent the birth. She disguised herself as Semele's nurse, . . . when Zeus first came to Semele he did not do so in the form of the lightning-bearing god of Heaven. The shape which Semele's secret husband had assumed was a mortal guise. Led astray by her pretended nurse, Semele asked Zeus to grant her just one wish. Zeus promised to do so, and when his beloved wished that he would appear to her as he did to Hera, he visited her with lightning. . . . The lightning struck her and she descended into the Underworld. Zeus rescued from her body the unripe fruit, the child Dionysos.

The Father sheltered the prematurely born god in his own thigh, . . . by sewing the child into it . . . his father bore him, when the proper time for his birth had come, far away to the east, on Mount Nysa. Zeus then . . . entrusted Dionysos to the divine nurses who were to look after him in the cave. . . . (*Plate* 23.)

When they had reared him to full stature, he went into the woods—so it was told—wreathed with ivy and laurel, but not yet with vine-leaves. He was accompanied by women, the nymphs of the woods: . . .

The story of Dionysos and Semele did not come to an end when she was struck by Zeus's lightning. . . . Semele had to be brought back from the Underworld by Dionysos. . . . [He] came to the Underworld in search of Semele. He needed a guide and pathfinder, and as a price for his service he had to promise complete female surrender. Only if he did this could he reach his mother and bring her back. He fulfilled his promise with the help of a phallus made of fig-wood, which he erected on this spot. . . . when Dionysos had brought Semele back and had made her immortal, he named her Thyone, "The ecstatically raging" . . . and took the goddess Thyone up to Heaven.

THE THUNDER RITE
(Omaha Indian)[10]

The first initiation takes place on the fourth day after birth. Before it takes place, the child is regarded as part of its mother, it has no separate existence, no personal name. The rite is one of introduction to the cosmos. To the sun and moon, the thunder and the clouds, the hills, the earth, the beasts, the water, the formal announcement is made that a new life is among them; they are asked, or rather adjured, to accept and cherish it. The refrain after each clause comes:

> Consent ye, consent ye all, I implore.

The second rite comes when the child is between two and three years old. It is specially significant in relation to the notion of Wa-*kon*-da. When the child first speaks, first walks, it is regarded as a manifestation of life, of Wa-*kon*-da. The speaking and walking are in fact called Wa-*kon*-da. It is only these *first* manifestations that are so called. If later a child falls sick and gets better the restored life is never called Wa-*kon*-da. This second ceremony differs from the first in that it is also an initiation into the tribe. It takes place 'after the first thunder in the springtime, when the grass is well up and the birds singing.'

The only ritual necessary for the child, boy or girl, is a pair of new moccasins, now to be worn for the first time. Great sanctity attaches to these moccasins, they cannot be given away or exchanged. The mother comes with her child to the sacred hut set up for the purpose, but the child must enter it alone, bearing his moccasins. Then follow six incantations, each ending with a roll of mimic thunder in a minor key. During the first song powers are invoked to come from the four cardinal points. During the second song a tuft of hair is shorn from the crown of the child's head and laid by the priest in a sacred case: but as we learn from the words of the song addressed to the Thunder as Grandfather, the lock and with it the life of the child pass into the keeping of the Thunder:

> Grandfather! there far above, on high,
> The hair like a shadow dark flashes before you.

In the third song it is proclaimed that the power of earth as well as life lies with Wa-*kon*-da:

> What time I will, then only then,
> A man lies dead a gruesome thing,
> What time I will, then, suddenly,
> A man lies dead a gruesome thing.
> (The Thunder rolls.)

The fourth song accompanies the putting on of the moccasins; its gist is:

> In this place has the truth been declared to you,
> Now therefore arise! go forth in its strength.

So far the main element of the rite is consecration to the thundergod, the supreme Wa-*kon*-da. Next comes a ceremony the gist of which, like the earlier ceremony, is to naturalize the child in the universe. Boys only are consecrated to the thunder-spirit, who is also the war-spirit; but the next ceremony is open to girls. It is called Dhi-ku-wi*n*-he, 'Turning the child.' The priest takes the child to the east of the fire in the hut, then lifting it by the shoulders carries it to the south, lets its feet rest on a stone or buffalo skull, a sort of omphalos placed there for the purpose. There the priest turns the child completely round, then carries it to the west, the north, the east again, turning it upon the stone at each point while the fifth song is sung:

> Turned by the winds goes the one I send yonder,
> Yonder he goes who is whirled by the wind,
> Goes where the four hills of life and the four winds are standing,
> There in the midst of the winds do I send him,
> Into the midst of the winds, standing there.
> (The Thunder rolls.)

The stone and grass laid on it and the buffalo skull stand for earth; the four hills are the four stages of life. Up till now the child bore its cradle name. It now takes its *ni-ki-e* name which relates it to its gens. After the turning of the child its *ni-ki-e* name is announced by the priest with a kind of primitive *Benedicite omnia opera*:

Ye hills, grass, trees—ye creeping things both great and small—
I bid you hear! This child has thrown away its cradle name. *Hi-e.*

The ceremony ends with a fire invocation. The priest picks up the bunches of grass, dashes them to the ground, where they burst into flames, and as the flames light up the sacred lodge the child is dismissed, while the priest sings:

O hot red fire hasten,
O haste ye flames to come,
Come speedily to help me.

PROCESSION OF THE HOLY GRAIL
(English)[11]

At the last came in fair procession, as it were, four seneschals, and as the last passed the door was the palace filled—nor were it fitting that I say more. In the sight of all there paced into the hall two maidens fair and graceful, bearing two candlesticks; behind each maid there came a youth, and the twain held between them a sharp spear. After these came other two maidens, fair in form and richly clad, who bare a salver of gold and precious stones, upon a silken cloth; and behind them, treading soft and slow, paced the fairest being whom since the world began God had wrought in woman's wise, perfect was she in form and feature, and richly clad withal. Before her she held on a rich cloth of samite a jewel wrought of red gold, in form of a base, whereon there stood another, of gold and gems, fashioned even as a reliquary that standeth upon an altar. This maiden bare upon her head a crown of gold, and behind her came another, wondrous fair, who wept and made lament, but the others spake never a word, only drew nigh unto the host, and bowed them low before him.

Sir Gawain might scarce trust his senses, for of a truth he knew the crowned maiden well, and that 'twas she who aforetime had spoken to him of the Grail, and bade him as he ever saw her again, with five maidens in her company, to fail not to ask what they did there—and thereof had he great desire.

As he mused thereon the four who bare spear and salver, the youths with the maidens, drew nigh and laid the spear upon the table, and the salver beneath it. Then before Sir Gawain's eyes there befell a great marvel, for the spear shed three great drops of blood into the salver that was beneath, and the old man, the host, took them straightway. Therewith came the maiden of whom I spake, and took the place of the other twain, and set the fair reliquary upon the table—that did Sir Gawain mark right well—he saw therein a bread, whereof the old man brake the third part, and ate.

With that might Sir Gawain no longer contain himself, but spake, saying, "Mine host, I pray ye for the sake of God, and by His Majesty, that ye tell me what meaneth this great company, and these marvels I behold?" And even as he spake all the folk, knights and ladies alike, who sat there, sprang from their seats with a great cry, and the sound as of great rejoicing. Straightway the host bade them again be seated as before, and make no sound until he bade, and this they did forthwith. . . .

"Sir Gawain, this marvel which is of God may not be known unto all, but shall be held secret, yet since ye have asked thereof, sweet kinsman and dear guest, I may not withhold the truth. 'Tis the Grail which ye now behold. Herein have ye won the world's praise, for manhood and courage alike have ye right well shown, in that ye have achieved this toilsome quest. Of the Grail may I say no more save that ye have seen it, and that great gladness hath come of this your question. For now are many set free from the sorrow they long had borne, and small hope had they of deliverance. Great confidence and trust had we all in Perceval, that he would learn the secret things of the Grail, yet hence did he depart even as a coward who ventured naught, and asked naught. Thus did his quest miscarry, and he learned not that which of a surety he should have learned. So had he freed many a mother's son from sore travail, who live, and yet are dead. Through the strife of kinsmen did this woe befall, when one brother smote the other for his land: and for that treason was the wrath of God shown on him and on all his kin, that all were alike lost. . . ."

BOSHKWADOSH (Plains Indian)[12]

A man who was alone in the world had wandered about from place to place until he was weary, and so laid himself down and fell asleep. In his sleep he heard a voice saying: "Nosis! Nosis! my grandchild! my grandchild!" and upon awakening, he actually heard it repeated; and, looking around, he discovered a tiny animal, hardly big enough to be seen with the naked eye. While speculating whether a voice could come from so diminutive a source, the animal cried again: "My grandson, I am Boshkwadosh. Tell me, why are you so desolate? Listen to me, and you shall find friends and be happy. You must take me up and bind me to your body, and never put me aside, and success will attend you through life."

The man took the little animal carefully up and placed him in a little sack, which he bound around his waist, when he set out in search of some one who would be a suitable companion for him. He walked a long distance without seeing man or animal. . . . and going over a hill he descried a large town in the centre of a plain. The town was divided by a wide road, and he noticed that the lodges on one side of the road were uninhabited, while on the other side they were filled with people. He walked without hesitation into the town, when the people all rushed out from their lodges, crying: "Why, here is Anishinaba, the being we have heard so much about! See his eyes, and his teeth in a half-circle, the Wyaukenarbedaid! How queer he is formed!" Amidst their shouting, the king's son appeared, the Mudjèkewis, and, greeting him with great kindness, conducted him to his father's lodge, where he was received by the king with much attention, and was presented one of the king's beautiful daughters. Anishinaba—for this was this man's name—soon discovered that these people passed much of their time in play and sports and trials of strength; and, after he was refreshed and rested, they invited him to join with them in these amusements. The first trial they desired him to make was that of frost. At some distance from the village there was a large body of frozen water, and the trial consisted in lying down naked on this ice and seeing who could endure the longest.

Anishinaba, accompanied by two young men, went out and laid his face upon the ice, according to their directions, the young men doing the same. At first there was much laughter between the youths, and they would call out to him, with many jests and jeers, to which he made no answer. He felt a manifest warmth from the belt, and was quite sure of his success.

About midnight, finding the two young men were quiet, he called to them in return: "What!" said he, "are you benumbed already? I am just beginning to feel the cold." All was still. Having waited until daybreak, he went to them, and found them both quite dead; but, to his great surprise, they were transformed to buffalo cows. He tied them together, however, and carried them in triumph to the village; but his victory was hailed with pleasure by Mudjèkewis only, for all the others had wished his death. This did not disturb Anishinaba, especially as, through his victory, two persons were mysteriously added to the silent lodges on the uninhabited side of the village. Anishinaba now was invited to another trial, which was of speed, in which he was equally successful, being borne as upon wings to the goal, outspeeding all others with the swiftness of the ka-ka-ke (the sparrow-hawk).

The villagers, however, were not yet convinced of his superior prowess, and desired him once more to go through the trial of frost. Previous to the trial he laid down to rest, untying his belt, which he placed beneath his head. Anishinaba slept some time. On awakening, he sprang up hastily and, feeling full of vigor and courage, hastened to the ice without recalling the taking off the belt. Then, alas, the cold entered his body, and by morning he was frozen to death.

Mudjèkewis bemoaned the fate of his friend; and the wife of Anishinaba was inconsolable. As she lay in her lodge in deep sorrow, she heard a groan, which was many times repeated through the night. In the morning she went to the place from whence she thought the sound might have issued, and there, within the grass, she found the belt, with the mystic sack. "*Aubishin,*—untie me!" cried a voice from the sack; and, as she carefully examined it for the seam, the voice continued to vociferate, "*Aubishin! Aubishin!*" At last, having succeeded in opening the sack, she was surprised to see a little naked animal, smaller than a newborn mouse, without a vestige of hair, except at the tip of its tail. The little beast was so weak that it could crawl only a little way and then rest. At each rest, however, it would shake itself, and, at every shake it grew in dimensions, until, finally, it became as large as a dog, when it ran quickly to the village, and in great haste collected the bones of Anishinaba, which were strewn in the different lodges; and as fast as they were collected, he adjusted them together in their natural position, until, at length, he had formed a complete skeleton; when he placed himself before it and uttered a hollow, low, continuous howl, at which the bones united themselves compactly together. He then modulated his howl, when the bones knit together. The third howl brought sinews upon the bones; the fourth and softest howl brought flesh. He then turned his head upwards, looking into the sky, and gave a howl that caused the people of the village to tremble, and the earth itself shook; then breath entered the body. Taking a few respirations Anishinaba arose, saying: "Hy, kow! I have overslept myself. I shall be too late for the trial."

"Trial!" said the mysterious animal; "you neglected my advice, and were defeated. You were frozen to death, and your body broken into fragments; for, when you undertook the trial of frost, you ungratefully forgot me; but by my skill I have returned you to life, and now I will declare myself to you."

Thereupon the mysterious animal shook himself many times; when, at every shake, he grew larger and larger, until he seemed to touch the sky. "I should fill the earth, were I to exert my utmost power, and all therein would not satisfy the desires of my appetite. It is useless, therefore, for me to exhibit my strength, and henceforth I give unto you power over all animals. They shall be your food, as they all belong to me." So saying, the marvellous creature vanished from sight.

ORIGIN OF O-PE-CHE, THE ROBIN REDBREAST (American Indian)[13]

It was the desire of an ambitious hunter that his only son should obtain a powerful guardian spirit, and, when the proper time arrived for the lad to fast, he gave him minute directions for his conduct, bidding him be courageous and acquit himself with a manly spirit. Whereupon the young lad went into the se-ra-lo, or vapor-bath lodge,—which is apart from others and contains hot stones, upon which is poured cold water until the lodge is filled with steam,—and having remained within this lodge as long as necessary, came out and plunged into the cold water of the river. This process he repeated twice, and then went, accompanied by his father, to a secret lodge within the deep shades of the forest, which had been expressly prepared for him, where he laid himself down upon a mat woven by his mother, covering his face in silence, upon which his father took his departure, promising to visit him on the morning of each day. Each succeeding morning for eight days the hunter presented himself before his son, when he would give him kind words of encouragement, commending him for his perseverance. On the eighth day the lad's strength failed rapidly and he lay totally unable to rise or move, while his limbs had the rigidity of one about to die. On the ninth he addressed his father with this appeal: "My father, my dreams are not good; the spirits who visit me are unfavorable to your wish. Permit me to break my fast, and another time I will try again. I have no strength to endure longer."

The lad covered his face again and lay perfectly still, neither moving nor speaking until the eleventh day, when he again faintly whispered his request. "Tomorrow," answered the father, "I will come early in the morning, and bring you food." Silence and obedience were all that remained to the lad. He seemed like one who was dead, and it was only by closely watching that it could be perceived that he breathed. Day glided into night, and night into day, but time was unmarked by him. He lay motionless, while the forest trees bent and whispered in the breeze, and the river ran its hasty course, in whose sparkling waters he had plunged in the full strength of dawning manhood. The twelfth morning came, and at its earliest dawn the hunter appeared with the promised repast.

On drawing near to the lodge he heard sounds from within, as if of someone talking. Stooping to look through the small opening he discovered his son sitting up, and in the act of painting his breast and shoulders as far as his hands could reach, while he was muttering to himself: "My father has destroyed me; he would not listen to my requests. I shall be forever happy, for I have been obedient to him even beyond my strength. My guardian spirit is not the one I sought; but he is just and pitiful, and has given me another shape."

At this the father broke into the lodge, exclaiming: "Ningwis! Ningwis!—My son! my son! leave me not, leave me not!" But the lad, on the instant, even as the old man spoke, was transformed into a beautiful bird,—the O-pe-che, the Robin-Redbreast —and flew to the top of the lodge, where he addressed his father in these words: "Mourn not my change, I shall be happier thus than I should be as a man. I could not gratify your pride as a warrior, but I will cheer you with my song and strive to produce in you the buoyancy I feel. I am now forever free from cares and pains such as mankind endure. My food is furnished by the fields and mountains, and my path is in the sweet, bright air."

Thus speaking he spread his wings and flew away.

But O-pe-che delights, say the old wise men, to live near the lodges of his people. Often he takes a stand on the highest branch of a tree, and to foretell someone's coming he cries *n'doan-watch-e-go, n'doan-watch-e-go;* but when his prediction proves false, he flies down and hides in the thick rushes, crying, *che! che! che! che!*

INITIATION AS
PSYCHIC LIBERATION:*
THE MYTHS

Although there are no formal myths of shamanism, this type of initiation, expressing the experience of psychic liberation, is so important in the mythic paraphernalia of primitive man that any discussion of initiation would be incomplete without some account of its characteristics. Authentic shamanistic experiences derived from primitive sources are told in Shamanic Initiation *and* Crashing Thunder's *account,* The Road of Life and Death. *A veiled but distinctly discernible reference to shamanism is reported in* The Valley of Dry Bones, *while* The Death of Odin *conveys the spirit of mantic wisdom combined with inspired action to be learned in this type of death and rebirth pattern.* The Big Lord of Lives *is an account of shamanism in ancient China, with its sober ending. In the Hindu myths* Nachiketas and Yama *and* Sāvitrī, *shamanism is used as a method of liberation in a truly religious sense.*

J.L.H.

SHAMANIC INITIATION (Siberian)¹

"A person cannot become a shaman if there have been no shamans in his sib," the Tungus shaman Semyonov Semyon declared, . . .

* See Introduction, pp. 60 to 65.

"When I shamanize," the shaman continued, "the spirit of my deceased brother Ilya comes and speaks through my mouth. My shaman forefathers, too, have forced me to walk the path of shamanism. Before I commenced to shamanize, I lay sick for a whole year: I became a shaman at the age of fifteen. The sickness that forced me to this path showed itself in a swelling of my body and frequent spells of fainting. When I began to sing, however, the sickness usually disappeared.

"After that, my ancestors began to shamanize with me. They stood me up like a block of wood and shot at me with their bows until I lost consciousness. They cut up my flesh, separated my bones, counted them, and ate my flesh raw. When they counted the bones they found one too many; had there been too few, I could not have become a shaman. And while they were performing this rite, I ate and drank nothing for the whole summer. But at the end the shaman spirits drank the blood of a reindeer and gave me some to drink, too. After these events, the shaman has less blood and looks pale.

"The same thing happens to every Tungus shaman.* Only after his shaman ancestors have cut up his body in this way and separated his bones can he begin to practice. . . .

"Up above there is a certain tree where the souls of the shamans are reared, before they attain their powers. And on the boughs of this tree are nests in which the souls lie and are attended. The name of the tree is 'Tuuru.' The higher the nest in this tree, the stronger will the shaman be who is raised in it, the more will he know, and the farther will he see.

"The rim of a shaman's drum is cut from a living larch. The larch is left alive and standing in recollection and honor of the tree Tuuru, where the soul of the shaman was raised. . . .

"According to our belief, the soul of the shaman† climbs up

* See Introduction, p. 61.
[† "The shaman is, therefore, the man who can die, and then return to life, many times . . . . Through his initiation, the shaman learns . . . what he must do when his soul abandons his body—and, first of all, how to orient himself in the unknown regions which he enters during his ecstasy. He knows the road to the center of the world, the hole in the sky through which he can fly up to the highest Heaven, or the aperture in the earth through which he can descend to Hell. . . . All this he learned . . . under the guidance of the master shamans." (*Plate* 26.) *Birth and Rebirth*, Eliade.²]

this tree to God when he shamanizes. For the tree grows during the rite and invisibly reaches the summit of heaven." . . .

THE ROAD OF LIFE AND DEATH
(Winnebago Indian)[3]

Crashing-Thunder steps forward and speaks: . . .

From the time I was a young child I had had a brother-in-law named Thunder-Cloud. He was living his third life as a human being. Many years ago he had lived on this earth, joined the Medicine Rite and adhered strictly to all its precepts. . . . Finally, after reaching a ripe old age, he died. Properly and humbly he had progressed along the Road of the Sacred Rite. That now was finished. Up above, where all those go who have heeded the injunctions of the Rite, he went. There, in this new home, he lived and there he married.

After living there some time, he prepared to come back to earth. Once a month he fasted and all the different spirits whom Earthmaker had created, gave him their blessings. And so, in the course of time, he was born again on earth, born as a human being. Here on this earth he fasted again and the spirits above, who dwelt where Earthmaker sits, all bestowed their blessings upon him. Thus he became a holy man, a shaman, in fact the reincarnation of the North-Spirit.

In the course of time he became my brother-in-law and I went along with him when he was on his errands, doctoring.

Once I, myself, fell ill and he treated me. As soon as he came, my father arose with his tobacco and made him an offering. . . .

And he, my brother-in-law, for whom tobacco was being poured, accepted what we gave and exerted his powers that I might become well again. Standing above me he then recounted his fasting experience:

"Brother-in-law, this is how I learned to cure human beings. I was carried up to the spirit-village of those who live in the sky, a doctor's village, and there I was instructed as follows. A dead and rotten log, almost completely covered with weeds, was placed in the middle of the lodge. This log I was to treat as though it were a sick human being. I breathed upon the log and the spirits in the lodge breathed with me. Twice, three times, four times, we did the same. Finally the log that had seemed dead was transformed into a young man, who arose and walked away. 'Human being,' said the spirits, 'you are indeed a holy person!'

"Brother-in-law, from the middle of the ocean, the spirits came after me, from a shaman's village situated there. They, too, bestowed their powers upon me and they, too, made me try my powers. They asked me to blow upon waves they had created, all of them as large as the ocean, and I blew upon them and they became as quiet as water in a small saucer. . . . Then the spirits created a choppy ocean, where the waves piled one upon the other furiously and I was told to blow upon it. I did so and that ocean of waves, mighty as it was, subsided and became quiet.

" 'Human being,' they said, 'thus will you always act. There will indeed be nothing that you cannot accomplish. No matter what illness one of your fellow-men may happen to have, you will be able to cure it.' . . ."

Then my brother-in-law sang, breathed upon me and finally squirted some water upon my chest. "All of this I have told you," he said to me, "is quite true and is very holy. Indeed, you will get well."

Thunder-Cloud steps forward and speaks:

. . . It is I, Thunder-Cloud, who speaks, I who am now on earth for the third time, I who am now repeating experiences that I well remember from my previous existences.

Once, many, many years ago I lived with people who had twenty camps. When I was but a young boy . . . our village was attacked by an enemy war party and we were all killed. . . . All I knew and felt was that I was running about just as I had been accustomed to do. Not until I saw a heap of bodies piled upon the ground, mine among them, did I realize that I was really dead. No one was present to bury us. There on the ground we lay and rotted.

Then I was taken to the place where the sun sets and I lived happily for some time with an old couple. In this particular village of spiritland the inhabitants have the best of times . . . after a few years, the thought ran through my mind that I would like to return to earth. . . .

So I went to the chief and I told him my desires. . . "Go, my son, and obtain your full revenge upon those who killed all your relatives and you."

Thus was I brought back to earth again. Now it did not seem to me that I entered a woman's womb. Indeed I felt that I had somehow been brought into a room, a room where I remained sitting continuously. Never, throughout all this period, did I lose consciousness. Always, I was keenly aware of what was happening outside. . . . Noise made by some little children came to my ears and I decided to go outside . . . it seemed to me, that I was making my way through a door into the open. I stumbled through, and a sudden rush of cold air struck me so bitterly that I began to cry. So, in fact, it appeared. Actually, of course, I was being born from a woman's womb. . . .

I was taught to fast in order to prepare myself adequately and completely for warfare, for my purpose in returning to this earth. In due course of time I went on the war path. I did so repeatedly until I had taken full revenge for the death of myself and my dear relatives. . . .

I finally died of old age. . . .

This was the second time that I had known death. . . . When they buried me it was not as they do now. . . .

There in the grave I lay and rotted.

As I was lying there, rotting, I heard someone speak to me saying, "Come, we must leave now!" Obediently I arose and we walked, the two of us, in the direction of the sun where lies the village of the dead. There all the people are gay and enjoy themselves. . . . Four nights I was told I would have to stay in the village, but they meant four years.

When my stay was over I was taken up to the home of Earthmaker. There, at his own home, I saw him and talked to him, face to face, even as now I speak to you. The spirits, too, I saw. In fact I was one of them. Then I came back again to this world. Here I am.

DEATH OF ODIN (Icelandic)[4]

By wounding and hanging himself from the branches of the world tree Odin was accomplishing a magic rite, the purpose of which was his own rejuvenation. . . . With an effort . . . he managed to lift the runes, and was immediately set free by their magic power . . . and discovered that he was filled with new vigor and youth. Mimir gave him a few sips of hydromel and again Odin became wise in word and fruitful in deed. Thus was his resurrection accomplished.—Larousse Encyclopedia of Mythology.[5]

I'm aware that I hung
on the windy tree,
  swung there nights all of nine;
gashed with a blade
bloodied for Odin,
  myself an offering to myself
knotted to that tree
no man knows
  whither the root of it runs.

None gave me bread
none gave me drink,
  down to the depths I peered
to snatch up runes
with a roaring screech
  and fall in a dizzied faint!

Well being I won
and wisdom too,
  I grew and joyed in my growth;
from a word to a word
I was led to a word
  from a deed to another deed.

THE BIG LORD OF LIVES (Chinese)[6]

The gates of Heaven are open wide;
Off I ride, borne on a dark cloud!

May the gusty winds be my vanguard,
May sharp showers sprinkle the dust!
The Lord wheels in his flight, he is coming down;
I will cross K'ung-sang* and attend upon you.
But all over the Nine Provinces there are people in throngs;
Why think that his task is among us?
High he flies, peacefully winging;
On pure air borne aloft he handles Yin and Yang.
I and the Lord, solemn and reverent,
On our way to God across the Nine Hills.
He trails his spirit-garment,
Dangles his girdle-gems.
One Yin for every Yang;
The crowd does not understand what we are doing.
I pluck the sparse-hemp's lovely flower,
Meaning to send it to him from whom I am separated.
Age creeps on apace, all will soon be over;
Not to draw nearer is to drift further apart.
He has driven his dragon chariot, loudly rumbling;
High up he gallops into Heaven.
Binding cassia-branches a long while I stay;
Ch'iang! The more I think of him, the sadder I grow,
The sadder I grow; but what does sadness help?
If only it could be forever as this time it was!
But man's fate is fixed;
From meetings and partings none can ever escape.

    I take the outline of the song to be as follows:
The gates of Heaven are open, which means that the god is about
to leave Heaven and descend. The shaman, as usual, goes out
to meet him. She remembers, however, that China is a large country and hardly dares hope that the god will descend in her direction.
    The god is "handling" Yin and Yang, the two primordial
principles, corresponding to shade and sunshine, female and male,
soul and body, and so on. . . . He is adjusting them—keeping them
in due balance, which will ensure good health, good weather . . .

   * K'ung-sang means "hollow mulberry-tree." Various heroes were born
miraculously out of such a tree.

and so forth. The shaman* joins him and is permitted to help him in his task, which consists in making sure that there is "one Yin for every Yang." . . . The last eleven lines [reveal that] the god has abandoned his devotee and she is left, as usual, in melancholy and desolation.

TEACHING OF THE IDENTITY OF LIFE AND DEATH (Zen Buddhist)[7]

Dogo went with his Disciple Zengen to a certain house to offer condolences for someone's death. Zengen rapped on the coffin and said to Dogo, "Is he alive or dead?" Dogo replied, "I do not say he is alive; I do not say he is dead." Zengen then asked, "Why don't you tell me (one way or the other)?" Dogo answered, "I will not say! I will not say!" On their way back to the temple, Zengen said, "Master! do tell me! If you don't, I'll knock you down." Dogo replied, "Strike me if you like—but you won't get a word out of me." Zengen thereupon struck him. Afterwards, when Dogo was dead, Zengen went to Sekiso [another of his disciples], and told him what had happened. Sekiso said, "I do not say he was alive, I do not say he was dead." Zengen asked, "Why don't you tell me?" Sekiso said, "I will not say! I will not say!" Zengen suddenly realized the truth.

NACHIKETAS AND YAMA (Indian)[8]

From the time of the Upanishads [800 B.C. and after] India rejects the world as it is and devaluates life as it reveals itself to the eyes of the

* From the *Kuo yu* or *Narrative of the States* (Fourth century B. C.). [A minister of State says] "Anciently, men and spirits did not intermingle. At that time there were certain persons who were so perspicacious, single-minded, and reverential that their understanding enabled them to make meaningful collation of what lies above and below, and their insight to illumine what is distant and profound. Therefore the spirits would descend into them. The possessors of such powers were, if men, called hsi (shamans), and, if women, wu (shamannesses). It is they who . . . handled religious matters."

sage—ephemeral, painful, illusory. Such a conception leads neither to nihilism nor to pessimism. This world is rejected, this life depreciated, because it is known that something else exists, beyond becoming, beyond temporality, beyond suffering. In religious terms, it could almost be said that India rejects the profane cosmos and profane life, because it thirsts for a sacred world and a sacred mode of being.—Yoga: Immortality and Freedom, *Eliade.*⁹

There was a cowherd of the name of Vajashrava; desiring a gift from the gods, he made offerings of all he owned. But the kine he had were old, yielding no milk and worthless; not such as might buy the worshipper a place in Heaven. Vajashrava had a son; he would have his father make a worthier offering. To his sire he spoke: "To which god wilt thou offer me?" "To Death I give thee."

Nachiketas thought: "I shall be neither the first nor last that fares to Yama. Yet what will he do with me? It shall be with me as with others; like grass a man decays, like grass he springeth up again." So Nachiketas went his way to Death's wide home, and waited there three days; for Death was on a journey. When Death returned his servants said: "A Brahman guest burns like a fire: Nachiketas waits three days unwelcomed; do thou soothe him with an offering of water, for all is lost to him in whose abode a Brahman waits unfed."

Then Death spake to Nachiketas: "Since thou, an honored guest, hast waited in my house three days unfed, ask of me three boons in return, and I shall grant them." Then first he prayed: "Grant to my father peace and to know and welcome me when I return." Death answered: "Be it so."

Nachiketas asked again: "In Heaven-world the folk are quit of thee; there is neither hunger, . . . nor fear of death. Reveal to me the sacred fire that leads to Heaven." Then Death described the sacred fire—what stones for its altar, and how disposed; and Nachiketas said it over, learning the lesson taught by Death. Death spoke again: "I grant thee, furthermore, that this sacred fire be known for ever by thy name; thine is the fire that leads to Heaven, thy second boon."

Nachiketas asked again: "The great mystery of what cometh after death; he is, some say; others say, he is no more. This great doubt I ask thee to resolve." Death replied: "Even the gods of old knew not this; this is a matter hard to be learnt; ask me, O Nachiketas, any other boon, though it be a hundred sons, or untold wealth, . . . or length of days. All that a man can desire shall be thine, . . . only ask not of death." Nachiketas answered: "What avails wealth whenas thou dost appear? How shall a man delight in life, however long, when he has beheld the bliss of those who perish not? This doubt of the Great Hereafter I ask thee to resolve; no other boon I ask."

Death replied: "Duty is one, delight another; these twain draw a man in diverse paths. Well is it for him that chooses duty; he goes astray who seeks delight. These twain, wisdom and folly, point to diverse ends. Well has Nachiketas spoken, seeking wisdom, not goaded by desires. Even the learned abide in delusion, blind led by the blind; while to the fool is naught revealed. This world, and no other, he thinketh; and so cometh again and again into my power.

"But he is great who tells of the One, of whom the many may never hear, whom the many, though they hear, may not know; a marvel is he who knoweth the Brahman. Untold is he, no path leads to him.

"Having heard and well grasped him with insight, attaining to that subtle One, a mortal is gladdened and rejoices for good cause. Wide is the gate for Nachiketas, methinks."

Nachiketas answered:

"Other than good, other than evil, other than formless or than forms, other than past or future—declare thou That." Death resumed:

"That goal of sacred wisdom, of goodly works and faith, is *Om!* This word is Brahman, the supreme. He who doth comprehend this word, whatsoever he desires is his. For that Singer is not born, nor does he ever die. He came not anywhere, nor anything was he. Unborn, eternal, everlasting, ancient; unslain is he, though the body be slain. If the slayer thinks he slays, or the slain deems he is slain, they err; That neither slayeth nor is slain.

"Smaller than small, greater than great, the Self indwells in every creature's heart.

"Sitting, he travels far; lying, he speedeth everywhere; who knoweth him hath no more grief.

"This Self is not obtainable by explanation, nor by intellection, nor by much hearkening to scripture; whom he chooses, to him That is revealed. But he that knoweth that all things are Self, for him what grief, what delusion lingers, knowing all things are That One?

"When all desires that linger in the heart are driven forth, then mortal is made immortal, he becometh Brahman.

"When every knot of the heart is loose then doth he win immortal Being. Thus far the teaching."

Thus having learnt the wisdom taught by Death, and finding Brahman, Nachiketas* was freed from death. So verily shall he be free who knoweth that Supreme Self.

THE VALLEY OF DRY BONES
(Christian)[11]

The hand of the Lord was upon me, and carried me out in the Spirit of the Lord, and set me down in the midst of the valley which was full of bones, and caused me to pass by them round about: and behold, there were very many in the open valley; and lo, they were very dry.

And he said unto me, Son of man, can these bones live? and I answered, O Lord, thou knowest.

Again he said unto me, Prophesy upon these bones, and say unto them, O ye dry bones, hear the word of the Lord. Thus saith the Lord God unto these bones; Behold, I will cause breath to enter into you, and ye shall live: and I will lay sinews upon you, and will bring up flesh upon you, and cover your skin, and put breath in you, and ye shall live; and ye shall know that I am the Lord.

* ["Herodotus . . . gives a symbolic account of the descent into Hades and the return to the human world of King Rhampsinitus [of Egypt] . . . the most ancient recorded parallel now known exists in the Rig Veda [1500-1200 B.C.] . . . where the boy mentioned is the same boy Nachiketas . . . That this primeval Hades legend was interpreted esoterically as teaching a rebirth doctrine is confirmed by the ancient Katha Upanishad, the story of Nachiketas being used . . . to convey the highest Vedāntic teachings concerning birth, life and death." *Tibetan Book of the Dead,* ed. Evans-Wentz.[10]

So I prophesied as I was commanded: and as I prophesied, there was a noise, and behold a shaking, and the bones came together, bone to his bone. And when I beheld, lo, the sinews and the flesh came upon them, and the skin covered them above: but there was no breath in them.

Then said he unto me, Prophesy unto the wind, prophesy, son of man, and say to the wind, Thus saith the Lord God: Come

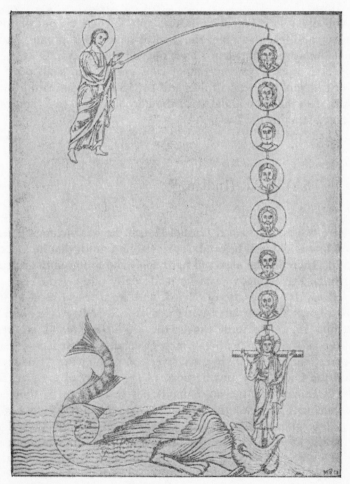

Fig. 14—Capture of the Leviathan with the sevenfold tackle of the line of David, with the crucifix as bait.

from the four winds, O breath, and breathe upon these slain, that they might live.

So I prophesied as he commanded me, and the breath came into them, and they lived, and stood up upon their feet, an exceeding great army.

Then he said unto me, Son of man these bones are the whole house of Israel: behold, they say, Our bones are dried, and our hope is lost; we are cut off for our parts. Therefore prophesy and say unto them, Thus saith the Lord God: Behold, O my people, I will open your graves, and cause you to come up out of your graves, and bring you into the land of Israel. And ye shall know that I am the Lord, when I have opened your graves, O my people, and brought you up out of your graves, and shall put my Spirit in you, and ye shall live, and I shall place you in your own land: then shall you know that I the Lord have spoken it, and performed it, saith the Lord. . . .

Ezekiel

SĀVITRĪ (Indian) [12]

There was a king named Lord-of-Horses; he was virtuous, generous, brave, and well-beloved. It grieved him much that he had no child. Therefore he observed hard vows and followed the rule of hermits. For eighteen years he made daily offerings to Fire, recited *mantras* in praise of Sāvitrī, and ate a frugal meal at the sixth hour. Then at last Sāvitrī was pleased and revealed herself to him in visible form within the sacrificial fire. "I am well pleased," she said, "with thy asceticism, thy well-kept vows, thy veneration. Ask, great king, whatever boon thou wilt." "Goddess," said the king, "may sons be born to me worthy of my race, for the Brāhmans tell me much merit lies in children. If thou art pleased with me, I ask this boon." Sāvitrī replied: "O king, knowing thy wish, I have spoken already with Brahmā that thou shouldst have sons. Through his favour there shall be born to thee a glorious daughter. Thou shouldst not answer again: this is the grandsire's gift, who is well pleased with thy devotion." The king bowed down and prayed. "So be it," he said, and Sāvitrī vanished. It was not long before his queen bore him a shining girl with lotus eyes. Forasmuch as she was the gift of the goddess Sā-vitrī, the wife of Brahmā, she was named Sāvitrī with all due ceremony, and she grew in grace and loveliness like unto Shrī herself. Like a golden image the people thought her, saying: "A goddess has come amongst us." But none dared wed that lady of the lotus eyes, for the radiant splendour and the ardent spirit that were in her daunted every suitor.

One holiday, after her service of the gods, she came before her father with an offering of flowers. She touched his feet, and stood at his side with folded hands. Then the king was sad, seeing his daughter of marriageable age and yet unwooed. He said to her: "My daughter, the time for thy bestowal has come; yet none seek thee. Do thou, therefore, choose for thyself a husband who shall be thy equal. Choose whom thou wilt; I shall reflect and give thee unto him, for a father that giveth not his daughter is disgraced. Act thou therefore so that we may not meet with the censure of the gods."

Then Sāvitrī meekly bowed to her father's feet and went forth with her attendants. Mounting a royal car she visited the forest hermitages of the sages. Worshipping the feet of those revered saints, she roamed through all the forests till she found her lord.

One day when her father sat in open court, conversing with the counsellors, Sāvitrī returned, and, seeing her father seated beside the *rishi* Nārada, bowed to his feet and greeted him. Then Nārada said: "Why dost thou delay to wed the girl, who is of marriageable age?" The king replied: "It was for this that she went forth, and even now she returns. Hear whom she has chosen for her husband." So saying, he turned to Sāvitrī, commanding her to relate all that had befallen her.

Standing with folded hands before the king and sage, she answered: "There was a virtuous king of the Shālwas, Dyumatsena by name. He grew blind; then an ancient foe wrested the kingdom from his hands, and he, with his wife and little child, went forth into the woods, where he practised the austerities appropriate to the hermit life. The child, his son, grew up in that forest hermitage. He is worthy to be my husband; him have I accepted in my heart as lord."

Then Nārada exclaimed: "Greatly amiss has Sāvitrī done in taking for her lord this boy, whose name is Satyavān; albeit I know him well, and he excels in all good qualities. Even as a child he took delight in horses and would model them in clay or draw their pictures; wherefore he has been named Horse-painter."

The king asked: "Has this Prince Satyavān intelligence, forgiveness, courage, energy?" Nārada replied: "In energy he is like the sun, in wisdom like Brihaspati, brave like the king of gods, forgiving as the earth herself. Eke he is liberal, truthful, and fair to look upon."

Then the king inquired again: "Tell me now what are his faults." Nārada answered: "He hath one defect that overwhelms all his virtues, and that fault is irremediable. It is fated that he will die within a year."

Then the king addressed his daughter: "Do thou, O Sāvitrī, fair girl, choose for thyself another lord; for thou hast heard the words of Nārada." But Sāvitrī answered: "The die can fall but once; a daughter can only once be given away; once only may it be said: 'I give away!' Forsooth, be life short or long, be he virtuous or vicious, I have chosen my husband once for all. I shall not choose twice. A thing is first thought of in the heart, then it is spoken, then it is done; my mind is witness thereof." Then Nārada said to the king: "Thy daughter's heart is unwavering; she may not be turned from the right way. Moreover, none excelleth Satyavān in virtue; the marriage has my approval." The king, with folded hands, answered again: "Whatsoever thou dost command is to be done." Nārada said again: "May peace attend the gift of Sāvitrī. I shall now go on my ways; be it well with all;" and therewith he ascended again to Heaven.

On an auspicious day King Lord-of-Horses with Sāvitrī fared to the hermitage of Dyumatsena. Entering on foot, he found the royal sage seated in contemplation beneath a noble tree; him the king reverenced duly, with presents meet for holy men, and announced the purpose of his visit. Dyumatsena answered: "But how may thy daughter, delicately nurtured, lead this hard forest life with us, practising austerity and following the rule of hermits?" The king replied: "Thou shouldst not speak such words to us; for my daughter knoweth, like myself, that happiness and sorrow come and go, and neither endures. Thou shouldst not

PLATE 25. *Ur-rammu Stele.*

PLATE 26. *Sorcerer of Trois Frères.*

PLATE 27. *Jadeite bowl of a shaman.*

PLATE 28. *Snake Goddess.*

PLATE 29. *Buddha and Seven Serpents.*

PLATE 30. *Bodhisattva.*

PLATE 31. *The God Vishnu in fish incarnation.*

PLATE 32. *Kolquhaludi's Emergence.*

disregard my offer." It was arranged accordingly, and in the presence of the twice-born sages of the forest hermitages Sāvitrī was
given to Satyavān. When her father had departed she laid aside
her jewels and garbed herself in bark and brown. She delighted
all by her gentleness and self-denial, her generosity and sweet
speech. But the words of Nārada were ever present in her mind.

At length the hour appointed for the death of Satyavān approached; when he had but four days more to live Sāvitrī fasted
day and night, observing the penance of "Three Nights." By the
third day Sāvitrī was faint and weak, and she spent the last unhappy night in miserable reflections on her husband's coming
death. In the morning she fulfilled the usual rites, and came to
stand before the Brāhmans and her husband's father and mother,
and they for her helping prayed that she might never be a widow.

Satyavān went out into the woods with axe in hand, suspect-
ing nothing, to bring home wood for the sacrificial fire. Sāvitrī
prayed to go with him, and he consented, if his parents also permitted it. She prayed them sweetly to allow it, saying that she
could not bear to stay behind and that she desired exceedingly
to see the blossoming trees. Dyumatsena gave her leave, saying:
"Since Sāvitrī was given by her father to be my daughter-in-law
I cannot remember that she has asked for anything at all. Now,
therefore, let her prayer be granted. But do not," he added, "hin-
der Satyavān's sacred labour."

So Sāvitrī departed with her lord, seeming to smile, but
heavy-hearted; for, remembering Nārada's words, she pictured him
already dead. With half her heart she mourned, expectant of his
end; with half she answered him with smiles, as they passed beside
the sacred streams and goodly trees. Presently he fell to work, and
as he hewed at the branches of a mighty tree he grew sick and
faint, and came to his wife complaining that his head was racked
with darting pains and that he would sleep awhile. Sāvitrī sat
on the ground and laid his head upon her lap; that was the appointed time of Satyavān's death. Immediately Sāvitrī beheld a
shining ruddy deity, dark and red of eye and terrible to look
upon; he bore a noose in his hand. He stood and gazed at Satyavān. Then Sāvitrī rose and asked him humbly who he might be
and what he sought to do. "I am Yama, Lord of Death," he answered, "and I have come for Satyavān, whose appointed span

of life is ended." So saying, Yama drew forth the soul from Satyavān's body, bound in the noose, and altogether helpless; therewith
he departed toward the south, leaving the body cold and lifeless.

Sāvitrī followed close; but Yama said: "Desist, O Sāvitrī.
Return, perform thy husband's funeral rites. Thou mayst come
no farther." But she answered: "Whither my lord is brought or
goeth of his own will I shall follow; this is the lasting law. The
way is open to me because of my obedience and virtue. Lo, the
wise have said that friendship is seven-paced. Relying on friendship thus contracted, I shall say thee somewhat more. Thou dost
order me to follow another rule than that of wife; thou wouldst
make of me a widow, following not the domestic rule. But the
four rules are for those who have not attained their purpose, true
religious merit. It is otherwise with me; for I have reached the
truth by fulfilment of the duty of a wife alone. It needs not to
make of me a widow." Yama replied: "Thou sayest well, and well
thou pleasest me. Ask now a boon, whatsoever thou wilt, except
thy husband's life." She prayed that Dyumatsena should regain
his sight and health, and Yama granted it. Still Sāvitrī would not
return, saying that she would follow still her lord, and, besides,
that friendship with the virtuous must ever bear good fruit. Yama
admitted the truth of this, and granted her another boon; she
asked that her father should regain his kingdom. Yama gave his
promise that it should be accomplished and commanded Sāvitrī
to return. Still she refused, and spoke of the duty of the great and
good to protect and aid all those who seek their help. Yama then
granted her a third boon, that her father should have a hundred
sons. Still Sāvitrī persisted. "Thou art called the Lord of Justice,"
she said, "and men ever trust the righteous; for it is goodness of
heart alone that inspireth the confidence of every creature." When
Yama granted another boon, save and except the life of Satyavān,
Sāvitrī prayed for a hundred sons born of herself and Satyavān.
Yama replied: "Thou shalt, O Lady, obtain a hundred sons, re-
nowned and mighty, giving thee great delight. But thou hast come
too far; now I pray thee to return." But she again praised the
righteous. "It is the righteous," she said, "who support the earth
by their austere life; they protect all." Again Yama was propitiated by Sāvitrī's edifying words, and he granted another boon.
But now Sāvitrī answered: "O giver of honour, what thou hast

already granted cannot come to pass without union with my husband; therefore I ask his life together with the other boons. Without him I am but dead, without him I do not even desire happiness. Thou hast given me a hundred sons, and yet dost take away my lord, without whom I may not live. I ask his life, that thy words may be accomplished."

The Yama yielded and gave back Satyavān, promising him prosperity and a life of four centuries, and descendants who should all be kings. Granting all that Sāvitrī asked, the Lord of the ancestors went his way. Then Sāvitrī returned to Satyavān's body, and she lifted his head upon her lap; behold, he came to life, like one returning home from sojourn in a strange land. "I have slept overlong," he said; "why didst thou not awake me? Where is that dark being who would have carried me away?" Sāvitrī answered: "Thou hast slept long. Yama has gone his way. Thou art recovered; rise, if thou canst, for night is falling."

Then those two returned, walking through heavy night along the forest paths.

Meanwhile Dyumatsena and his wife and all the sages remained in grief. Yet the Brāhmans were of good hope, for they deemed that Sāvitrī's virtue must avail even against fate, and they gave words of comfort to the king. Moreover, Dyumatsena suddenly regained his sight, and all took this for an omen of good fortune, betokening the safety of Satyavān. Then Sāvitrī and Satyavān returned through the dark night, and found the Brāhmans and the king seated beside the fire. Warm was their welcome and keen the questioning; then Sāvitrī related all that had befallen, and all saluted her; then, forasmuch as it was late, all went to their own abodes.

Next day at dawn there came ambassadors from Shālwa to say that the usurper had been slain, and the people invited Dyumatsena to return and be again their king. So he returned to Shālwa and lived long; and he had a hundred sons. Sāvitrī and Satyavān had also the hundred sons bestowed by Yama. Thus did Sāvitrī by her goodness alone raise from a poor estate to the highest fortune herself, her parents, and her lord, and all those descended from them.

MYTHS OF RESURRECTION*

In The Death of Balder, *we find a myth which contains features of the yearly death and rebirth of a vegetation god found in the Babylonian, Egyptian, and Greek myths. But Balder does not return yearly from the underworld; he must wait until the old order has been destroyed and a new one arises. This suggests the change from rebirth to resurrection found in a typical series of myths and religious beliefs.*

The best-known version of resurrection is the story of Christ, as told in THE GOSPEL OF JOHN. *Characteristic of the Christian tradition, with its Old Testament background, is the belief in a Last Judgment with a final end of the world* (eschaton), *ending in resurrection for the blessed "when the dead shall arise." Significant passages representing this transcendent faith, with its capacity also to perform miracles (as in the story of Elijah), are told in the group of stories from the Bible.*

In contrast to this type of patriarchalism, with its admixture of shamanism, there is a series of stories from India representing resurrection as a process of evolution in which human loyalties, humility, and compassion are the virtues chiefly required to attain a blessed state of being. In this religious archetype we find especially the conception of yoga *as a means of attaining liberation. This is derived from that kind of tribal wisdom I have described as shamanism, and is a way of finding the direction for the soul's journey shown in* Black Elk Speaks.

* See Introduction, pp. 66 to 73.

*Finally, we have the mysterious power of the feminine in
connection with resurrection, as represented in the tale of* The
Temple Cat, *pointing out the contrast between this and the much
more direct and much more common masculine stories of ascent
or the need to pass a significant series of tests or rites of passage.
Usually this theme is reserved for the rites of rebirth associated
with the moon and the cycle of nature. There are, however,
esoteric versions of the theme which intermingle themes of rebirth and resurrection, showing there may be a need to reconcile
these two opposite principles in a mythological sense.*

J.L.H.

THE DEATH OF BALDER (Icelandic)[1]

Now I must tell you of events which to the gods seemed most omi-
nous. It all began like this: Balder the God dreamed premonitory
dreams touching the safety of his life. When he told the gods his
dreams they pooled their suggestions and it was decided to seek
protection for Balder from every conceivable kind of hurt; and
to this end Frigg exacted oaths from fire and water, iron and
every sort of metal, stones, earth, trees, diseases, beasts, birds,
poisons and serpents, that they would never harm Balder. And
when all this had been seen to, it became a sport and a pastime
at their meetings for him to stand up . . . while all the others
either shot at him or cut and thrust or merely threw stones. No
matter what they did, he never took the slightest harm . . .

Loki . . . saw all this and liked it the worse when Balder was
never injured. Disguised as an old crone, he went to see Frigg at
Fensalir. Frigg asked the old woman if she knew what the gods
were doing at their meeting today? She said they were all shooting at Balder without hurting him a bit. Frigg explained, "Neither
weapon nor wand will ever wound Balder, I have their given
word—all of them." The old crone croaked, "Do you mean to say
every single thing has given its oath to protect Balder from harm?"
"As a matter of fact," Frigg said, "there is one young sprout growing in a wood over to the west of Valhalla (they call it Mistletoe)
far too immature for me to ask it to swear oaths."

The "old crone" turned on "her" heel at once, but Loki cut the mistletoe down and took it with him to the meeting. Hoor stood away on the edge of the ring of gods because he was blind. Loki whispered to him, "Why aren't you shooting at Balder?" And he replied, "Because I can't see where he is; and another thing—I have nothing to throw." Then said Loki, "Do as the others are doing and show honor to Balder as they do. I'll guide you to where he is standing: here, pitch this shaft at him."

Hoor took the mistletoe and threw it at Balder just as Loki told him. The shaft flew full at him and he fell down dead to the ground—the cruelest tragedy that ever happened to gods and men.

As soon as Balder dropped, the gods were dumb-struck . . . and they looked the one at the other with but a single thought in their heads, "Who did this shameful thing?" which no one could avenge. They thought they had taken every precaution, and when the gods did find their voices the first sounds they made were wails of affliction. . . . Odin had the bitterest grief to bear since his knowledge was the keener of how portentous to the gods was the slaying and loss of Balder.

When the gods had composed themselves a little, Frigg spoke up, "Who is there," she asked, "on our side who will earn the love and undying gratitude of all the gods by riding down the road to hel and trying to find the ghost of Balder, who will ask the ransom Hel desires—provided she is willing to allow Balder to come back home to Asgard?"

He who is called Hermodr the Swift, a son of Odin, said he was ready to go.

Then Odin's horse Sleipnir was led from the stables; Hermodr strode into the saddle and galloped away.

The gods lifted up Balder's corpse and carried it down to the sea shore. Balder's ship was called Hringhorni. This was the greatest of all vessels which the gods were about to launch, and amidships they built Balder's funeral pyre, only to find they were unable to budge the boat. So they sent into Giantland for a giantess called Hyrrokkin who came astride a wolf with a viper for a bridle. As she leapt off her steed, Odin shouted up four berserkers to manage the brute, which they were quite unable to control until they stunned it. Hyrrokkin stepped up to the ship's prow and heaved it ahead at the first short, sharp shove, so that the sparks feathered up from the rollers and the ground trembled. Thor was suddenly enraged and flew to his hammer intending to smash open her skull; but the gods pacified him for her sake. Then Balder's body was carried out onto the ship, and when his wife, Nanna the daughter of Nep, saw it she cried out in her grief and anguish; she was born in the fire and she perished in the fire. Thor then stepped in front and blessed the pyre with Mullicrusher, and at the same time a dwarf named Litr ran in under his feet; Thor lunged at him savagely with his toe, flinging him into the midst of the blaze and he burned to death.

All manner of people gathered for the burning; first let me mention Odin, and with him Frigg and his Valkyries and his ravens; Frey, and drawing his chariot the two boars called Golden-topping; Freys with her cats; then thronged a great host of frost giants and hill trolls. Odin flung into the fire his gold ring called Draupnir the Dropper: it had a supernatural power in that every ninth night there dropped from it eight other such rings of equal weight. Balder's horse in full harness had already been laid on the pyre.

But to speak now of Hermodr: he rode nine days and nights down ravines ever darker and deeper, meeting no one, until he came to the banks of the river Gjoll which he followed as far as the Gjoll Bridge: this bridge is roofed with burning gold. Modgudr is the maiden's name who guards the bridge. She asked him his name or lineage, saying only the day before five droves of dead men had passed over the bridge, "but the bridge echoed less under them than you. Anyway, you haven't the pallor of a dead man: why are you riding down the Hel Way?"

He replied, "I ride to hel to seek out Balder. You don't happen to have set eyes on Balder on the road to hel?"

She said Balder had already ridden over Gjoll Bridge, "and the road to hel lies down still and to the north."

Hermodr galloped on until he came to Hel Gate Bars, where he stepped down from his horse and tightened the girths. He mounted again and plunged his spurs into the animal's flanks. The stallion leapt so high there was plenty of twilight between him and the bars. And Hermodr rode on to the hall of Hel where he got down and went in to see his brother Balder sitting on a throne. Hermodr stayed with him that night.

Next morning Hermodr begged Hel to let Balder ride back home with him and went on to tell how greatly the gods were grieving. Hel said it would soon be put to the test that Balder was so beloved by all as they make out: "If every single creature up in heaven, dead or alive, really mourns him then he shall be restored to the gods. He stays with Hel if but one alone speaks against him or refuses to mourn."

Hermodr stood up and Balder saw him outside and he pulled off the ring Draupnir and sent it back to Odin for a memento, while Nanna sent some linen and many other gifts to Frigg, and to Fulla a golden ring.

Then rode Hermodr back to Asgard and related all his news, everything he had seen and everything he had heard.

At once, the gods sent messengers to every corner of heaven asking all to weep Balder un-dead, and everything did so, both men and beasts, earth, stones, trees, and every metal. . . . When at last the messengers came home, having pursued their errand diligently, they passed to a cave where an old witch was crouching. Her name was Pokk and they asked her to mourn for Balder, but she chanted:

> Pokk must drop
> only dry tears
> for the beautiful Balder's burial:
> living or dead
> I loved not the churl's son;
> let Hel hold what she has.

Everybody guessed this must have been Loki who had done so much evil among the gods.

THE REVELATION OF ST. JOHN
THE DIVINE (Christian)[2]

And I saw an angel come down from heaven, having the key of the bottomless pit and a great chain in his hand.

And he laid hold on the dragon, that old serpent, which is the Devil, and Satan, and bound him a thousand years,

And cast him into the bottomless pit, and shut him up, and set a seal upon him, that he should deceive the nations no more, till the thousand years should be fulfilled; and after that he must be loosed a little season.

And I saw thrones, and they sat upon them, and judgment was given unto them: and I saw the souls of them that were beheaded for the witness of Jesus, and for the word of God, and which had not worshipped the beast, neither his image, neither had received his mark upon their foreheads, or in their hands; and they lived and reigned with Christ a thousand years.

But the rest of the dead lived not again until the thousand years were finished. This is the first resurrection.

Blessed and holy is he that hath part in the first resurrection: on such the second death hath no power, but they shall be priests of God and of Christ, and shall reign with him a thousand years.

And when the thousand years are expired, Satan shall be loosed out of his prison,

And shall go out to deceive the nations which are in the four quarters of the earth, Gog and Magog, to gather them together to battle: the number of whom is as the sand of the sea.

And they went up on the breadth of the earth, and compassed the camp of the saints about, and the beloved city: and fire came down from God out of heaven and devoured them.

And the devil that deceived them was cast into the lake of fire and brimstone, where the beast and the false prophet are, and shall be tormented day and night for ever and ever.

And I saw a great white throne, and him that sat on it, from whose face the earth and the heaven fled away; and there was found no place for them.

And I saw the dead, small and great, stand before God; and the books were opened: and another book was opened, which is the book of life: and the dead were judged out of those things which were written in the books, according to their works.

And the sea gave up the dead which were in it; and death and hell delivered up the dead which were in them: and they were judged every man according to their works.

And death and hell were cast into the lake of fire. This is the second death.

FIG. 15—Apocalypse. 16th-century woodcut.

And whosoever was not found written in the book of life was cast into the lake of fire. . . .

But the fearful, and unbelieving, and the abominable, and murderers, and whoremongers, and sorcerers, and idolaters, and all liars, shall have their part in the lake which burneth with fire and brimstone: which is the second death. . . .

And he shewed me a pure river of water of life, clear as crystal, proceeding out of the throne of God and of the Lamb.

In the midst of the street of it, and on either side of the river, was there the tree of life, which bare twelve manner of fruits, and yielded her fruit every month: and the leaves of the tree were for the healing of the nations.

And there shall be no more curse: but the throne of God and of the Lamb shall be in it; and his servants shall serve him:

And they shall see his face; and his name shall be in their foreheads.

And there shall be no night there; and they need no candle, neither light of the sun; for the Lord God giveth them light: and they shall reign for ever and ever.

I KINGS, CHAP. 17 (Christian)[3]

And it came to pass after these things, that the son of the woman, the mistress of the house, fell sick; and his sickness was so sore, that there was no breath left in him.

And she said unto Elijah, What have I to do with thee, O thou man of God? art thou come unto me to call my sin to remembrance, and to slay my son?

And he said unto her, Give me thy son. And he took him out of her bosom, and carried him up into a loft, where he abode, and laid him upon his own bed.

And he cried unto the Lord, and said, O Lord my God, hast thou also brought evil upon the widow with whom I sojourn, by slaying her son?

And he stretched himself upon the child three times, and cried unto the Lord, and said, O Lord my God, I pray thee, let this child's soul come into him again.

And the Lord heard the voice of Elijah; and the soul of the child came into him again, and he revived.

And Elijah took the child, and brought him down out of the

chamber into the house, and delivered him unto his mother: and Elijah said, See, thy son liveth.

And the woman said to Elijah, Now by this I know that thou art a man of God, and that the word of the Lord in thy mouth is truth.

FIG. 16—The ascension of Elijah. Early Christian mural painting in the Lucian churchyard, Rome.

JOB, CHAP. 14 (Christian)[4]

Man that is born of a woman is of few days, and full of trouble.

He cometh forth like a flower, and is cut down: he fleeth also as a shadow, and continueth not.

And dost thou open thine eyes upon such an one, and bringest me into judgment with thee?

Who can bring a clean thing out of an unclean? not one.

Seeing his days are determined, the number of his months are with thee, thou hast appointed his bounds that he cannot pass:

Turn from him, that he may rest, till he shall accomplish, as an hireling, his day.

For there is hope of a tree, if it be cut down, that it will sprout again, and that the tender branch thereof will not cease.

Though the root thereof wax old in the earth, and the stock thereof die in the ground;

Yet through the scent of water it will bud, and bring forth boughs like a plant.

But man dieth, and wasteth away: yea, man giveth up the ghost, and where is he?

As the waters fail from the sea, and the flood decayeth and drieth up:

So man lieth down, and riseth not: till the heavens be no more, they shall not awake, nor be raised out of their sleep.

O that thou wouldest hide me in the grave, that thou wouldest keep me secret, until thy wrath be past, that thou wouldest appoint me a set time, and remember me!

If a man die, shall he live again? all the days of my appointed time will I wait, till my change come.

GOSPEL ACCORDING TO ST. JOHN, CHAP. 20 (Christian)[5]

The first day of the week cometh Mary Magdalene early, when it was yet dark, unto the sepulchre, and seeth the stone taken away from the sepulchre.

Then she runneth, and cometh to Simon Peter, and to the other disciple, whom Jesus loved, and saith unto them, They have taken away the Lord out of the sepulchre, and we know not where they have laid him.

Peter therefore went forth, and that other disciple, and came to the sepulchre.

So they ran both together: and the other disciple did outrun Peter, and came first to the sepulchre.

And he stooping down, and looking in, saw the linen clothes lying; yet went he not in.

Then cometh Simon Peter following him, and went into the sepulchre, and seeth the linen clothes lie,

And the napkin, that was about his head, not lying with the linen clothes, but wrapped together in a place by itself.

Then went in also that other disciple, which came first to the sepulchre, and he saw, and believed.

For as yet they knew not the scripture, that he must rise again from the dead.

Then the disciples went away again unto their own home.

But Mary stood without at the sepulchre weeping: and as she wept, she stooped down, and looked into the sepulchre,

And seeth two angels in white sitting, the one at the head, and the other at the feet, where the body of Jesus had lain.

And they say unto her, Woman, why weepest thou? She saith unto them, Because they have taken away my Lord, and I know not where they have laid him.

And when she had thus said, she turned herself back, and saw Jesus standing, and knew not that it was Jesus.

Jesus saith unto her, Woman, why weepest thou? whom seekest thou? She, supposing him to be the gardener, saith unto him, Sir, if thou have borne him hence, tell me where thou hast laid him, and I will take him away.

Jesus saith unto her, Mary. She turned herself, and saith unto him, Rabboni; which is to say, Master.

Jesus saith unto her, Touch me not; for I am not yet ascended to my Father: but go to my brethren, and say unto them, I ascend unto my Father, and your Father; and to my God, and your God.

Mary Magdalene came and told the disciples that she had seen the Lord, and that he had spoken these things unto her.

Then the same day at evening, being the first day of the week, when the doors were shut where the disciples were assembled for fear of the Jews, came Jesus and stood in the midst, and saith unto them, Peace be unto you.

And when he had so said, he shewed unto them his hands and his side. Then were the disciples glad, when they saw the Lord.

Then said Jesus to them again, Peace be unto you: as my Father hath sent me, even so send I you.

And when he had said this, he breathed on them, and saith unto them, Receive ye the Holy Ghost:

Whose soever sins ye remit, they are remitted unto them; and whose soever sins ye retain, they are retained.

But Thomas, one of the twelve, called Didymus, was not with them when Jesus came.

The other disciples therefore said unto him, We have seen the Lord. But he said unto them, Except I shall see in his hands the print of the nails, and put my finger into the print of the nails, and thrust my hand into his side, I will not believe.

And after eight days again his disciples were within, and Thomas with them: then came Jesus, the doors being shut, and stood in the midst, and said, Peace be unto you.

Then saith he to Thomas, Reach hither thy finger, and behold my hands; and reach hither thy hand, and thrust it into my side: and be not faithless, but believing.

And Thomas answered and said unto him, My Lord and my God.

Jesus saith unto him, Thomas, because thou hast seen me, thou hast believed: blessed are they that have not seen, and yet have believed.

THE MYSTERY OF THE CROSS

(Gnostic, c. 2ND Century)[6]

Our Lord stood in the midst of the cave and filled it with light and said, "To the multitude below, in Jerusalem [? the Jerusalem Below—the physical world], I am being crucified, and pierced with lances and reeds, and gall and vinegar is given Me to drink; to thee now I speak, and hearken to My words. 'Twas I who put it in thy heart to ascend this mount, that thou mightest hear what disciple must learn from Master, and man from God."

And having thus spoken, He showed me a cross of light set up, and about the cross a great multitude, and therein one form and one likeness; and on the cross another multitude, not having one form, and I saw the Lord Himself above the cross, not having any shape, but only a voice; and a voice not such as was familiar to us, but a sweet and kind voice and one truly of God, saying unto me: "John, it is needful that one should hear these things from Me; for I have need of one who will hear. This cross of light is sometimes called the Word by Me for your sakes, sometimes Mind, sometimes Jesus, sometimes Christ, sometimes Door, sometimes Way, sometimes Bread, sometimes Seed, sometimes

Resurrection, sometimes Son, sometimes Father, sometimes Spirit, sometimes Life, sometimes Truth, sometimes Faith, sometimes Grace.

Now these things it is called as toward men; but as to what it is in truth, as conceived of in itself and as spoken of to thee— it is the marking off (delimitation) of all things, the firm necessity of those things which are fixed and were unsettled, the harmony of Wisdom. And whereas it is Wisdom in harmony (or fitly ordered), there are on the Right and Left Powers, Principalities, Sources and Daemons, Energies, Threats, Wrath, Accusers, Satan, and [Below] the Lower Root from which hath proceeded the nature of the things in genesis.

This, then, is the cross which fixed all things apart by Reason, and marked off the things that come from genesis, the things below it, and then compacted all into one whole.

This is not the cross of wood which thou wilt see when thou hast descended; nor am I He that is upon the cross, whom now thou seest not but only hearest a voice.

By the others, the many, I have been thought to be what I am not, though I am not what I was. And they will [still] say of Me what is base and not worthy of Me.

As, therefore, the Place of Rest is neither seen nor spoken of, much more shall I, the Lord of that Place, be neither seen nor spoken of.

Now the multitude of one aspect that is about the cross is the lower nature, and those whom thou seest on the cross, if they have not one form, it is because not yet hath every Limb of Him who came down been gathered together. But when the upper nature shall be taken up, and the race which is repairing to Me, in obedience to My voice; then that which [as yet] hears Me not, shall become as thou art, and shall no longer be what it now is, but above them [of the world] even as I am now. For so long as thou callest not thyself Mine, I am not what I am. But if hearing thou hearkenest unto Me, then shalt thou be as I am, and I shall be what I was, when I have thee as I am with Myself. For from this thou art. Pay no attention, then, to the many, and them outside the mystery think little of; for know that I am wholly with the Father and the Father with Me.

Nothing therefore of the things which they will say of Me

have I suffered; nay, that suffering also which I showed unto thee and unto the rest in the dance, I will that it be called a mystery. For what thou seest that did I show thee; but what I am that I alone know, and none else. Suffer me then to keep that which is Mine own, and that which is thine behold thou through Me, and

FIG. 17—The Risen Christ as symbol of the *filius philosophorum.*

behold Me in truth that I am, not what I said, but what thou art able to know, for thou art kin to Me.

Thou hearest that I suffered, yet I suffered not; that I suffered not, yet did I suffer; that I was pierced, yet was I not smitten; that I was hanged, yet was I not hanged; that blood flowed from Me, yet it flowed not. In a word those things that they say of Me, I had not, and the things that they say not, those I suffered. Now what they are I will shadow forth (riddle) for thee, for I know that thou wilt understand.

See thou therefore in Me the slaying of a Word (Logos), the piercing of a Word, the blood of a Word, the wounding of a Word, the hanging of a Word, the passion of a Word, the nailing [? fixing or joining] of a Word, the death of a Word. And by a Word I mean Man. First, then, understand the Word, then shalt thou understand the Lord, and thirdly the Man, and what is His passion."

THE DEATH OF BUDDHA (Indian)[7]

Then the Exalted One [Buddha] entered into the first stage of rapture. And rising out of the first stage he passed into the second. And rising out of the second he passed into the third. And rising out of the third stage he passed into the fourth. And rising out of the fourth stage of rapture, he entered into the state of mind to which the infinity of space is alone present. And passing out of the mere consciousness of the infinity of space he entered into the state of mind to which the infinity of thought is alone present. And passing out of the mere consciousness of the infinity of thought he entered into a state of mind to which nothing at all was specially present. And passing out of the consciousness of no special object he fell into a state between consciousness and unconsciousness. And passing out of the state between consciousness and unconciousness he fell into a state in which the consciousness both of sensations and of ideas had wholly passed away.

Then the venerable Ananda said to the venerable Anuruddha:

"O my lord, O Anuruddha, the Exalted One is dead!"

"Nay! Brother Ananda, the Exalted One is not dead. He has

entered into that state in which both sensations and ideas have ceased to be!" *(Plate 29.)*

Then the Exalted One, passing out of the state in which both sensations and ideas have ceased to be, entered into the state between consciousness and unconsciousness. And passing out of the state between consciousness and unconsciousness he entered into the state of mind to which nothing at all is specially present. And passing out of the consciousness of no special object he entered into the state of mind to which the infinity of thought is alone present. And passing out of the mere consciousness of the infinity of thought he entered into the state of mind to which the infinity of space is alone present. And passing out of the mere consciousness of the infinity of space he entered into the fourth stage of rapture. And passing out of the fourth stage he entered into the third. And passing out of the third stage he entered into the second. And passing out of the second he entered into the first. And passing out of the first stage of rapture he entered into the second. And passing out of the second stage he entered into the third. And passing out of the third stage he entered into the fourth stage of rapture. And passing out of the last stage of rapture he immediately expired.

THE BODHISATTVA PRINCE (Indian)[8]

When the Buddha was about to pass away . . . and his disciples were weeping, He said to them, "The world being transitory and death inevitable for all living things, the time for my departure has come. But weep not; for twelve years after my departure, from a lotus blossom on the Dhanakosha Lake, . . . Urgyān, there will be born one who will be much wiser and more spiritually powerful than Myself. He will be called Padma-Sambhava, and by him the Esoteric Doctrine will be established."

In the country of Urgyān, . . . there was the great city of Jatumati, containing a palace called "Emerald Palace" wherein dwelt King Indra-bodhi. Although possessed of vast worldly wealth and power . . . Indra-bodhi was blind. . . . When his only son and heir died and famine immediately thereafter weakened his kingdom, Indra-bodhi wept, overcome with misfortune. . . .

Oppressed with the thought of being heirless, the King made offerings and prayers to the deities of all the prevailing faiths, but, no son being vouchsafed to him, he lost confidence in every religion. Then, one day he went to the roof of his palace and beat the summoning drum; and, when all the people had come, he addressed the assembled priests thus: "Hear me, each of you! I have made prayer to the deities and the guardian spirits of this land and offerings to the Trinity, but I have not been blessed with a son. Religion is, therefore, devoid of truth; and I command that within seven days ye destroy every one of these deities and guardian spirits. Otherwise, ye shall know my punishment."

The priests, in consternation, hurriedly collected materials for the performance of a ceremony of burnt offerings. The deities and guardian spirits, filled with anger, sent storms of wind, hail, and blood; and throughout Urgyān the inhabitants were as frightened as fish are when taken from the water and placed upon dry sand. In great pity, Avalokiteshvara made appeal to the Buddha Amitābha, in . . . Heaven, to protect the suffering people.

Thereupon, the Buddha Amitābha thought, "Let me take birth in the Dhanakosha Lake"; and there went forth from His tongue a ray of red light, which like a meteor, entered the centre of the lake. Where the ray entered the water, there appeared a small island covered with golden-coloured grass whence flowed three springs of the colour of turquoise; and from the centre of the island there sprang forth a lotus blossom. Simultaneously the Buddha Amitābha, (Plate 30) with great radiance, emitted from His heart a five-pointed dorje,* and the dorje fell into the centre of the lotus blossom.

. . . The King dreamt that he held in his hand a five-pointed dorje which emitted radiance so great that all the kingdom was illuminated. Upon awakening, the King was so happy that he worshipped the Trinity; and the deities and guardian spirits appeared and made humble submission to him. . . .

Gods appeared in the heavens and prophesied: "Hail! Hail! the Lord Amitābha, Protector of Mankind, shall take birth as a Divine Incarnation from a lotus blossom amidst the Jewel Lake, and he will be worthy to become thy son. Suffer no harm

* One of the chief ritual objects of Tibetan Buddhism, has come to be called the *lamas'* sceptre. Esoterically, the word . . . has many meanings. *Tibetan Book of Great Liberation*, p. 107.

to befall Him and give Him thy protection. Thereby, every good will come to thee. . . ."

The King noticed a rainbow of five colours over the . . . Lake, although there were no clouds and the sun was shining brightly. And the King said to the minister, "Please go and ascertain what there is in that lake yonder."

"How is it that thou, being blind, canst see this?" asked the minister. "I appealed to the wish-granting gem and my sight* was restored," replied the King. . . .

The King and his minister went to the lake, and, taking a small boat, reached the place over which the rainbow shone. There they beheld a fragrant lotus blossom, the circumference of which exceeded that of one's body and circled arms, and seated at the centre of the blossom a fair rosy-cheeked little boy resembling the Lord Buddha, holding in his right hand a tiny lotus blossom and in his left hand a tiny holy-water pot, and in the folds of the left arm a tiny three-pronged staff.

The King felt much veneration for the self-born babe; and in excess of joy, he wept. He asked the child, "Who are thy father and mother, . . . and why art thou here?" The child answered, "My father is Wisdom and my mother is the Voidness. My country is the country of *Dharma*. I am of no cast and no creed. I am sustained by perplexity; and I am here to destroy Lust, Anger, and Sloth." When the child had ceased speaking, the King's right eye was no longer blind. Overwhelmed with joy, the King named the child "The Lake-born Dorje," and he and the minister made obeisance to the child.

DEATH (Chinese)[9]

When Chuang Tzu was going to Ch'u he saw by the roadside a skull, clean and bare, but with every bone in its place. Touching it gently with his chariot-whip he bent over it and asked it saying, "Sir, was it some insatiable ambition that drove you to transgress the law and brought you to this? Was it the fall of a kingdom, the blow of an executioner's axe that brought you to this? Or had

* [The wish-granting gem presented to the King by the *Nagas* (serpents) who dwelt under the oceans healed his left eye.]

you done some shameful deed and could not face the reproaches of father and mother, of wife and child, and so were brought to this? Was it hunger and cold that brought you to this, or was it that the springs and autumns of your span had in their due course carried you to this?"

Having thus addressed the skull, he put it under his head as a pillow and went to sleep. At midnight the skull appeared to him in a dream and said to him, "All that you said to me—your glib, commonplace chatter—is just what I should expect from a live man, showing as it does in every phrase a mind hampered by trammels from which we dead are entirely free. Would you like to hear a word or two about the dead?"

"I certainly should," said Chuang Tzu.

"Among the dead," said the skull, "none is king, none is subject, there is no division of the seasons; for us the whole world is spring, the whole world is autumn. No monarch on his throne has joy greater than ours."

Chuang Tzu did not believe this. "Suppose," he said, "I could get the Clerk of Destinies to make your frame anew, to clothe your bones once more with flesh and skin, send you back to father and mother, wife and child, friends and home, I do not think you would refuse."

A deep frown furrowed the skeleton's brow. "How can you imagine," it asked, "that I would cast away joy greater than that of a king upon his throne, only to go back again to the toils of the living world?"

CHUANG TZU

BLACK ELK* SPEAKS (Dakota Indian)[10]

Soon the young men who were watching for the coming of the *wakan* (holy) person announced that they saw something in the distance approaching them in a beautiful manner, and then sud-

---

* Black Elk [an old priest] belonged to the Oglala [Sioux] division of the Teton Dakota. . . . The Dakota were established in the sixteenth century on the headwaters of the Mississippi, and in the seventeenth century were driven westward from Minnesota by their powerful enemies the Chippewa.
—*Sacred Pipe*, Brown[11]

denly she entered the lodge, walked around sun-wise, and stood in front of Standing Hollow Horn. She took from her back the bundle, and holding it with both hands in front of the chief, said: "Behold this and always love it! It is very sacred, and you must treat it as such. No impure man should ever be allowed to see it, for within this bundle there is a sacred pipe. (*Plate* 27.) With this you will, during the winters to come, send your voices to *Wakan-Tanka,* your Father and Grandfather (The Great Spirit, identical to the Christian Godhead, or the Hindu *Brahma-Nirguna*)."

After the mysterious woman said this, she took from the bundle a pipe, and also a small round stone which she placed upon the ground. Holding the pipe up with its stem to the heavens, she said: "With this sacred pipe you will walk upon the Earth; for the Earth is your Grandmother and Mother, and she is sacred. Every step that is taken upon Her should be as a prayer. The bowl of this pipe is of red stone; it is the Earth. Carved in the stone and facing the center is the buffalo calf who represents all the four-leggeds who live upon your Mother. The stem of the pipe is wood, and this represents all that grows upon the Earth. And these twelve feathers which hang here where the stem fits the bowl are from . . . the Spotted Eagle, and they represent . . . all the wingeds of the air. All these peoples, and all the things of the universe, are joined to you who smoke the pipe—all send their voices to *Wakan-Tanka,* the Great Spirit. When you pray with this pipe, you pray for and with everything. . . .

"From above *Wakan-Tanka* has given you this sacred pipe, so that through it you may have knowledge. . . . But now before I leave I wish to give you instructions for the first rite in which your people will use this pipe.

"It should be for you a sacred day when one of your people dies. You must then keep his soul as I shall teach you, and through this you will gain much power; for if this soul is kept, it will increase in you your concern and love for your neighbor. So long as the person, in his soul, is kept with your people, through him you will be able to send your voice to *Wakan-Tanka*." . . .

Turning again to Standing Hollow Horn, she said: "Behold this pipe! Always remember how sacred it is, and treat it as such, for it will take you to the end. Remember, in me there are four ages.* I am leaving now, but I shall look back upon your people in every age, and at the end I shall return."

Moving around the lodge in a sun-wise manner, the mysterious woman left, . . . she looked back towards the people and sat down. When she rose the people were amazed to see that she had become a young red and brown buffalo calf. Then this calf walked farther, lay down and rolled, looking back at the people, and when she got up she was a white buffalo. Again the white buffalo walked farther . . . becoming now a black buffalo. This buffalo . . . stopped, and after bowing to each of the four quarters of the universe, disappeared over the hill. . . .

By keeping a soul according to the proper rites, as given to us by the White Buffalo Cow Woman . . . one so purifies it that it and the Spirit become one, and it is thus able to return to the "place" where it was born—*Wakan-Tanka*—and need not wander about the earth as is the case with the souls of the bad people; further, the keeping of a soul helps us to remember death and also *Wakan-Tanka*, who is above all dying.†

[At a rite given over the body of a dead child the sacred pipe was lit and smoked and many prayers were said.]

A bundle was then made containing the body of the child, and the men took this to a high place away from the camp and placed it upon a scaffold set up in a tree. When they returned, High Hollow Horn went into the tipi with the father of the child, in order to teach him how he must prepare himself . . . [to] become a holy man.

"You are now keeping the soul of your son," High Hollow Horn said, "who is not dead, but is with you. From now on you must live in a sacred manner, for your son will be in this tipi until his soul is released . . . there should always be harmony in your

* According to Siouan mythology, it is believed that at the beginning of a cycle a buffalo was placed at the west in order to hold back the waters. Every year this buffalo loses one hair, and every age he loses one leg. When all his hair and all four legs are gone, then the waters rush in once again, and the cycle comes to an end.

† "It is good," Black Elk said, "to have a reminder of death before us, for it helps us to understand the impermanence of life on this earth, and this understanding may aid us in preparing for our own death. He who is well prepared is he who knows that he is nothing compared with *Wakan-Tanka*, who is everything; then he knows that world which is real."

lodge, for all these things have an influence on the soul which is being purified here.

"Your hands are *wakan* . . . your eyes are *wakan*. . . . Your mouth is *wakan,* and every word you say should reflect this holy state in which you are now living. . . . Every day and night your son will be with you; look after his soul all the time. . . . From this day on you will be *wakan,* and as I have taught you, so you too will now be able to teach others. The sacred pipe will go a long way, even to the end, and so will the soul of your son. . . ."

Before the soul of the child is released, all the people gather together, for everyone participates in this great rite, which can best be called The Making of Sacredness . . . the keeper of the soul . . . appoints the special day, . . . the helpers make a large ceremonial lodge . . . and cover the earth inside with sacred sage.

The helper of the keeper of the soul then takes a pipe, and holding it up to the heavens, he cries: "Behold, O *Wakan-Tanka!* We are now about to do Thy will. With all the sacred beings of the universe, we offer to You this pipe!"

The helper then takes a pinch of the sacred tobacco . . . and holding it and the stem of the pipe towards the west, he cries: "With this *wakan* tobacco, we place You in the pipe, O winged Power of the west. We are about to send our voices to *Wakan-Tanka,* and we wish You to help us! . . .

[Then offering tobacco and prayers to the four other directions he ends his prayer by saying to sacred Earth, the sixth direction:]

"We and all who move upon You are sending our voices to *Wakan-Tanka!* All together as one we cry: 'Help us!' "

When the pipe has thus been filled with all the Powers and with all that there is in the universe,* it is given to the keeper of the soul, who takes it and, crying as he walks, goes to the tipi of the keeper of the most sacred pipe, and holding out the pipe with its stem pointing toward the south, he places it in the hands of the keeper of the pipe.

---

* In filling a pipe, all space (represented by the offerings to the powers of the six directions) and all things (represented by the grains of tobacco) are contracted within a single point (the bowl or heart of the pipe) , so that the pipe . . . is the universe . . . it is also man, and the one who fills a pipe should identify himself with it, thus not only establishing the center of the universe, but also his own center . . . .

"Hi Ho! Hi Ho! Thanks!" the holy man says as he takes the pipe, "this pipe which you have brought to me is really as sacred as the original pipe which was given to us by the White Buffalo Cow Woman. . . .

"They are really the same. But this pipe which you have now brought is especially sacred, for I see that there has been placed within it the whole universe. What is it that you wish?"

"We wish you to smoke this pipe and then to lead the rites for releasing the soul of my young son. We wish you to bring with you the original *wakan* pipe which you are keeping."

"*How, hetchetu welo*," the holy man replied, "I will come!"
. . .

The two men . . . walk sun-wise around and sit at the west of the lodge, opposite the door. The wife of the keeper of the soul then goes to her tipi, crying as she walks, picks up the sacred bundle, and returns to the lodge, where she stands in front of the keeper of the sacred pipe, placing the bundle in his . . . hands. "Thanks! Thanks!" the holy keeper says, and then he speaks to the soul within the bundle:

"You, O soul, were with your people, but soon you will leave. . . . Today your Father, *Wakan-Tanka*, is bending down to see you. . . . All your relatives love you. . . . You and the holy woman of the four ages, who brought to us the sacred pipe, are now together here in this lodge. . . . Behold! This is the sacred day!" . . .

One of the helpers then goes to the fire at the center of the tipi and . . . picks up a glowing coal and places it in front of the keeper of the pipe. . . .

The bowl of the pipe is placed over the smoke, in such a way that this smoke passes through the pipe, coming out the end of the stem which is held toward heaven. In this manner *Wakan-Tanka* is the first to smoke, and the pipe is purified. As he does this, the "keeper of the pipe" prays.

"O *Wakan-Tanka*, behold the pipe! The smoke from this herb will cover everything upon earth, and will reach even to the heavens . . . now I place within its bowl the sacred [tobacco]. You have taught us that the round bowl of the pipe is the very center of the universe and the heart of man! O *Wakan-Tanka*, bend down to look upon us today; look upon Thy pipe with which we are about to send a voice, along with the winged peoples, the four-leggeds, and all the fruits of our Mother Earth. All that you have made will join us in sending this voice!"

As he fills the pipe, the holy keeper makes the ritual offerings of tobacco to the six directions, [and prays], . . .

". . . We are about to release a soul who is to travel upon Your path; through this soul we are sending a voice to *Wakan-Tanka*! Help us to send this voice. . . ."

[A prayer is then offered to the sacred White Swan and the Spotted Eagle and the six directions and] in this manner, the whole universe was placed in the pipe, and then, turning to the people, the keeper of the pipe says: "Since we have done all this correctly, the soul should have a good journey, and it will help our people to increase and to walk the sacred path in a manner pleasing to *Wakan-Tanka*."

And then to the soul he says: "O you soul, my grandchild, you are the root of this great rite; from you will grow much that is *wakan*. . . . You are as the root of the *wakan* tree which is at the center of our nation's hoop. May this tree bloom! . . . look back upon your people as you travel upon the great path!" . . .

The keeper of the pipe then walks around to the south and picking up the "soul bundle," says to it: "Grandchild, you are about to leave on a great journey. Your father and mother and all your relatives have loved you. Soon they will be happy."

The father of the child then embraces the sacred bundle . . . the keeper says to him: "You loved your son. . . . The sacred influence of your son's soul will be upon the people; it is as a tree that will always bloom." . . . Then, holding the bundle up towards the heavens, he cries: "Always look back upon your people, that they may walk the sacred path with firm steps!"

This, the keeper cries four times as he walked towards the door of the lodge, and, as he stops the fourth time just outside the door, he cries with a very shrill voice: "Behold your people! Look back upon them!"

The moment the bundle passes out of the "lodge",* the soul is released; it has departed on the "spirit trail" leading to *Wakan-Tanka*. . . .

* . . . The tipi is the universe, the cosmos; and the space outside the tipi is symbolically the Infinite, or *Wakan-Tanka*.

THE PRIEST'S SOUL (Irish)[12]

In former days there were great schools in Ireland, where every sort of learning was taught to the people, and even the poorest had more knowledge at that time than many a gentleman has now. . . .

Now, at this time there was a little boy learning at one of them who was a wonder to everyone for his cleverness. His parents were only laboring people, and of course poor; but young as he was, . . . no king's or lord's son could come up to him in learning. Even the masters were put to shame. . . . When he grew up his poor father and mother were so proud of him that they resolved to make him a priest . . . though they nearly starved themselves to get the money. Well, such another learned man was not in Ireland, and he was [so] great in argument . . . that no one could stand before him. Even the bishops tried to talk to him, but he showed them at once they knew nothing at all.

Now, there were no schoolmasters in those times, but it was the priests taught the people; and as this man was the cleverest in Ireland, all the foreign kings sent their sons to him. . . . So he grew very proud, and began to forget how low he had been, and worst of all, even to forget God, who had made him what he was. And the pride of arguing got hold of him, so that from one thing to another he went on to prove that there was no Purgatory, . . . no Hell, . . . no Heaven, and then no God; and at last that men had no souls but were no more than a dog or a cow, and when they died there was an end of them. "Whoever saw a soul?" he would say. "If you can show me one, I will believe." No one could make any answer to this; and at last they all came to believe that as there was no other world, everyone might do what they liked in this; the priest setting the example, for he took a beautiful young girl to wife. . . . It was a great scandal, yet no one dared to say a word, for all the kings' sons were on his side, and would have slaughtered anyone who tried to prevent his wicked goings-on. Poor boys; they all believed in him. . . . In this way his notions began to spread about, and the whole world was going to the bad, when one night an angel came down from Heaven, and told the priest he had but twenty-four hours to live. He began to tremble, and asked for a little more time.

But the angel was stiff. . . .

"What do you want time for, you sinner?" he asked.

"Oh, sir, have pity on my poor soul!" urged the priest.

"Oh, no! You have a soul, then," said the angel. "Pray, how did you find that out?"

"It has been fluttering in me ever since you appeared," answered the priest. . . .

"What good was all your learning, when it could not tell you that you had a soul?" [said the angel].

"Ah, my lord," said the priest, "if I am to die, tell me how soon I may be in Heaven?"

"Never," replied the angel. "You denied there was a Heaven."

"Then, my lord, may I go to Purgatory?"

"You denied Purgatory also; you must go straight to Hell," said the angel.

"But, my lord, I denied Hell also," answered the priest, "so you can't send me there either."

The angel was a little puzzled.

"Well," said he, "I'll tell you what I can do for you. You may either live now on earth for a hundred years, enjoying every pleasure, and then be cast into Hell for ever; or you may die in twenty-four hours in the most horrible torments, and pass through Purgatory, there to remain till the Day of Judgment, if only you can find some one person that believes, and through his belief mercy will be vouchsafed to you, and your soul will be saved." . . .

"I will have death in the twenty-four hours," he said, "so that my soul may be saved at last."

On this the angel . . . left him.

Then immediately the priest entered the large room where all the scholars and the kings' sons were seated, and called out to them:

"Now, tell me the truth, and let none fear to contradict me; tell me what is your belief—have men souls?"

"Master," they answered, "once we believed that men had souls; but thanks to your teaching, we believe so no longer. There is no Hell, and no Heaven, and no God. This is our belief, for it is thus you taught us."

Then the priest grew pale with fear, and cried out: "Listen! I taught you a lie. There is a God, and man has an immortal soul. I believe now all I denied before."

But the shouts of laughter that rose up drowned the priest's voice, for they thought he was only trying them for argument.

"Prove it, master," they cried. "Prove it. Who has ever seen God? Who has ever seen the soul?" . . .

The priest stood up to answer them. . . . All his eloquence, all his powers of argument had gone from him; and he could do nothing but wring his hands and cry out, "There is a God! . . . . Lord have mercy on my soul!"

And they all began to mock him and repeat his own words that he had taught them:

"Show him to us; show us your God." And he fled from them groaning with agony, for he saw that none believed; and how, then, could his soul be saved? . . .

Then despair came on him, and he rushed from the house, and began to ask everyone he met if they believed. But the same answer came from one and all: "We believe only what you have taught us," for his doctrine had spread far and wide through the country.

Then he grew half mad with fear, . . . and he flung himself down on the ground in a lonesome spot, and wept and groaned in terror, for the time was coming fast when he must die.

Just then a little child came by. "God save you kindly," said the child to him.

The priest started up.

"Do you believe in God?" he asked.

"I have come from a far country to learn about him," said the child. "Will your honor direct me to the best school they have in these parts?"

"The best school and the best teacher is close by," said the priest, and he named himself.

"Oh, not to that man," answered the child, "for I am told he denies God, and Heaven, and Hell, and even that man has a soul, because he cannot see it; but I would soon put him down."

The priest looked at him earnestly. "How?" he inquired.

"Why," said the child, "I would ask him if he believed he had life to show me his life."

"But he could not do that, my child," said the priest. "Life cannot be seen; we have it, but it is invisible."

"Then if we have life, though we cannot see it, we may also have a soul, though it is invisible," answered the child.

When the priest heard him speak these words, he fell down on his knees before him, weeping for joy, for now he knew his soul was safe; he had met one at last that believed. And he told the child his whole story—all his wickedness, and pride, and blasphemy against the great God; and how the angel had come to him, and told him of the only way in which he could be saved, through the faith and prayers of someone that believed.

"Now, then," he said to the child, "take this penknife and strike it into my breast, and go on stabbing the flesh until you see the paleness of death on my face. Then watch—for a living

Fig. 18—The Soul Goes to Heaven: the seven angels with the six keys, standing for the six works of charity, with which they open heaven and receive the soul into heaven. 16th-century woodcut.

thing will soar up from my body as I die, and you will then know that my soul has ascended to the presence of God. And when you see this thing, . . . call on all my scholars to come and see that the soul of their master has left the body, . . . that there is a God who punishes sin, and a Heaven, and a Hell, and that man has an immortal soul destined for eternal happiness or misery."

"I will pray," said the child, "to have courage to do this work." And he kneeled down and prayed. Then he rose and took the penknife and struck it into the priest's heart, and struck and struck again till all the flesh was lacerated; but still the priest lived, though the agony was horrible, for he could not die until the twenty-four hours had expired.

At last the agony seemed to cease, and the stillness of death settled on his face. Then the child, who was watching, saw a beautiful living creature, with four snow-white wings, mount from the dead man's body into the air and go fluttering round his head.

So he ran to bring the scholars; and when they saw it, they all knew it was the soul of their master; and they watched with wonder and awe until it passed from sight into the clouds.

And this was the first butterfly that was ever seen in Ireland; and now all men know that the butterflies are the souls of the dead, waiting for the moment when they may enter Purgatory, and so pass through torture to purification and peace.

THE TEMPLE CAT (Khmer)[13]

When, with the malevolent moon, the barbarian Siamese Thais* came to the mountains of the Sun, Mun-Ha was living in the Temple of Lai-Tsun: Mun-Ha, the most precious among the most precious, for whom the god Song-Hio had woven the beard of gold. This venerable priest had ever lived in rapt contemplation of Tsun-Kyanksé, the goddess with eyes of sapphire who presided over the transmutation of souls about to receive their dues, whose searching gaze none could evade. Mun-Ha had an oracle who

* The Indian brahmins were the bitter enemies of the people of Khmer and their beloved kittahs. From the commencement of the eighteenth century they . . . pursued and massacred their priests. . . .

dictated his decisions, and this was his cat Sinh, whom the kittahs (priests) fervently revered.

Seated close to his dread master, Sinh lived in the contemplation of the goddess. The beautiful animal! His eyes were yellow like gold from the reflection of the metallic beard of Mun-Ha, yellow like the amber body of the goddess with the sapphire eyes.

One night, at the rising of the moon, the Thais menacingly approached the sacred Temple. Then, invoking destiny, Mun-Ha died, weighed down by years and anguish. He died in the presence of his goddess; close beside him was his divine cat, and the kittahs lamented their cruel loss. But suddenly, the miracle of immediate transmutation took place. Sinh bounded on to the holy Throne. Supported on the head of his stricken master he faced the goddess. His four feet, brown as the earth, his four feet which contacted the venerable skull, whitened to the claws, to the toe-tips, thus purified by the touch of the puissant dead.

Sinh turned towards the South Door his imperious gaze, in which could be read an imperative order, possessed of an invincible force the kittahs obeyed. Then they closed on the ancestral enemy the bronze doors of the holy Temple, and passing by their subterranean tunnel they routed the profane invaders.

Sinh refused all nourishment, and would not quit his Throne. He continued standing erect and facing the goddess—mysterious priest——fixing his steadfast gaze on her eyes of sapphire, partaking of their fire and sweetness.

Seven days after the death of Mun-Ha, erect on his purified feet of white, without lowering an eyelash, he died. Thus was borne away towards Tsun-Kyanksé the soul of Mun-Ha, which was too perfect for earth. But, for the last time, his look turned slowly towards the South Door.

Seven days after the death of Sinh the kittahs assembled before Tsun-Kyanksé to choose the successor of Mun-Ha. Then—Oh wonder!—there came in slow procession the hundred cats of the Temple. Their feet were gloved in white; their snowy hair emitted the reflection of gold, and the topazes of their eyes had changed to sapphires.

The kittahs fell prostrate in an attitude of devout fear, and waited. Did they not know that the souls of their masters inhabited the harmonious forms of the sacred animals? And these, solemn and grave, surrounded Legoa—the most youthful of the priests—and so revealed the will of Heaven. When a sacred cat dies in the temple of Lao-Tsun, the soul of a kittah re-enters— to quit no more—the mysterious paradise of Song-Hio, the god of gold. Unhappy are those who even involuntarily hasten the end of these formidable and venerable cats: the most dreadful torments are reserved for them, that the soul in pain may be appeased.

APPENDIX

FURTHER EXAMPLES OF
THE THEME OF DEATH
AND REBIRTH IN POETRY

P*oets more than prose writers express clearly and poignantly the mythological theme of death and its archetypal corollary, rebirth, or of the quest for the certainty of an after-life, namely, resurrection.*

J.L.H.

In the following lines, Emily Dickinson[1] expresses resistance to death simply and beautifully.

> Drowning is not so pitiful
>   As the attempt to rise.
> Three times, 't is said, a sinking man
>   Comes up to face the skies,
> And then declines forever
>   To that abhorred abode
> Where hope and he part company,—
>   For he is grasped of God.
> The Maker's cordial visage,
>   However good to see,
> Is shunned, we must admit it,
>   Like an adversity.

The return from death to life is vividly presented in this poem by Emily Dickinson.[2]

Just lost when I was saved!
    Just felt the world go by!
Just girt me for the onset with eternity,
When breath blew back,
And on the other side
I heard recede the disappointed tide!

Therefore, as one returned, I feel,
Odd secrets of the line to tell!
Some sailor, skirting foreign shores,
Some pale reporter from the awful doors
Before the seal!

Next time, to stay!
Next time, the things to see
By ear unheard,
Unscrutinized by eye.

Next time, to tarry,
While the ages steal,—
Slow tramp the centuries,
And the cycles wheel.

Samuel Taylor Coleridge[3] *reveals rebirth as redemption from a curse in this extract from* The Rime of the Ancient Mariner.

. . . An orphan's curse would drag to hell
A spirit from on high;
But oh! more horrible than that
Is the curse in a dead man's eye!

Seven days, seven nights, I saw that curse,
And yet I could not die.

The moving Moon went up the sky,
And no where did abide:
Softly she was going up,
And a star or two beside—

Her beams bemocked the sultry main,
Like April hoar-frost spread;
But where the ship's huge shadow lay,
The charméd water burnt away
A still and awful red.

Beyond the shadow of the ship,
I watched the water-snakes:
They moved in tracks of shining white,
And when they reared, the elfish light
Fell off in hoary flakes.

Within the shadow of the ship
I watched their rich attire:
Blue, glossy green, and velvet black,
They coiled and swam; and every track
Was a flash of golden fire.

O happy living things! no tongue
Their beauty might declare:
A spring of love gushed from my heart,
And I blessed them unaware:
Sure my kind saint took pity on me,
And I blessed them unaware.

The self-same moment I could pray;
And from my neck so free
The Albatross fell off, and sank
Like lead into the sea.

In Darest Thou Now O Soul, *Walt Whitman*[4] *speaks eloquently of the acceptance of death.*

Darest thou now O soul,
Walk out with me toward the unknown region,
Where neither ground is for the feet nor any path to follow?

No map there, nor guide,
Nor voice sounding, nor touch of human hand,
Nor face with blooming flesh, nor lips, nor eyes, are in that land.

I know it not O soul,
Nor dost thou, all is a blank before us,
All waits undream'd of in that region, that inaccessible land.

Till when the ties loosen,
All but the ties eternal, Time and Space,
Nor darkness, gravitation, sense, nor any bounds bounding us.

Then we burst forth, we float,
In Time and Space O soul, prepared for them,
Equal, equipt at last, (O joy! O fruit of all!) them to fulfil O soul.

NOTES ON THE PLATES

REFERENCES

INDEX

NOTES ON THE PLATES

trinitarian, transcendent symbol characteristic of
Christianity. Celtic book cover, 8th century A.D.

7. The Goddess Innina [Inanna]. Susa, 2nd half of 3rd mill.

Plates 1–7 follow page 102.

8. Lilith, Crowned Goddess of the Underworld (the Great
   Mother). An archetypal image for the unredeemed
   aspect of the feminine godhead. The owl and birdlike
   features of the goddess represent both her death-deal-
   ing power to annul the creative masculine principle
   and the feminine principle of fertility. Baked clay
   high relief. Sumer, c. 2000 B.C.

9. Ishtar-Venus, with crescent moon headdress representing rebirth. Parthian, c. 1st-2nd century A.D.

10. Assyrian Vegetation God. Assur, 2nd half of 2nd
    mill.

11. Isis with outstretched wings. The Egyptian Great
    Mother in her aspect as spiritual protectress. The two
    Anubis dogs on either side are openers of the way into
    and out of the realm of death. The nine rays of the
    sun, beneath the stool on which the goddess kneels,
    represent her new life. The Sarcophagus of Taho.

12a. The impersonator of Tezcatlipoca arrayed in his
     finery.

12b. The sacrifice of the youth impersonating the god
     Tezcatlipoca. His heart, which has been torn out by
     the priest, is held up to the sun as an offering.

13. The Great Mother. A man with the headdress of a hare
    lies sleeping in a position suggesting birth. In this
    mythology, the hare denotes the moon and its power
    of bringing new life by way of the unconscious. Terra-
    cotta figure, Campeche, Mexico.

14. Demeter and Kore. Demeter holds the ears of wheat
    and Kore holds the torches to illuminate the mystery
    of rebirth as celebrated in the underground rite of
    the Eleusinian Mysteries. Stone relief, Eleusis, 5th
    century B.C.

15. Pārvatī, the Thunder Goddess. South India, late 11th or early 12th century A.D.

Plates 8–15 follow page 134.

16. Wheel of Mother Nature. From a French manuscript.
17. Ancestor image. Atchin, New Hebrides.
18. Gilgamesh with herb of immortality. The rod of worldly power is in his left hand and the plant of immortality in his right. Relief, a palace of Assurnasirpal II (885-860 B.C.). Nimrud, Assyria.
19. Coffin of Amenapet. The seven scenes within the coffin represent the seven stages of initiation showing that death was thought to require an initiation into the next life. 19th dynasty, Egypt.
20. Wall painting from Tomb of Rameses IX. The king (as dead sun god) journeys through darkness, represented by the serpent. In this rite of passage he "gathers from his past forms a new energy for a new birth" indicated by the erect phallus (now seen only as a mutilation), outstretched arms, and the rising serpent. The sacred scarab beetle emerging from the sun symbolizes the reborn state. Valley of the Kings, Egypt.
21. Baptism of King Seti I. Baptism as rite of initiation where the king-initiate is purified by water whose drops are in the form of the ankh cross or sign of life, symbolic of the Water of Life. The masters of initiation are two contrasting bird-headed deities—Horus, the hawk-headed figure (representing outer achievement of a heroic nature) and Thoth, the ibis-headed one (representing inner knowledge and wisdom). Bas-relief from Temple of Abydos, Egypt.
22. Le Baptême. Mosaic. Eglise de Daphni, 11th century.
23. Birth of Dionysus. The infant is reborn from the thigh of Zeus and springs into the arms of Hermes. Antique bas-relief in Vatican Museum, Rome.
24. The Moon Boat. Seven female figures standing in a crescent-shaped boat suggestive of the moon. This symbolizes an inner journey of initiation through waters of

the underworld ruled by the moon or moon goddess. Therefore it probably symbolizes a woman's initiation.

Plates 16–24 follow page 166.

25. Ur-rammu Stele. The ladder of seven rungs suggests initiation leading from lower to higher realms of consciousness, in a religious ceremony associated with watering a sacred tree in the presence of a king or deity. Above are shown traces of a similar throne with the king-initiate in the center. Above him is the conjunction of crescent moon and sun symbolizing the union of masculine and feminine principles as the central meaning of initiation. Bas-relief, 3rd dynasty of Ur, c. 2070-1960 B.C.

26. The Sorcerer of Trois Frères. He is dressed in a composite animal costume symbolizing the master of initiation. Paleolithic rock engraving from Cave of the Trois Frères, France.

27. Jadeite bowl of a shaman. A contemplative god-like being, representative of the shaman's power of transformation, is seated upon the head and curved beak of a thunderbird. This is a mythical symbol of supreme power (such as Zeus's thunderbolt) for overcoming monsters of the deep and promoting initiation into the realm of the spirit. Pacific Coast Salish.

28. Snake Goddess. The serpents and pointed hat are symbols of transcendence associated with psychic development. North Syria (?), c. 1500 B.C.

29. Buddha and Seven Serpents. Buddha's attainment of inner liberation through assimilation of the wisdom represented by the seven naga serpents. Angkor Vat, Cambodia, 11th century.

30. Bodhisattva. The attainment of the higher initiation represented in the halo of the saint by seven Buddhas of Perfection. Chinese stone sculpture, Sui dynasty, late 6th century A.D.

31. The God Vishnu in his fish incarnation. 18th-century Indian miniature.

32. Kolquhaludi's Emergence. Example of the theme of Jonah and the Whale in which a man experiences death and rebirth in being swallowed and then cast ashore by a sea monster (in this case a salmon) as a punishment for sin. This represents initiation as an unconscious threshold experience. Haida Indian black slate dish. Victoria, B.C.

Plates 25–32 follow page 198.

REFERENCES

INTRODUCTION

I. The Fear of Death

1. Erich Neumann, *Mystical Man*, Eranos-Jahrbuch XVI, 1959, p. 44, tr. Manheim (New York: Analytical Psychology Club Publication, Spring, 1961).
2. *Ibid.*, p. 45.

II. Death and Rebirth as Cosmic Pattern: The Dance of Shiva

1. Ananda Coomaraswamy, *The Dance of Shiva* (New York: Farrar, Straus & Cudahy, Inc., 1957), p. 76.
2. Heinrich Zimmer, *Myths and Symbols in Indian Art and Civilization*, ed. Joseph Campbell (New York: Bollingen Series VI, 1946), p. 172.
3. *Ibid.*, p. 173.
4. *Ibid.*, p. 175.
5. Mircea Eliade, *Yoga: Immortality and Freedom* (New York: Bollingen Series LVI, 1958), p. 4.
6. *Ibid.*, p. 119.
7. C. G. Jung, *Modern Psychology*, tr. E. T. H. Leeluies (Zurich: C. G. Jung Institute, 1934), pp. 17-22.
8. Thomas Mann, *The Living Thoughts of Schopenhauer* (New York: Longmans Green & Co., Inc., 1939), introduction.

III. Death and Rebirth as Cycles of Nature: The Descent of Inanna

1. C. G. Jung and K. Kerényi, *Essays on a Science of Mythology* (New York: Bollingen Series XXII, 1949), p. 3.

2. M. Esther Harding, *Women's Mysteries* (New York: Pantheon, rev. ed. 1955), p. 158.

3. T. G. Pinches, "Tammuz," *Hastings Encyclopedia of Religion and Ethics* (New York: Charles Scribner's Sons, 1909), Vol. XII, p. 189.

4. Thomas Mann, *Joseph and His Brothers* (New York: Alfred A. Knopf, Inc., 1936).

5. Erich Neumann, *The Great Mother* (New York: Bollingen Series XLVII, 1955), p. 160.

6. C. G. Jung, *Symbols of Transformation* (New York: Bollingen Series XX, *The Collected Works of C. G. Jung*, Vol. 5, 1956); Harding, *op. cit.* and *The Way of All Women* (New York: Longmans, Green & Co., Inc., 1932); C. G. Jung, *Two Essays in Analytical Psychology* (New York: Bollingen Series XX, *The Collected Works of C. G. Jung*, Vol. 7, 1953); Gerhart Adler, *Studies in Analytical Psychology* (New York: W. W. Norton & Co., 1948).

7. Jane Ellen Harrison, *Prolegomena to the Study of Greek Religion* (3rd ed.; London: Cambridge University Press, 1922), p. 273.

8. Mircea Eliade, *Myths, Dreams and Mysteries* (New York: Harper Brothers, 1960), p. 182.

9. *Ibid.*

10. *Ibid.*, pp. 176-77.

11. Mircea Eliade, *Images and Symbols* (New York: Sheed and Ward, 1961), p. 127.

12. *Ibid.*, p. 148.

13. Harding, *Women's Mysteries*, p. 240.

14. Richard Wilhelm, tr., Cary F. Baynes, *The I Ching or Book of Changes* (New York: Bollingen Series XIX, 1950), Vol. I, pp. 9-10.

V. Initiation as a Spiritual Education

1. Arnold Van Gennep, *Rites of Passage* (Chicago: University of Chicago Press, 1959). Book as whole, especially introduction.

2. K. Kerényi, "Mysteries of the Cabeiroi" in Joseph Campbell, ed. *Papers from the Eranos Yearbooks*, Vol. 2, *The Mysteries* (New York: Bollingen Series XXX, 1955), pp. 38-39.

3. Mircea Eliade, *Birth and Rebirth* (New York: Harper and Brothers, 1958), p. 77.

4. John Layard, "The Malekulan Journey of the Dead" in Joseph Campbell, ed. *Papers from the Eranos Yearbooks*, Vol. 4, *Spiritual Disciplines* (New York: Bollingen Series XXX, 1960), pp. 138-39.

5. C. G. Jung, "Psychological Aspects of the Mother Archetype" in *Basic Writings of C. G. Jung* (New York: Modern Library, 1959), pp. 327ff.

6. C. G. Jung, *Seminar Notes* (Zurich: C. G. Jung Institute Publication, 1929-1930), p. 18.

7. Van Gennep, *op. cit.*

8. W. F. Jackson Knight, *Cumaean Gates* (London: Oxford University Press, 1936), p. 143, as quoted by M. R. W. Cruttwell.

9. Paul Schmitt, "Ancient Mysteries and Their Transformation" in Campbell, ed. *The Mysteries,* p. 95.
10. *Ibid.,* p. 96 (cf. Van Gennep, *op. cit.*).
11. Jane Ellen Harrison, *Themis: A Study of the Social Origins of Greek Religion* (London: Cambridge University Press, 1912).
12. Schmitt, *op. cit.,* p. 103.

VI. Initiation as Psychic Liberation: The Magic Flight

1. Eliade, *Birth and Rebirth,* p. 96.
2. Mircea Eliade, *Le Chamanisme et les techniques archäiques de l'extase* (Paris: Payot, 1951), p. 101.
3. *Job,* Chap. 19.
4. *Ibid.*
5. *Colossians* 1: 18.
6. Eliade, *Chamanisme,* p. 118.
7. *Ibid.,* p. 119.
8. *Ibid.,* p. 118.
9. *Ibid.,* p. 102.
10. *Ibid.,* p. 106.
11. *Ibid.*
12. *Ibid.,* p. 108.

VII. Resurrection and Rebirth in the Process of Individuation

1. Joseph Campbell, "The Symbol Without Meaning," *Eranos-Yahrbuch* XXVI (Zurich: Rhein-Verlag) pp. 454-55.
2. *Ibid.*
3. *Ibid.*
4. *Ibid,* p. 455.
5. C. G. Jung, "Rosarium Philosophorum" (The Psychology of Transference), *The Practice of Psychotherapy* (New York: Bollingen Series XX, *The Collected Works of C. G. Jung,* Vol. 16, 1954). Final chap.
6. C. G. Jung, "Dream Symbols of the Individuation Process" in Campbell, ed., *Spiritual Disciplines,* p. 350.

MYTHS OF DEATH, REBIRTH, AND RESURRECTION

Death and Rebirth as Cosmic Pattern

1. Jessie L. Weston, *From Ritual to Romance* (Garden City, New York: Doubleday-Anchor Books, 1957).
2. Mircea Eliade, *The Myth of the Eternal Return* (New York: Bollingen Series XLVI, 1954).

3. Joseph Campbell, *The Masks of God* (New York: Viking Press, 1959).
4. Ananda Coomaraswamy, *The Dance of Shiva* (New York: Farrar, Straus & Cudahy, Inc., 1957), pp. 66-78.
5. Heinrich Zimmer, *The Art of Indian Asia*, ed. Joseph Campbell (New York: Bollingen Series XXXIX, 1955), p. 122.
6. P. Thomas, *Epics, Myths and Legends of India* (8th ed.; Bombay: D. B. Taraporevala Sons & Co., Ltd., n.d.) . p. 4–6.
7. Zimmer, *Myths and Symbols in Indian Art and Civilization*, pp. 3-10.
8. Alfonso Caso, *The Aztecs*, tr. Lowell Dunham (Norman, Oklahoma: University of Oklahoma Press, 1958), pp. 14-15.
9. Laurette Sejourne, *Burning Water* (New York: Vanguard Press, 1957), p. 72.
10. Brian Branston, *Gods of the North* (New York and London: Thames and Hudson Ltd., 1955), p. 277.
11. Finnur Jonsson, ed. *Snorra Edda* [i.e. The Prose Edda] (Reykjavík, 1907), "Gylfaginning" LII.
12. *Ibid.*, "Gylfaginning" LII, LIII.
13. Heinrich Zimmer, *The King and the Corpse* (New York: Bollingen Series XI, 1948), pp. 285-93.
14. Dr. Papus, *The Tarot of the Bohemians* (London: William Rider & Son, Ltd., 1919), pp. 157-58.
15. J. E. Cirlot, *A Dictionary of Symbols* (New York: Philosophical Library, 1962), pp. 310-11.

Death and Rebirth as Cycles of Nature

1. James B. Pritchard, ed. *Ancient Near Eastern Texts* (Rev. ed.; Princeton: Princeton University Press, 1955), pp. 53-57.
2. Samuel Noah Kramer, *Sumerian Mythology* (Rev. ed.; New York: Harper and Brothers, 1961), pp. 7-8. Harper Torchbook.
3. Pritchard, *op. cit.*, p. 52.
4. Samuel Noah Kramer, ed. *Mythologies of the Ancient World* (Chicago: Quadrangle Books, Inc., 1961), pp. 10; 108-15.
5. A. Klasens, *In the Museum of Antiquities at Leiden* (Leiden: E. J. Brill, 1952) , pp. 54–58.
6. S. Langdon, *Babylonian Epic of Creation* (Oxford: Clarendon Press, 1923) , pp. 53–56.
7. Jack Finegan, *Light from the Ancient Past* (Princeton: Princeton University Press, 1959), pp. 106-07.
8. Henri Frankfort, *Ancient Egyptian Religions* (New York: Columbia University Press, 1948), pp. 109, 110.
9. C. Kerényi, *The Gods of the Greeks* (London and New York: Thames and Hudson, 1951), pp. 89-90.
10. Funk and Wagnalls, *Standard Dictionary of Folklore, Mythology and Legend* (New York: Funk and Wagnalls Co., 1949), Vol. I, p. 90.
11. L. Schmitz, *Keightley's Classical Mythology* (London: G. Bell and Sons, Ltd., 1896). pp. 126-27.

12. *Ibid.*, pp. 152-56.
13. Padraic Colum, *Myths of the World* (New York: The Macmillan Co., 1930; New York: Grosset and Dunlap, 1959), pp. 179-84.
14. E. Dale Saunders, "Japanese Mythology," in Kramer, ed. *Mythologies of the Ancient World*, pp. 420-22.
15. Fray Bernardino de Sahagun, "The Ceremonies," Part III, *Florentine Codex*, Book II, tr. Arthur J. O. Anderson and Charles E. Dibble (Santa Fe: The School of American Research and The University of Utah, 1951), pp. 64-68.
16. Sejourne, *op. cit.*, pp. 162-63.
17. *Ibid.*, p. 165.
18. Paul Radin and James J. Sweeney, eds. *African Folktales and Sculpture* (New York: Bollingen Series XXXII, 1952), p. 272.
19. Grimm Brothers, *Grimm's Fairy Tales* (New York: Pantheon Books, Inc., 1944), pp. 94-97.

Initiation as a Spiritual Education

1. Layard, *op. cit.*, pp. 119-28.
2. Alexander Heidel, *The Gilgamesh Epic and Old Testament Parallels* (2nd ed.; Chicago: University of Chicago Press, 1954), pp. 18, 65-92.
3. Pritchard, *op. cit.*, p. 88.
4. G. R. S. Mead, *The Hymn of the Robe of Glory* (London and Benares: The Theosophical Publishing Society, 1908), Vol. X, "Echoes from the Gnosis," pp. 15-29.
5. Alan W. Watts, *Myth and Ritual in Christianity* (New York: Vanguard Press, 1953), pp. 177-80.
6. Sahagun, *op. cit.*, "The Origin of the Gods," Part IV, Book III, pp. 13-36.
7. Sejourne, *op. cit.*, p. 58.
8. *East of the Sun and West of the Moon—Old Tales from the North* (New York: George H. Doran Co., n.d.), p. 53.
9. Kerényi, *Gods of the Greeks*, pp. 252-59.
10. Harrison, *Themis*, pp. 69-71.
11. Jessie L. Weston, tr., *Sir Gawain at the Grail Castle* (London: David Nutt, Publisher, 1903), pp. 40-43.
12. Ellen Russell Emerson, *Indian Myths or Legends, Traditions, and Symbols of the Aborigines of America* (Boston: James H. Osgood & Co., 1884), pp. 413-15.
13. *Ibid.*, pp. 210-11.

Initiation as Psychic Liberation

1. Campbell, *The Masks of God*, pp. 251-52.
2. Eliade, *Birth and Rebirth*, p. 95.
3. Paul Radin, *The Road of Life and Death* (New York: Bollingen Series V, 1945), pp. 1-9.
4. Branston, *op. cit.*, p. 115.

5. Larousse, *Larousse Encyclopedia of Mythology* (New York: Prometheus Press, 1959), p. 261.
6. Arthur Waley, *The Nine Songs,* "A Study of Shamanism in Ancient China" (London: George Allen & Unwin Ltd., 1955), pp. 37-38.
7. R. H. Blyth, *Zen in English Literature* (Tokyo: The Hokuseido Press, 1948), p. 340.
8. Nivedita and Coomaraswamy, *Myths of the Hindus and Buddhists* (London: George G. Harrap & Co., 1914), pp. 332ff.
9. Eliade, *Yoga: Immortality and Freedom,* p. 10.
10. W. Y. Evans-Wentz, ed. *The Tibetan Book of the Dead* (3rd ed.; London: Oxford University Press, 1957), pp. N. 45-46.
11. Robert O. Ballou, ed. *The Bible of the World* (New York: The Viking Press, Inc., 1939), p. 989.
12. Nivedita and Coomaraswamy, *op. cit.,* pp. 345-52.

Myths of Resurrection

1. Branston, *op. cit.,* chap. X, pp. 269-75.
2. *The Holy Bible,* King James Version (Garden City, New York: Garden City Publishing Co., Inc., 1940), chap. 20-22, pp. 993-94.
3. *Ibid.,* pp. 320-21.
4. *Ibid.,* p. 452.
5. *Ibid.,* chap. 20.
6. G. R. S. Mead, *Fragments of a Faith Forgotten* (The Gnostics) (New Hyde Park, New York: University Books, Inc., n.d.), pp. 435-38.
7. Ballou, *op. cit.,* p. 240.
8. W. Y. Evans-Wentz, *The Tibetan Book of the Great Liberation* (London: Oxford University Press, 1954), p. 105.
9. Arthur Waley, *Three Ways of Thought in Ancient China* (New York: The Macmillan Co., 1939; Garden City, New York: Doubleday-Anchor Books, 1956), pp. 30-31.
10. Joseph Epes Brown, *The Sacred Pipe, Black Elk's Account of the Seven Rites of the Oglala Sioux* (Norman, Oklahoma: University of Oklahoma Press, 1953), pp. 4-29.
11. *Ibid.,* p. xi.
12. Lady Wilde, "Ancient Legends of Ireland" in *Irish Folk Stories and Fairy Tales,* William Butler Yeats, ed. (New York: Grosset & Dunlap, n.d.), pp. 197-201.
13. W. Oldfield Henry, *The Cat in the Mysteries of Magic and Religion,* tr. from the French of Marcelle Adam (New York: Wehman Bros., 1956), p. 131.

Appendix

1. Emily Dickinson, *The Complete Poems of Emily Dickinson* (London: Martin Secker, 1928), pp. 50-51.
2. *Ibid.,* p. 47.

3. *The Poems of Samuel Taylor Coleridge* (London: Oxford University Press, 1924), pp. 197-98.
4. Walt Whitman, "Leaves of Grass" in *Walt Whitman: Complete Poetry and Selected Prose and Letters,* Emory Holloway, ed. (London: The Nonesuch Press, n.d.), p. 399.

INDEX

Note: Page references in italics are to the text of specific myths in the anthology.

Dreams
agree with religious teachings
of past, 31
colors in, 34-38
initiation rites symbolized in,
51-52, 57, 70-73
of Joseph, 21
labyrinths in, 44-47
in psychotherapy, 13
author's cases, 34-40, 44-46,
70-73
serpents (snakes) in, 34-39,
43-46
"sliding into" water in, 49
Drowning, 235
ritualized, 49-50

Education, initiation as, 41-59,
139-83
Ego
Self as independent of, 13-14
transformation of consciousness of, 41, 50, 54, 59
in dream symbolism, 51, 57
Egyptian myths
hymn to Aton, *114-16*
See also Isis
Eleusinian Mysteries, 18, 58, 59,
120-21
Eliade, Mircea, 43, 77
on Earth Mother, 27, 28
on Hinduism, 10-13, 191-92
on shamanism, 62, 64, 185n.
Eliot, T. S., *The Cocktail Party*,
48
Engagement and disengagement
in modern individuals, 68-73
in types of initiation, 66-68
Ereshkigal, 26, *103-4*
Eros, 78
European myths
of the Holy Grail, 49, 52, 54-
58, *177-78*
of Lemminkainen (Finnish),
121-27
of the priest's soul (Irish),
226-30

European myths—*Continued*
of Prince Lindworm, 140, *167-
172*
of three snake-leaves, *135-38*
See also Greeks—myths of;
Icelandic myths
Evergreen tree, 99-100
Ezekiel, *194-96*

Female Devouring Ghost, 44, 45,
142
Femininity, *see* Masculinity and
femininity; Mother god-
desses
Fenris Wolf, *90-93*
Fertility myths, 16-17, 99-100;
see also specific myths
Finnish myth of Lemminkainen, *121-27*
Frazer, Sir James, 18
Freud, Sigmund, 23
libido of, 12

Gender, confusion of, 24; *see
also* Masculinity and
femininity
Gilgamesh, 49, 50, 52-53, 72,
139-40, *143-52*
Gnosticism
resurrection in, *213-16*
symbolism of pearl in, 29-30,
153-60
Good and evil
in folk art, 100
as subordinate to higher law,
10, 18
Grail myth, 49, 52, 54-58, *177-78*
Great Mother, *see* Mother goddesses
Greeks
incorporation in thought of,
66
myths of
Aphrodite and Adonis, 17,
19, *118-19*
Artemis (Mountain
Mother), 17, *118*